D0984328

INNOVATIONS TO GROUP PSYCHOTHERAPY

Third Printing

INNOVATIONS TO GROUP PSYCHOTHERAPY

Edited by

GEORGE M. GAZDA, Ed.D.

Professor of Education
University of Georgia
Athens, Georgia
Department of Psychiatry and Neurology
Medical College of Georgia
Augusta, Georgia

CHARLES C THOMAS • PUBLISHER
Springfield • Illinois • U.S.A.

Published and Distributed Throughout the World by
CHARLES C THOMAS • PUBLISHER
Bannerstone House
301-327 East Lawrence Avenue, Springfield, Illinois, U.S.A.
Natchez Plantation House
735 North Atlantic Boulevard, Fort Lauderdale, Florida, U.S.A.

© *1968, by* CHARLES C THOMAS • PUBLISHER

Library of Congress Catalog Card Number: 68-13755

First Printing, 1968
Second Printing, 1970
Third Printing, 1971

With THOMAS BOOKS careful attention is given to all details of manufacturing and design. It is the Publisher's desire to present books that are satisfactory as to their physical qualities and artistic possibilities and appropriate for their particular use. THOMAS BOOKS will be true to those laws of quality that assure a good name and good will.

Printed in the United States of America
R-1

CONTRIBUTORS

JOHN BEEBE, III, M.D. *United States Public Health Service, San Francisco, California.*

RAYMOND J. CORSINI, PH.D. *Counselor, Family Counseling Center of Hawaii; Psychologist Alcoholism Clinic, Department of Public Health; Lecturer, University of Hawaii, Honolulu, Hawaii.*

GEORGE M. GAZDA, ED.D. *Professor of Education, University of Georgia, Athens, Georgia, and Department of Psychiatry and Neurology, Medical College of Georgia, Augusta, Georgia.*

EUGENE T. GENDLIN, PH.D. *Associate Professor, Department of Psychology, University of Chicago, Chicago, Illinois.*

JACK R. GIBB, PH.D. *Organizational Consultant, Private Practice, La Jolla, California.*

LORRAINE M. GIBB, M.A. *Organizational Consultant, Private Practice, La Jolla, California.*

HAIM G. GINOTT, ED.D. *Adjunct Associate Professor of Psychology, Graduate School of Arts and Science, New York University, New York City; Associate Clinical Professor, Post-doctoral Program in Psychotherapy, Adelphi University, Garden City, New York.*

O. HOBART MOWRER, PH.D. *Research Professor of Psychology, University of Illinois, Urbana, Illinois.*

VIRGINIA M. SATIR, M.A. *ASCW Director, Family Project Mental Research Institute, Palo Alto, California.*

FREDERICK H. STOLLER, PH.D. *Senior Research Associate, Youth Studies Center, University of Southern California, Los Angeles, California.*

To Barbara and David

PREFACE

THIS book contains eight innovations to group psychotherapy. In a clinical practice characterized by a proliferation of new theories and methods, selecting positions to be representative of the many innovations presented a real dilemma. The positions selected for inclusion herein were selected because they presented, first of all, a new and unique method of group psychotherapy that reflected a strong theoretical rationale and, therefore, held promise of enduring rather than representing someone's soon to be forgotten, fly-by-night scheme.

In attempting to determine the relative permanency of the position, the prospective contributor's stature was a deciding factor. Each position or chapter has been prepared either by the originator of the position or one considered to be among the originators. Thus, each chapter represents a firsthand or primary source rather than a secondhand interpretation. Some of the positions are so current that they also represent the most recent and most complete expositions of the theoretical rationale and methods.

Finally, the chapter selections were chosen so as to reflect representative coverage of the following recent trends in group psychotherapy: accelerated treatment—represented by Corsini's immediate therapy in groups and Stoller's version of marathon group therapy; potential for mass treatment—represented by leaderless groups or, in this book, Gibbs' TORI process, and Mowrer's integrity therapy; greater therapist involvement—represented by Gendlin's version of experiential group psychotherapy; use of special communications media—represented by Stoller's focused feedback with video tape; the increased emphasis on the treatment of a family as a therapy group—represented by Satir's conjoint family therapy; and the application of new methods of treating children in groups—represented by Ginott's group psychotherapy with preadolescents. It is the plan and the wish of the editor that these selections be truly the best and most representative of innovations to group psychotherapy.

There is one obvious omission from the selection, and I feel that the method and the reason for its omission should be given. The method is the use in therapy groups of LSD and similar drugs. At the time of the organization of this volume, the legality of the use of LSD was being challenged seriously; therefore, the editor did not wish to advertise a procedure, the scientific value of which was in serious question.

The brief introductory chapter was prepared by the editor in an attempt to provide a framework for the introduction and assimilation of the eight innovative positions. In this chapter the problems of defining group psychotherapy were discussed and a means for defining group psychotherapy was presented, its history was traced briefly and some of the notables in its history were cited, and some conclusions were drawn concerning the future of group psychotherapy.

This book was prepared to assist in the improvement of the current practice of group psychotherapy and, hopefully, to stimulate research and still other innovations and improvements by making available to the student and practitioner, alike, some of the most promising recent innovations to group psychotherapy. It is my wish that the contributors of this book and I have been of some small assistance in this endeavor.

GEORGE M. GAZDA, ED.D.

ACKNOWLEDGMENTS

SEVERAL persons have assisted me in the various aspects of the preparation of this volume. First of all, I should like to express my sincere appreciation to the contributors for their chapter contributions, and also for their cooperation and tolerance when progress slowed. Secondly, my deep gratitude is extended to those unsung heroes, the faithful secretaries: Linda Wilkes, Wilma Forbes, Lillian Jewell, Janet Sumpter, and Ethel Epps. To Drs. Jonell Folds and Kathleen Davis for their unselfish assistance in proofreading, my most sincere appreciation. To my students for their encouragement and confidence in me, my thanks. Finally, my deepest appreciation to my wife, Barbara, and my son, David, for their forbearance, encouragement, and understanding during the preparation of the manuscript.

G.M.G.

CONTENTS

INNOVATIONS TO GROUP PSYCHOTHERAPY

I

GROUP PSYCHOTHERAPY:
ITS DEFINITION AND HISTORY

George M. Gazda

ONE who has followed the development of the group psychotherapy movement is likely to be struck by what appears, on the surface, to be a very presumptuous title for this book. A strong case can be made that, from its relatively recent inception, group psychotherapy has been a series of *innovations* and, as such, most positions would be eligible for inclusion in a book entitled *Innovations to Group Psychotherapy*. The following criteria were applied in the selection of positions included herein: first, the position must appear sound and contain the potential to endure; second, the position must be set forth by a person of high professional standing, and third, the position must be representative of one or more recent trends in group psychotherapy. These recent trends and the positions which were selected to represent them are as follows: accelerated treatment procedures—marathon group therapy and immediate therapy in groups; mass means for treatment—leaderless groups (TORI process) and integrity therapy; increased therapist involvement in treatment—experiential group psychotherapy; increased emphasis on treatment of a family as a therapy group—conjoint family therapy; new methods for working with preadolescents—innovations in group psychotherapy with preadolescents; and finally the use of special communications media—focused feedback with video tape.

The one significant recent innovation which is notably absent is the use of drugs, especially LSD, with group psychotherapy patients. At the time this book was organized, the use of LSD and similar drugs in the treatment of patients was under severe criticism and rather than encourage what might be an unprofessional practice, this position was not included.

In order to set the stage for the assimilation of the eight positions described in this volume, group psychotherapy is defined, its history is traced briefly, some of its most notable leaders are cited, and some conclusions are drawn in the remainder of this chapter.

DEFINITION OF GROUP PSYCHOTHERAPY

The manner in which one chooses to define group psychotherapy may determine his interpretation of its historical development. For example, if one uses Slavson's (1959) criteria for defining group psychotherapy, its history would begin in the 1930's rather than in 1905 with Pratt's class method or, as some suggest, even much earlier as with Mesmer's "suggestion" methods in the 1770's. For Slavson, a therapy group must be small in size (approximately eight); clients must be grouped on the basis of their nosological classification; leadership must be permissive and catalytic; and freedom of action and spontaneity of group members must be assured. When Slavson's criteria are applied to contemporary group psychotherapies, many versions would not qualify; nevertheless, they are today accepted forms of group psychotherapy.

Harms (1944) has defined three major categories of group psychotherapy: "(1) group therapy for one or more patients through one or more outside therapeutic agents; (2) therapy in psychopathology of the natural group and the social group; (3) internal therapeutic influence in artificial group settings" (p. 139). According to Harms (1944), most of the forms of group therapy practiced in the 1940's consisted of a single group therapist's influence upon a group of mentally ill patients (who frequently were not even grouped according to similarity of illness); the treatment given was often superficial and general since there was little opportunity to deal with specific individual problems. He felt that unless the patients were treated as a group based on a certain homogeneity of illness, the treatment did not deserve to be called group therapy. With respect to grouping according to homogeneity of illness, Harms seems to be in agreement with

Slavson's criteria; however, Harms' (1944) preferred use of the term "group" with "therapy" takes on the aura of "social engineering," *e.g.*, setting up mental institutions to be therapeutic groups, intervening in social pathological groups, environmental group therapy of placing an unhealthy person in a healthy family, and so on. Harms, then, appears to have envisioned group therapy as something quite different from a single therapist working with a small group of patients. His views are perhaps best represented in current versions of milieu therapy, family therapy, therapeutic social clubs and similar attempts resembling social engineering.

Since J. L. Moreno is given credit for coining the terms "group therapy" in 1931 (Z. Moreno, 1966) and "group psychotherapy" in 1932 (Corsini, 1957), one would expect his definitions to delimit current usage; however, in his attempt to clarify the issue he has chosen to give a general definition: "Group psychotherapy means simply to treat people in groups" (J. L. Moreno, 1962, p. 263). Corsini (1957) was to interpret Moreno's first definition to mean classifying members of a group, but Z. Moreno (1966) has countered that Corsini made an honest misinterpretation, and that J. L. Moreno's definition of 1931 is consistent with contemporary usage.

Gibb, Platts, and Miller (1951) have given different interpretations to Moreno's "group therapy" and "group psychotherapy." They state, "Moreno uses the term 'group therapy' for personality change which is a by-product of more primary group activities carried on for other purposes than therapy. He uses the term 'group psychotherapy' to designate the process by which a professional therapist guides a group in which the immediate and primary objective is the therapeutic welfare of the group" (p. 14). The interpretation by Gibb *et al.* (1951) of Moreno's "group psychotherapy" probably comes as close to approaching current acceptable usage of group psychotherapy as any other.

In general, group therapy and group psychotherapy are used synonymously in current discourse; group therapy has become the shortened version of group psychotherapy. However, the interpretation suggested by Gibb *et al.* (1951) demonstrates that some limited and specific meanings are assigned to the two different terms. Group therapy also is used, on occasion, to represent a more inclusive category of group procedures including physical therapy, recreational therapy, psychotherapy, and the like. In this sense, group psychotherapy would represent a special type of group therapy.

Our contemporary group therapies frequently represent adaptations of all our individual psychotherapies plus some varieties which may not have their counterparts in the individual psychotherapies. The group psychotherapies practiced today cut across and/or include all three of Harms' categories or types and, because of the rapid proliferation of group therapies, J. L. Moreno's (1962) general definition seems apropos if we apply Harms' three categories to refine the definition (see also Zerka Moreno's (1966), Summary of Definitions for additional treatment of this subject).

LEADERS OF THE GROUP PSYCHOTHERAPY MOVEMENT

Although it can be demonstrated that forms of group therapy have existed since the beginning of recorded history, the approaches to group psychotherapy presented in this volume have their roots in the more recent history of the 1900's; therefore, only the significant contributors and their contributions to this period of history will be cited. This brief tracing of the significant contributors to group therapy will be divided into the early period extending from 1905 to 1932, and the period of expansion extending from 1932 to the present.

EARLY PERIOD 1905-1932

The author will not enter into the already crowded field of writers who have taken sides with respect to *the person* who should be considered *the father* of group psychotherapy, since this seems wholly dependent upon the definition one is willing to accept for group psychotherapy. Slavson's (1959) definition, for example, rules out all practices prior to 1930 and the early years of that decade.

The early period includes Joseph H. Pratt's application of his "class method" to the treatment of tubercular patients to Moreno's introduction of the terms "group therapy" in 1931 and "group psychotherapy" in 1932. This period is perhaps best represented by the contributions of the following men: Pratt, Lazell, Marsh, Burrow, and Moreno.

J. H. PRATT. Dr. Pratt, as early as 1905 held group meetings with tuberculosis patients for the purpose of saving time in instructing them in hygienic practices (Hadden, 1955). It is generally accepted that Dr. Pratt did not at first understand the psychological impact on his patients of this group procedure. It is quite likely that Pratt began to understand and appreciate the psychotherapeutic effects of one person on another in his "class" or "thought control" approach to group therapy only *after* he had read Dejerine's work (perhaps as early as 1913).

E. W. LAZELL. Dr. Lazell, a psychiatrist, was one of the first to use group procedures—mainly didactic (inspirational) lectures to hospitalized schizophrenics. The first published account of Lazell's work was in 1921 which, apparently, was several years after he had been practicing group therapy.

L. C. MARSH. Marsh, first an Episcopal minister, entered the field of psychiatry at middle age. Along with Lazell, Marsh was one of the first to use group psychotherapy in mental hospitals. He used an inspirational, revival-like method of lectures, group discussions, music, art, dance, and other media to involve the patients with each other, and he met with all segments of the hospital staff to develop a therapeutic team—the forerunner of the milieu therapy approach. Perhaps Marsh can best be characterized by his famous motto, "By the crowd they have been broken; by the crowd they shall be healed."

T. BURROW. Trigant Burrow, like several other well-known followers of Freud, became dissatisfied with the lack of concern of psychoanalysis with the social forces affecting behavior. Thus, he developed group analysis which was his most significant contribution to group psychotherapy. Burrow's group analysis stressed the importance of studying man in relation to the group of which he is a part. After 1932 Burrow's efforts were devoted to the study of biological principles of group behavior which he named phyloanalysis. Phyloanalysis did not achieve widespread popularity, and Burrow's contributions to group psychotherapy after 1932 were minimal.

J. L. MORENO. Moreno is very likely the most colorful, controversial, and single-most influential person in the field of group psychotherapy. Moreno emigrated to the United States in 1925, but while still in Vienna he worked with prostitutes in groups. He states, "Modern group psychotherapy started in the sexual ghetto of Vienna, in a natural setting *in situ* 1913 . . ." (J. L. Moreno, 1966, p. 156).

Moreno introduced psychodrama into the United States in 1925; in 1931 he coined the term group therapy and in 1932 group psychotherapy; in 1931 he began to publish *Impromptu,* a journal concerned with dramatics and therapy; in 1936-37 he founded the journal *Sociometry; Sociatry* was founded in 1947, but was changed to *Group Psychotherapy* in 1949; in 1942 he founded the Sociometric and Psychodramatic Institutes and the first society of group psychotherapy (the American Society of Group Psychotherapy and Psychodrama) and became its first president; he organized the First International Committee on Group Psychotherapy in 1951 and was instrumental in organizing the First International Congress of Group Psychotherapy in 1954; he was elected president of the Second International Congress of Group Psychotherapy, 1957, the International Council of Group Psychotherapy, 1962, and the Third International Congress of Group Psychotherapy, 1963. In addition to the above accomplishments, Moreno has written numerous books and journal articles in the field of group psychodrama, group therapy, and sociometry. His latest work has been the editing of the *International Handbook of Group Psychotherapy.* Moreno continues to give leadership to the group psychotherapy movement although he is best known for his championing of psychodrama.

PERIOD OF EXPANSION: 1932 TO THE PRESENT

The total number of books, articles, and dissertations in the group psychotherapy literature for the twenty-five-year period preceeding 1931 was thirty-four; for the five-year period 1931-35, it was twenty; from 1936-40, it was sixty-nine; from 1941-45, it was two-hundred and three; and it increased to five-hundred and thirty-six during the next five-year period (Corsini, 1957). The annual review of group psychotherapy references published in the *International Journal of Group Psychotherapy* listed one-hundred and ninety-nine references for the year 1965 (MacLennan, Morse, and Goode, 1966). These figures represent a geometric increase in the growth of interest and contributions to the field of group psychotherapy. The tremendous year-to-year increase in the group psychotherapy literature was further reflected in the number of different contributors to the field. For the sake of brevity, only some of the most significant contributors will be cited for the period of expansion.

Paul Schilder and Louis Wender were two group therapists who were practicing during the latter part of the *early period* but did not publish their results until the middle and late thirties. Both of these psychiatrists pioneered the applications of psychoanalytic procedures to psychotic, hospitalized adult patients. Schilder also pioneered the use of group therapy with prison inmates, and Wender discovered the value of group meetings for discharged patients.

Samuel R. Slavson, an engineer by training, was one of the leading figures to emerge in the early thirties. Slavson, an analytically oriented group therapist, is probably best known for his development of activity group therapy. Slavson also organized the American Group Psychotherapy Association in 1943 and has been a leader of that organization as well as editor of its journal, *The International Journal of Group Psychotherapy*. Slavson has been one of the most prolific writers in the field of group psychotherapy.

Among the leaders in the application of group therapy techniques to play therapy with children have been F. Redl, Lauretta Bender, Gisela Konopka, Betty Gabriel, and Haim Ginott. Ginott has been instrumental in implementing new techniques in activity and play group therapies. He is the author of a very useful book on play therapy, *Group Psychotherapy with Children*.

Nathan Ackerman, a New York psychiatrist, has utilized analytic techniques with a wide variety of clientele and is particularly noted for group therapy with adolescents and for his pioneer work with family group therapy. Other leaders in the family group therapy movement are John Bell, Donald Jackson, and Virginia Satir. Satir has recently provided the field of family therapy with an interesting text, *Conjoint Family Therapy*.

Following in the tradition of Schilder and Wender, Alexander Wolf became one of the leading spokesman for psychoanalysis in groups. He uses it in his private practice and has also trained several psychiatrists in this method. He initiated the use of the "alternate session," *i.e.* the meeting of patients on alternate sessions without the therapist in attendance. E. K. Schwartz has collaborated with Wolf in producing numerous publications dealing with psychoanalysis in groups.

Helen Durkin in *The Group in Depth,* succinctly describes her analytic approach to group therapy. This book also provides a systematic description of other popular group therapies.

Rudolf Dreikurs, a Chicago psychiatrist trained by Adler, has applied Adlerian principles to group therapy. He is known especially for his work with family groups, child guidance, and the development of group therapy training centers. One of his recent collaborators is Manford Sonstegard, who, with Dreikurs, has applied Adlerian principles to group counseling in the school setting with children, parents, teachers, and other school personnel.

Raymond Corsini has given to the field of group therapy one of the most thorough accounts of its history in his *Methods of Group Psychotherapy.* Corsini has utilized psychodramatic approaches to group psychotherapy and has been the exponent of immediate group therapy. His *Methods of Group Psychotherapy,* published in 1957, is still a popular text in the field of group psychotherapy.

George Bach, a clinical psychologist in private practice in Beverly Hills, has been a leader in innovations in group psychotherapy. His book *Intensive Group Psychotherapy* represents one of the most complete treatments of the application of concepts of group dynamics to group therapy. Bach, a former student of Lewins, has recently been one of the pioneers of marathon group therapy. Jack Gibb, an eminent group dynamicist, is also applying group-dynamics research and theory to group psychotherapy; he has developed the TORI process to describe group procedures, including group therapy. Frederick Stoller, another California-based clinical psychologist, has been pioneering marathon group therapy with Bach and also has been one of the first to employ video with group psychotherapy; this he calls Focused Feedback, a technique developed around communications theory and principles.

The followers of Carl Rogers have not been without interest in the application of phenomenological psychology and client-centered principles to groups—witness the work of Thomas Gordon, Nicholas Hobbs, Walter Lifton, Charles Truax, and Eugene Gendlin. Gendlin, perhaps more than any of the others of the group cited, and perhaps more than Rogers himself, has championed the experiential approach to group psychotherapy. Gendlin's application of Rogerian principles appears to incorporate some of the principles of certain elder statesmen of experiential group therapy such as Carl Whitaker, Thomas Malone, and John Warkentin, who have taught and practiced this method at the Atlanta Psychiatric Clinic. This approach includes a greater involvement of the therapist: his values and feelings are also expressed and become a significant part of the treatment. Hugh Mullan and Max Rosenbaum's *Group Psychotherapy* presents a variation of the experiential approach advocated by the Atlanta group. Mullan has become one of the more articulate spokesman for the existential-experiential approach to group therapy. Thomas Hora, like Mullan, a New York psychiatrist, has become an advocate of existential group psychotherapy. Hora has combined his psychoanalytic training with communications theory and has produced a system of group psychotherapy similar to his counterparts in Europe. The trend toward greater therapist involvement with groups of patients growing out of the experiential-existential approaches may produce a new era in group psychotherapy. Its influence is very likely just beginning to be felt.

Although behavior theory applied to group therapy is just beginning to make its impact, the recent arrival in the United States from South Africa of Arnold Lazarus, a student of Wolpe and a leading exponent of behavior group therapy, will likely add leadership and zest to this movement. Lazarus, upon his arrival in the United States, assumed the post of Director of the Behavior Therapy Institute in Sausalito, California, but has most recently assumed an academic position in the Department of Behavioral Science at Temple University.

Several leading English group therapists are included below in this tracing of the history of group psychotherapy because of their influence on American group therapists. Joshua Bierer has been one of the most significant proponents of group psychotherapy in England. Bierer is probably best known for his development of the therapeutic social club, a type of self-help therapy group.

S. H. Foulkes in collaboration with E. J. Anthony is known for his utilization of Freudian concepts and the application of Lewin's field theory in the development of a group analytic psychotherapy.

W. R. Bion and a colleague, H. Ezriel, at the Tavistock Clinic have promoted the concept of the therapy group as an entity, as has J. D. Sutherland. Bion, in particular, has been the advocate of this concept. He is also well known for his concept of the "leadership by default" group approach to psychotherapy and his use of Kleinian concepts in a group-dynamics approach to group therapy. Bion's work has stimulated the interest of Herbert Thelen and his students at the University of Chicago. Dorothy Stock Whitaker and Morton Lieberman recently have combined the theory of Bion, Ezriel, and Foulkes with the "focal conflict" model of Thomas French and produced an intriguing book, *Psychotherapy Through the Group Process*.

A recent and comprehensive review of the history of group psychotherapy and contributions on an international scope has been written by Zerka Moreno, a leader in the field of group psychodrama and group psychotherapy in the United States. Her account can be found in Part II of *The International Handbook of Group Psychotherapy*.

The list of significant contributors to the field of group psychotherapy has now grown so lengthy that this volume cannot do justice to any of them and worse yet some important contributors have not been cited. Aside from the British group psychotherapists, no attempt has been made to cite the contributions of the growing number of foreign group psychotherapists.

CONCLUSIONS

J. L. Moreno has indicated that the changes brought about by the "third psychiatric revolution" were induced by the ". . . influence of cosmic and social forces" (1966, p. 152) and that the greatest contribution to the Third Psychiatric Revolution is being made through group and action methods, namely group psychotherapy and psychodrama. Whether or not group psychotherapy is making or will make the greatest contribution to the field of psychiatry during the third revolution, only history can record. Nevertheless, group psychotherapy has become almost as common a household expression as psychoanalysis—witness its current popularity in the popular magazines, for example. Also, note the proliferation of methods. Zerka Moreno, (1966) lists some forty-seven different approaches and in the same volume, Fine (1966) cites some eighteen different titles given to therapy groups by members of the psychology department of the St. Louis State Hospital Training Institute for Psychodrama and Group Psychotherapy. Inasmuch as it appears to be easier to attach names to group methods of therapy than to do so to individual therapies, this writer predicts a greater number of systems of group psychotherapy than the numerous varieties of individual methods of psychotherapy and, perhaps, if J. L. Moreno's (1966) mass psychiatry becomes a reality and the use of his suggested "two-way" television for psychodrama is perfected, we shall see the demise of the use of the adjective "group" and the substitution of the adjective "mass" to describe psychotherapies.

With the present popularity of group psychotherapy we are confronted with the immediate need for professional standards and a code of ethics. J. L. Moreno (1966) has proposed a code and a group oath in *The International Handbook of Group Psychotherapy* which he edited recently. In this handbook, Moreno had this to say about the popularity and rapid spread of group psychotherapy: "The movement has become easily the most popular and influential among the psychotherapies of our time. But in the rapid spread there is danger that the movement may go out of hand. The many trends and subforms, although a sign of productivity and progress, threaten to break it up from within into fragments" (p. 165). Thus, is formed the "threat and the promise" of group psychotherapy: Will its popularity contain within it the "seeds of its own destruction?" The answer to this question may very well depend upon the firmness of the foundation on which group psychotherapy is built. At the moment, we are more proficient in founding or naming varieties of group psychotherapy than we are in researching those now in existence. The theories and methods described in this volume have great appeal and appear to offer great promise, but with these, as with all other psychotherapies, let us be guided by research evidence rather than emotional appeal.

REFERENCES

CORSINI, R. J.: *Methods of Group Psychotherapy.* Chicago, James, 1957.

FINE, L.: The development and program of the St. Louis State Hospital Training Institute for Psychodrama and Group Psychotherapy. In J. L. Moreno (Ed.), *The International Handbook of Group Psychotherapy.* New York, Philosophical Lib., 1966, pp. 375-380.

GIBB, J. R.; PLATTS, GRACE N., and MILLER, LORRAINE F.: *Dynamics of Participative Groups.* St. Louis, Swift, 1951.

HADDEN, S. B.: Historic background of group psychotherapy. *Int J Group Psychother,* 5: 162-168, 1955.

HARMS, E.: Group therapy—Farce, fashion, or sociologically sound? *Nervous Child,* 4: 186-195, 1944.

MACLENNAN, BERYCE; MORSE, VIERA, and GOODE, P.: The group psychotherapy literature 1965. *Int J Group Psychother,* 16: 225-241, 1966.

MORENO, J. L.: Common ground for all group psychotherapists. What is a group psychotherapist? *Group Psychotherapy,* 15: 263-264, 1962.

MORENO, J. L. (Ed.): *The International Handbook of Group Psychotherapy.* New York, Philosophical Lib., 1966.

MORENO, ZERKA: Evolution and dynamics of the group psychotherapy movement. In J. L. Moreno (Ed.), *The International Handbook of Group Psychotherapy.* New York, Philosophical Lib., 1966, pp 27-125.

SLAVSON, S. R.: Parallelisms in the development of group psychotherapy. *Int J Group Psychother,* 9: 451-462, 1959.

II

IMMEDIATE THERAPY IN GROUPS

Raymond J. Corsini

PSYCHOTHERAPY ordinarily is conceived as essentially a long-term process which must necessarily take hundreds of hours to be of any value because of the resistance of personality to change. If the "problem" is "deep," then longer term therapy is said to be required, lasting for a period of several years. It is not uncommon to hear people say, "I started therapy but I had only about a thousand hours," or "I quit near the middle of the second year and really didn't finish." The writer knows one person who has been in psychoanalysis on and off for some thirty years and who has accumulated well over 10,000 hours, who states that her analysis is not yet completed.

How long should psychotherapy take? Of course there is no final answer, but if we use an analogy the problem may become clear. If a number of people are learning the same thing, the amount of time required for success will vary considerably whether it be understanding calculus, how to hula, or how to keep one's temper when provoked. Indeed, some individuals may never learn to do any of these three things to the extent they would wish. Suppose, in addition, that the individual being taught really does not want to learn; suppose that the more the teacher insists, cajoles, demonstrates, tries to allay anxiety, the more the student gets scared; this learning situation then becomes analogous to psychotherapy.

NEED PSYCHOTHERAPY BE INTERMINABLE?

Assuming that psychotherapy is a valid phenomenon, *i.e.* that worthwhile and lasting changes in thinking, feeling, and acting do occur as a result of systematic symbolic interaction between therapists and patients, is there any *necessary* relation between

15

the length of time that the process takes and results? One may be inclined to think the question foolish, since the answer seems so evident, but in dealing with human beings we cannot be too sure of anything. What holds for inanimate objects or for animals need not be valid for man. It may take hours to condition a rat to some symbol, but a man may see a woman for a fraction of a second and become hopelessly in love with her. A proposition in higher mathematics which may take most people dozens of hours to understand may be mastered in a matter of seconds by some genius. The typical person may require several hours to memorize a particular poem, but someone else may repeat it after reading it once. One child may require weeks to learn to swim, but another child jumps into the water and swims the first time in water.

Progress in psychotherapy is determined not only by the patient but also by the therapist. The therapist's preconceptions may affect rate of progress. If the therapist assumes his typical patient must be with him three years, and if the therapeutic process includes a thorough personality diagnosis, a medical checkup, a tryout period, a detailed history, establishment of a transference neurosis, working through of conflicts, catharsis, and such, the patient unconsciously may conform to the therapist's notions. A major problem in psychotherapy is that the therapist finds confirmation for what he is looking. Taught in one mode of thinking, he deals with his patients in the same manner, and just as he conformed to his training, so too his patients will conform.

The claim is made herein that psychotherapy need not be interminable, and that long-lasting, coordinated, ameliorative, desirable changes in personality, thinking, feeling, and behavior are possible under very short-term conditions. These changes can be as permanent, extensive, and of the same nature as long-term psychotherapy.

This chapter discusses immediate therapy in groups, a phenomenon previously discussed in two books (Corsini, 1957; 1965) and in a number of articles (Corsini, 1951a; 1951b; 1951c; 1952). Immediate therapy is perhaps best described as the phenomenon of rapid, conversion-like, constructive personality change subsequent to psychotherapy and depending on a peak experience reaction resulting from direct confrontation with the truth.

EXAMPLES OF IMMEDIATE THERAPY

About twenty-five years ago while working at Auburn Prison in New York State, I received a request for an interview. Our conversation went somewhat as follows: "I am being paroled next week, but before I leave I want to thank you for what you did for me." (To the best of my memory I had never seen this young man before.) "I used to think you 'bug doctors' were a lot of bull, but I only repeated what I heard and what I wanted to believe. Anyway, now I am grateful that the state employs you because you have completely changed my life."

"How?" I asked, wondering if he had confused me with someone else.

"After I left your office two years ago, I felt as though I could walk on air. I was excited and almost delirious. For a couple of days I just didn't talk to anyone. Then I stopped hanging around with the crowd of crooks I had been going with. I started associating with a much better element. I went back to school, and in less than a year I got a high school diploma—I completed three years' work in less than one year. And now I am taking college work by correspondence. I am also learning drafting and blueprint reading. On account of you I began writing to my parents, and they are delighted with what you did for me. They consider my change a miracle. I am much happier now, know I will make a success out of life, am realistic, and my whole criminal past is over. I am rehabilitated, a new man. I am telling you this so that you will realize that some people are grateful for what you do for them."

I replied, "I sure appreciate the compliment, but I am afraid you made a mistake. All I do is test people and sometimes give vocational advice, but what you have described is a complete personality change, and I am not a psychotherapist."

"It's you all right," my interviewee said, "but I don't blame you for not remembering me."

"How come I changed your life so, when I don't even remember you?" I asked.

My interviewee smiled, "It's what you told me. A sentence that literally changed my life."

"What was it?" I asked eagerly, visions of a new psychotherapeutic system and an article in *Reader's Digest* dancing in my head.

"You said, and I remember your exact words, 'You have a high IQ.'"

I used to tell the above as a kind of party story, not realizing its profound implications. Many years after the event I began to realize its meaning, after I had had some other cases of rapid, profound, and lasting personality changes based on apparently minor stimuli. I had tended to minimize these as "flights into health," but gradually I began to realize that there was for some people a "hot button" which pressed at the right time could produce enormous changes.

Certainly the statement, "You have a high IQ" has nothing in it of intrinsic therapeutic value. I have made that statement subsequently to hundreds of people, and none of them ever reported any personality change, although some did express considerable surprise. Why then did this statement so profoundly affect this young prisoner? It must have challenged some basic self-conception.

By a strange coincidence, about the time of the above-mentioned event I observed a number of cases of conversions in the opposite direction: from normality to abnormality (Corsini, 1945), but while I was able to generalize from good to bad, I did not at that time generalize from bad to good.

Some years later I was conducting a therapy group of self-referred prisoners. According to the rules of this group, any member could invite any other prisoner to attend one session. The new arrival could declare himself a part of the group and be considered a participant. Joe came into the group via this route. At the end of six weeks he had contributed almost nothing. We had a system of going "in rotation" with problems and he accepted his assignment reluctantly. However, the next session Joe told a story about his mother who, in effect, told him never to trust anyone. It seemed impossible to construct a psychodrama on this story, our usual practice. At that moment the idea of the "behind-the-back" technique was born, and I asked Joe whether he would just turn his back to the group so that we could discuss him. He did so reluctantly. The members, in rotation, began to discuss Joe, and each had only negative things to say about him. When we finished, Joe was asked to rejoin the group. He got up, faced us, and told us angrily what he thought of us. After spitting on the floor, he left the room indignantly. I thought this was the end of him as far as I was concerned, but I did not know that again immediate therapy had taken place.

Several weeks later Joe came to see me and told me that after the session he had not been able to sleep, had tossed and turned, and was quite upset by the group criticism. He asked whether the attack had been planned. I told him the whole matter had been spontaneous. He then wanted to know why people felt as they did about him. I told him that I did not know the answer. He asked to return to the group, but I refused. He asked for individual therapy, but I would not take him. He begged for help. I then told him if he would change his job from a kitchen helper (a soft job) to attendant for the seniles (the least desirable job in the institution) I would see him—after six months. He did change the jobs, did very well in the attendant's job, and when he came to see me after six months he seemed a new person. We both agreed that he had had his therapy and that he did not need anything else. He then stated that the shock of the session had been so powerful that it just changed all his thinking.

When we analyzed the reasons for his change from a "no-good bum" to a "nice guy," he insisted that what he had discovered about himself in the group had been a profound shock to him, since he had felt up to then he was no different from anyone else and a rather "nice guy" who had been pushed around a bit by life. As in the case of the man who learned he had a "high IQ," Joe learned that he was "no good." And this was a man who, by his own admission, did not have a friend in the world and whose modal crime was marrying women bigamously and then stealing their money!

In both cases the individuals were given "obvious" information. It seems incredible that a young man with an IQ of about 130 should think of himself as "stupid" or that a man who could generate universal dislike should think of himself as a "nice guy," but in both cases this was precisely the situation.

One additional case of immediate therapy illustrates the nature of problems in handling this technique. In an adult group, one member was a relatively prominent clergyman who periodically spent an evening at a house of prostitution. He was afraid he might be recognized, blackmailed, and thus bring shame to his family, but the urge was so strong that he visited this particular brothel about once every two weeks—with routine subsequent re-morse and apprehension. In the same group another member had three women pregnant. He was a sexual athlete, could have inter-course as often as six times a day, and it was his compulsion to have intercourse with a new woman daily. Aside from this, he was an extremely successful businessman.

The writer planned a psychodrama directed to the minister. In the first scene the minister was lying on the rug with one of the female members of the group when in burst his wife, a detective, and some laymen from his church's board. In the second scene his wife reproached him for the shame he had brought to her. In the third scene the church board held a hearing about him, and after pro and con discussion they decided to keep him but to transfer him. It was quite an exhausting session, and the writer was posi-tive that immediate therapy would occur. It did occur—but not to the minister! The businessman was so affected by the scene (he had played one of the minor supporting roles in the drama) that he immediately gave up his philandering, but the minister, to whom the scene had been directed, kept going to his assignations despite this attempt to stop him.

THE PHILOSOPHY OF IMMEDIATE THERAPY

Implicit in every therapeutic system is a value decision about man, superseding theory and technique. In the directive therapies the therapist is superior to the patient: the patient is the "stu-dent"; the therapist, the "teacher." In nondirective therapies, the patient is the therapist, and the therapist is the catalyst, or stage director, preparing the field in which the patient can explore and cure himself.

Neither of these two polar positions expresses the philosophy of immediate therapy. For lack of a better word, the philosophical position taken by the therapist is cooperative. Both individuals are free to express themselves, neither assumes command nor leadership nor superiority. Both are engaged in an effort in which either may take the lead or assume superiority in the quest of understanding the patient, trying to find out what is troubling him, and attempting to get to a solution. The therapist accepts the inviolability of the patient—at no time must he attempt anything without the consent, implicit, or explicit, of the patient.

This essential point did not come out of some preconception of man. It came from harsh reality. Soon after discovering the concept of immediate therapy, the writer began to develop a system of group psychotherapy in which the principles of immediate therapy were to be employed. The results from the first seemed spectacular—people were changing dramatically; enormous emotional reactions were elicited, and so forth. One day while in the middle of working with a patient who had been reluctant to participate "for his own good," this patient suddenly went psychotic! The meeting came to a halt, and attendants had to put him in a straight jacket. Within the same month another patient, who also had been reluctant to participate, likewise went psychotic. This time, however, it was the group and not the therapist which had put pressure on the patient. This second incident made it clear that immediate therapy was strong medicine! Troubled by these two incidents, I discussed them with a respected colleague who advised me to stop. This "meat-axe" therapy, he said, was very dangerous. The behind-the-back technique, he pointed out, was especially hazardous for people with paranoid tendencies. "Psychodrama could easily unhinge a person. Personality change had to be a slow process. It was unsafe to try to hurry things. The things I thought I was doing were only 'flights into health' by patients, who tried to escape my relentless and insistent demands." It was lucky, he told me, that I had talked with him so that I could stop my dangerous work in time.

Convinced, I determined to stop going in the direction I had been heading. Yes, perhaps I had done some people some good, but perhaps I had done much more harm. At the next session of the group I told them the story and informed them that from now on I would operate nondirectively. My decision met with strong opposition, both from those who had already gone through the experience of confrontation therapy and from patients who were waiting their turn! We argued the issue, and from the group I obtained understanding of the basic error we had made and got courage to try again. The error was simple: in the first case *I* had put pressure on a reluctant patient; in the second case the *group* had done so. Yes, immediate therapy *was* strong medicine, but was it not strong medicine that we were looking for? Strong medicine must be handled properly. The fact that two patients had been harmed was incidental. The solution was not to put any pressure on patients to participate; they had to make a free and uncoerced decision. The therapist must not be directive.

But immediate therapy could not function with a nondirective leader. The therapist had to be very active, had to participate fully, had to use his judgment, initiative, cleverness. How could the therapist function fully and dynamically and not be directive? How could the patient also function fully and dynamically if the therapist was to be nondirective?

The answer seemed clear in principle: so long as there was agreement, a free agreement on the part of the patient on what was to be done, then the therapist would be free to do whatever he would do. The concept of democratically working together on a specific problem seemed to be the answer. The patient was like a child sitting on a toy wagon. The therapist was going to push the wagon. The patient would point the wagon in whatever direction he wanted to go. He had freedom to choose the direction. But the therapist could push as far and as fast and as hard as he felt he should. The patient would decide where the problem was and what he wanted treated, and the therapist would operate at that point.

The patient must actually serve as a diagnostician as well as a therapist. The patient knows where it hurts, as it were, and knows the proper place to treat. The therapist has to become sensitive to the patient's perception of himself and has to be willing to follow any lead, no matter how unpromising, exactly as the patient develops it, and to follow this line to the bitter end.

The philosophy of immediate therapy that developed went something like this: Both the patient and the therapist were to function freely, but the therapist was limited in his operations within the sectors delimited by the patient. Moreover, the therapist should not function in any cajoling, leading, or demanding manner. But when the patient said "go" and pointed the way, the therapist could operate as freely and as strongly as he felt wise. The following analogy illustrates my point. A patient has a toothache and asks someone to look at his mouth. Then he states, "This is the offending tooth." Next, he says to the dentist, "Pull it." At this point the dentist can do what he thinks best to that particular tooth regardless of the patient's behavior during the tooth pulling.

This philosophy, put into action, has prevented any untoward occurrence in the subsequent years of use of methods intended to elicit immediate therapy. The therapist does what he can but only with the patient's expressed approval.

THE THEORY OF IMMEDIATE THERAPY

Therapists would do their professions a service if they could divest themselves of theories and operate in a common-sense manner: reporting facts, especially "critical incidents" upon which hypotheses could be established, later leading to theories of the kind that could be operationally investigated. However, such is the *Zeitgeist* that psychotherapists have assumed it necessary first to be indoctrinated in some theory and then to operate as though the theory were correct.

In a very real sense immediate therapy has no theory or, what may appear to be the same thing to some people, its theory is synthetic, since it is built upon parts of other peoples' theories. Below are a number of propositions, none of them to be defended at any great length here, which underlie immediate therapy.

1. Psychotherapy may be primarily directed to any one of the triad *cognition-emotions-behavior*. Psychoanalysis deals mostly with cognition; client-centered therapy deals with feelings; psychodrama operates in terms of behavior. In immediate therapy one can employ any one of the three, but preferably for fullest impact all three modalities should be stimulated simultaneously.

2. Psychotherapy essentially is a process of bringing into the open hidden fundamental conceptions, what Adlerians call "private logic." This "private logic" is composed of a connected series of "basic errors." Psychotherapy is fundamentally a matter of cognitive treatment. The emotions and the behavior are functions of thinking.

We do not change emotions or behavior directly; these changes are the consequences of modifying thinking.

3. The patient "knows" what is wrong with him but does not "understand" it. He has developed a series of fences that separate him from the truth. He has evolved a complex system for supporting his basic errors. In psychotherapy he goes through an approach-avoidance gradient: the closer he gets to the truth, the more he tries to avoid it. As the therapist closes in on him, he discovers new methods to avoid facing the truth. Psychotherapy is a process of trying to corner a wily quarry, who on the surface wants to change, but who is frightened of change.

4. The process of psychotherapy consists of learning—unlearning and relearning. But it has two phases: first, a Gestalt type "ah ha" kind of experience during which one "understands" what one "knows." This experience is "immediate"; when it happens, it happens rapidly. The second aspect of psychotherapy is trial-and-error, adaptive learning in which the individual develops new habit patterns. The first kind of learning properly is the function of psychotherapy. Psychotherapists should stop when the patient has achieved the first phase—understanding—and the patient should be permitted to work out his solution on his own. Dependency can occur at this point. Once the patient "understands," he should leave the group and "fly on his own."

5. The process of immediate therapy has these phases:

a. Understanding (in group therapy every patient is a therapist to every other patient) of the patient's *life style* (social stimulus value), and of the patient's *private logic* (self) gained via historical information, interviews, observations of the patient's behavior, analysis of dreams, hypnosis, analysis of early recollections, and the like. The writer prefers to use a system developed by Dreikurs (1963) which includes the taking of a family history and the elicitation of early recollections.

b. *Pari passu* the patient experiences a feeling of acceptance and belonging and identification with the group, and so begins to gain confidence.

c. The patient is manipulated, with his full knowledge and understanding, into a situation of anxiety via the establishment of an anticipatory set. A crisis-type situation is then developed which will break through his fences and defenses. The therapist attempts to achieve a cathartic moment, a peak experience, bringing the patient to a state of panic to be sustained to its absolute maximum.

d. When this peak is obtained, the patient is cast out of the group. This is the "moment of truth." Just as traumatic as the instance of birth or the moment of death, this "moment of truth" must be suffered alone.

e. The patient must be on his own following this "moment of truth." During this time, if immediate therapy has occurred, he will be in a state of great distress. Sleeplessness, operating in a mechanical manner, listlessness, irritability, partial dissociation, feelings of "jumping out of one's skin," and shock are common sequelae. Then, usually about twenty-four to forty-eight hours after the "moment of truth," (the peak experience), the patient suddenly "understands"; and peace, tranquility, calmness come over him. When he reenters the group, if immediate therapy has taken place, everyone immediately recognizes the fact, since the individual is so different that he literally seems to be a new person. It is almost as though his brain had been taken out and replaced by a new one.

f. The therapist must not keep his patient too long after this experience. This is not usually a problem since the typical patient, after experiencing immediate therapy, soon loses interest in the group and is eager to get on with the process of meeting real life. For the purpose of helping prepare new patients, it is good to have such "cured" individuals in the group, as well as to be certain that the change is not a "flight into health." Generally, such people should remain for at least two months after their experience.

6. It is possible for the patient to have one or two quanta-type jumps of improvement. These can be instances of "flight into health" but most often are partial examples of immediate therapy. This is another reason why the patient should be kept for at least two months after the "moment of truth," and why at least one more effort should be made to produce another peak experience. If therapy is complete, another peak experience, of course, will not be achieved.

Since the theory of immediate therapy is fragmentary and inchoate, some of its propositions are given a further elaboration below.

Every child develops a conception of self and a philosophy of life as a function of his interaction with the social environment. The concept of self and philosophy of life become the essence of the individual and determine his reactions to life, *i.e.* his emotional and behavioral components. How one feels (attitudes, opinions, values) and how one behaves (talks, walks, his habits) are a function of his interpretations of his experiences. Perceptions and conclusions are stored and become the source of future interpretations of new events, and are the essence of his personality.

One way to understand this "life style" is to know an individual's history, most importantly his very early years' experiences within his family. If we know, for example, that the patient was the baby of the family, pampered and spoiled by all, that he had frequent temper tantrums, that he had few friends as a child and preferred to read rather than play, and that when he played he tended to have one rather than several friends, we can begin to get some conception of the kind of person that he is. Another way to understand the patient's "private logic" is by analysis of early recollections, which Ruth Munroe (1955) has identified as the first of the projective techniques. The theory is that an individual's private logic or essential philosophy of life is fixed by these early memories, serving as "instances of the way life is" and thus permitting therapists as analysts to gain some understanding of the individual's basic thinking (Mosak, 1958).

This understanding gives the therapist a frame of reference for comprehending the dramatic moment of encounter that serves as the basis of immediate therapy. The patient is understood in depth, something that appears to be lacking, for example, in ordinary psychodrama (Corsini, 1945).

The patient has developed a personality (self concept = private logic and social stimulus value = life style) which operates to time-bind the individual's past and future in terms of the demands of the immediate present. If the individual is not functioning optimally, if in distress (guilt, tensions, anger, anxieties), or if functioning poorly (marital difficulties, job problems, social inadequacies), or, as is most common, in trouble both subjectively and objectively, the most effective way of helping him is to get him to see himself as he really is. One must try to get him to understand his philosophy of life, his private logic, and his basic errors. He must understand that what he had accepted as "basic truth" about himself and others is nothing but a "fiction," a story he has told himself over and over again, but one that is not true. In this respect immediate therapy comes close to Ellis' (1963) rational-emotive therapy.

We view personality as a fiction composed by the patient, reinforced by his memories, and then impressed on others by the patient's behavior. The therapist's problem is to change the fiction that causes the patient distress or which causes distress to others, to another better fiction, but closer to the truth. Psychotherapy helps the patient understand the truth, which has the effect of changing him *to an already existing form*. This central theoretical point explains why we can have an overnight change. Personality is a series of independent layers. The current one, like the skin of a snake, can be shed to reveal another complete skin beneath.

Possibly the simplest example of this comes from the following recently reported case. George, a retiring, shy inmate in a training school, complained, "Everybody picks on me. . . ." The treatment consisted of George playing the role of King Kong for fifteen minutes, "terrorizing" the members of the therapy group, including the two adult therapists. When seen the next week he was black and blue. He explained that he had been fighting almost everybody. He then said, "When you think you are weak, they pick on you. Now that they know I am not going to take any crap from anybody they leave me alone."

Little George discovered that if you look and act frightened, people will pick on you; if you think you are weak and powerless, you will convey this information to the world. But George had to find out what he probably already knew—he had to learn to understand what he knew. The "moment of truth" which helped him to break through his prior habit patterns only occurred as a result of the crisis-type situation in which he was placed. This moment of truth directed itself to a basic error in his thinking.

The conception of diagnosis in immediate therapy refers to the location of the major area of difficulty. Suppose that a person has a splinter in his hand. A doctor may press various areas of the skin and when the splinter is touched the patient and doctor learn precisely where it is. In the employment of immediate therapy when the patient gains the confidence to go ahead, he inevitably selects a problem that refers directly to his central or basic error. We shall discuss this issue more directly later.

Since it is difficult to decide whether at this point the theory of immediate therapy is clear, perhaps another short formulation will help. The therapist wants to get to understand the patient in depth, in terms of his history and his concepts; he wants to see the patient in action in a social scene; he wants the patient to gain confidence that he can change. When the therapist understands the patient's history and his ways of operating, and when he thinks the patient has the courage to go ahead, he begins to arrange some situation likely to get close to the individual's self-concept in order to expose dramatically the individual's basic errors. The therapist knows by the patient's reaction when he has hit the "hot button." Only when the patient is upset to an extreme degree by a peak experience will immediate therapy occur. At the absolute moment of greatest tension, the contrived situation is ended, and the patient is cast out of the group to suffer and to work out his problem alone.

During the postsession period the individual is usually upset, settles the issue of his basic error, readjusts himself, and immediately tends to find peace and assume a new personality. This usually occurs instantaneously from the point of view of the patient, overnight from the point of view of observers, and from one session to another from the point of view of group-therapy members. The patient subjectively becomes aware of the *truth*, *i.e.* he is really intelligent; he is really a no-good bum; he provokes others' hostilities by his behavior, and so forth. This *truth* is usually "obvious"—and to the patient often becomes a process of accepting what he already knows.

THE TECHNIQUE OF IMMEDIATE THERAPY

The essence of this immediate therapy is confrontation: a dramatic meeting of the self. The therapist desires the following conditions, none of them especially novel.

1. The patient should be in complete charge of his case. The therapist does not make decisions for the patient. The therapist makes no demands.
2. The patient understands there is complete equality between himself and the therapist and other patients. Any attempts at subservience or superiority are to be squelched.
3. The therapist plays the role of himself as honestly and as forthrightly as possible, talking at a gut level about his own feelings and reactions, but always keeping within the context of the group rather than in terms of his outside problems. "I am bothered by you, puzzled and quite upset," the therapist may say—if this is

how he feels. The therapist must strive for fullest honesty, fullest expression, fullest openness.

4. The patient is to be informed of everything; there are to be no surprises. Nothing is held back from him.

5. The therapist does not push anyone, but he does push himself. He desires to be busy all the time, getting and giving information, setting up situations, directing role-playing scenes, thinking up ideas, and the like.

6. Periodically, the usual type of aggressive session (to be described later) is modified to a completely nondirective meeting during which the therapist plays the role of another patient.

Some of the phases in psychodramatic group therapy are the following:

1. After the usual initial period of getting to know one another, the therapist interviews each patient in the group to get a history. The other members ask questions to complete the history. The patient is further interviewed and an analysis of his early recollections is made. A case conference involving the whole group, led by the therapist, attempts to elicit the individual's *life style* and *private logic*.

This "diagnostic" phase helps establish equality, lets each person understand each of the others, generates a feeling of sympathy and empathy, and serves to dispel antagonism or competition between members.

We thus have a series of case history takings and projective testings, with case conferences. The gains are cognitive and attitudinal. Each patient feels he is a therapist, begins to like the other members, and compassion and altruism tend to occur. A kind of round-robin, follow-the-leader situation develops in that everybody in the group goes through an initiation procedure, and even the most reluctant and withdrawn are forced by the social pressure in the group to participate. Since each person receives equal attention, equality is established, and the person who tends to be overaggressive or underassertive learns in a subtle way that all get equal treatment.

The preparatory phase is conducted in a spirit of inquiry. The therapist asks the questions and then leads the group, seminar-wise, in trying to understand the patient's *life style* and *private logic*, how he operates (social stimulus), and how he feels and thinks about himself (self).

2. The active treatment phase has a variety of subphases depending on the judgment of the therapist, the opinions of the patients, and the problem of the patient who serves as the subject of the deeper inquiry.

One of the first aspects of this phase is an explanation of what is to come. The therapist says somewhat as follows: "Psychotherapy is a process, sometimes of learning what we already know. People have a tendency to fight, usually unconsciously, against self-improvement. It is hard for us to really understand ourselves or to make changes. One way to do both is to have a dramatic confrontation with ourselves: perhaps to be told how we appear to others, perhaps to recount some very important experiences, and sometimes to reenact important situations. I serve as a guide and will show you various methods we can use, but only you can show us where to work. For example, there is a technique known as the behind-the-back technique, which I would like to tell you about, and perhaps one of you would like to volunteer to try it out, after you know what it is all about. . . ."

If one obtains a volunteer, the next step is to induce situational anxiety. This seems to be essential for immediate therapy to occur. Anxiety is generally obtained by telling the volunteer that he will be in the limelight the following session. This gives the subject a week to worry about what he is to do. Unless the patient is concerned about his presentation, there can be little hope that immediate therapy will occur.

The next element is the collaboration between the group, the therapist, and the patient during the presentation. The patient, in effect, is told that now is the time "to put up or shut up" and the group, in effect, is told that now is their turn to help the patient realize himself. The therapist plays a delicate role of directing but not leading the patient. In effect the therapist does only what the patient wants, but does it in his own way. He can use all his ingenuity, courage, and skill, but he must not overwhelm the patient in any manner.

Whatever the procedure used, whether a long monologue, the behind-the-back technique, or role-playing, the therapist attempts to drive the patient to a climax of emotionalism, and then when he thinks he has gotten to the farthest point, suddenly stops the action and sends the patient out of the group.

3. The next phase is the patient's solitary reaction. The patient tends to be stunned, upset, and otherwise shaken. The patient eventually readjusts himself and then gains insight, peace, and otherwise achieves immediate therapy.

This "reconstruction phase" is diminished if the patient is permitted to stay in the group. For this reason, as soon as the subject has achieved this raw emotional climax, regardless of how upset he is, he must be sent out of the group. "Nursing" or other forms of sympathy must not be permitted. The reconstruction is done alone.

4. The next phase is the recapitulation period. At the next session the patient is asked for his summary of what happened to him, how he feels, whether he has changed, and so on; and then each member of the group is asked to comment. The recapitulation is very important since every member is aware he will be asked to discuss the chief protagonist of the prior session, and consequently he tends to keep that person in mind during the week.

5. The final phase is found during the patient's further stay in the group. The therapist notices the patient's behavior and comments on it. When immediate therapy has occurred, the patient is different and seems to be "clear." From being a complainer he becomes a helper; his pessimism becomes realism; he participates and cooperates. In some cases the change is partial. Immediate therapy is not always an all-or-none situation, although it often appears to be. In some cases, the further rounding-out occurs as a result of discussions; in some rare cases, the patient requires another similar treatment. In such cases the first treatment tends to accomplish just a little; but in the second instance we find the big leap forward.

FURTHER EXAMPLES OF IMMEDIATE THERAPY

If an individual experiences a conversion-type change subsequent to some stimulus, the sole "cause" of the change is not the stimulus, but also the readiness of the individual to change. However, the stimulus is important, but not essential to the change. In the theory of personality inherent in this discussion, personality change is seen as saltatory rather than as straight-line in nature. Since resistance tends to prohibit any progress, our procedure is to outwit the resistance, as it were, and permit one big rapid gain rather than a number of small gains. Consequently, in the use of this method, the therapist, without forcing things, attempts to set up the situation to permit the patient to experience a great big bang. Perhaps the best way to explain the flexible technique is to give a few detailed case histories, concentrating mostly on the therapist's thinking and functioning.

MARIE. Marie was brought to an alcoholism clinic by a physician who had treated her for extreme debility following a prolonged period of heavy drinking and no eating. When first seen by the writer she was gaunt and pale. This woman of thirty had lost weight and was down from her usual one hundred and thirty pounds to eighty-five pounds, as close to skin and bones as anyone I had ever seen. She was listless, dispirited, polite, weak, soft-spoken; her head hung down; her eyes were closed, and she gave the appearance of extreme depression. She answered appropriately, but without any elaboration. Her typical remarks were of this nature: "Yes, doctor," "Twice," "I don't know," "I took off and went to California and stayed with a girl friend"—minimum information.

Her history was obtained with some difficulty. She was the older of two children, and her younger brother was a hemophiliac, who occupied her parents' attention and was inordinately spoiled. She was supposed to be the older sister in every sense and was tied down to her brother. Her father was cold and devoted only to his business and to drinking. Her mother was a hard worker and unaffectionate. Marie had few friends and spent most of her time daydreaming. When she was eighteen, her father informed her she would not go to college but would have to work in the family business. She then got into the family car and drove to another state one thousand miles away. Enroute she met a man who raped her. After several months she returned to a wedding in the family, and after leaving the wedding with a family friend, she was raped by him. One night she went out with some friends on a blind date and spent the evening in bed with her date. The next day she married this man. The marriage lasted four months. The husband was supported by his family and had no intention of ever working. She divorced him and left, this time ending up in a small town in the same state. She went to a Catholic church for help and the pastor, on hearing her problem, took her in as a clerk, permitting her to sleep in the rectory. Pregnant, she began working from twelve to fourteen hours a day, rarely leaving the rectory. She began drinking at this time. She had her baby, gave it away, and then began serious drinking to the point she could no longer function. One of the younger priests advanced her money to take an alcoholism cure in another city. When she came back, he tried to counsel her, but she soon slipped back into her drinking, and during this period they became lovers. Her family discovered her whereabouts, and for several months the following situation existed: Her priest-counselor-lover played all three roles; her family tried to get her to come back; she tried to work herself to exhaustion. She drank heavily so she could sleep, since, from her point of view, her major problem was her inability to sleep.

One night Marie and her priest-lover absconded and flew to another state some two thousand miles away where they got married—but her alcoholism increased and her weight decreased. Finally her husband called in a physician who treated her with vitamins and tranquilizers. When released from the doctor's care, the same drinking pattern reestablished itself, and this time she was hospitalized. The same thing occurred once again, and it was following a second hospitalization that she was put into psychotherapy.

At the alcoholism clinic she was put on Antabuse® as well as tranquilizers. Her husband administered the medication. During the time seen at the clinic, she continued to lose weight, and at the time of immediate therapy she had lost another ten per cent of her weight and weighed seventy-eight pounds. The clinic physician was seriously considering hospitalizing her so she could get intravenous feeding, since she was obviously on her way to death by starvation. When asked about food she simply replied, "I am not hungry."

Because of her serious condition, group therapy did not seem indicated, and individual therapy was attempted, but nothing seemed to get through to this young woman, who seemed more dead than alive. Her weight during individual therapy kept decreasing. Finally, she was asked whether she would like to enter group therapy. She answered, "Whatever you say, doctor." The theory of group therapy and the concept of immediate therapy were explained, and she accepted the information without evidence that she understood.

During the group sessions she sat in a corner, did not participate unless asked a direct question, but sat head bowed for the most part in what might have looked to the casual observer as a deep depression. At this time she was on Antabuse and was not drinking, but her weight continued to drop.

At one session every member was asked to state his major problem. When it came to Marie's turn, she simply said, "I am married to a priest." She was then asked to bring up something for the next session for discussion or dramatization. When the following session arrived, she confessed that she had nothing to bring up. When asked what bothered her most she referred once again to her marriage.

At this point the idea of what followed came to the writer's mind. A bit of analysis of the therapist's thinking about the case may explain his behavior and also may explain the immediate therapy that followed.

Marie's history led me to the belief that her major "problem" was her high standards. Brought up in a strongly religious family, her sexual life was in direct contradiction to her standards. Her suicidal drinking seemed to be related to her divorce, giving up her baby, and her love affair and marriage. The type of drinking as well as her refusal to communicate openly seemed to be expressing this thought, "I am no good. I should not live." When she openly stated her problem was "I am married to a priest," I decided to attack the problem at this point. In the group was Pete, a Catholic, who also had a marital-religious problem. Divorced, he had remarried a Catholic woman. Both Pete and his second wife attended church services every week, but neither could partake of the sacraments. Pete's drinking was stated by him to be in reaction to his belief he would go to hell when he died.

The group was in existence about a year. Pete had been in the group about three months; Marie, about six weeks. Marie knew from observing prior sessions that the main subject of any session might produce rather strenuous activities. After she stated her problem, the following occurred:

THERAPIST. Pete, I'd like to ask you to play a role opposite Marie. I won't tell you what it is for a moment, but it will be very important and it could help Marie. Will you accept?

PETE. If it will help Marie, sure.

THERAPIST. O.K., now the rest of you—this is serious. This situation may really shake up Marie. Marie, are you ready? (*Her eyes opened; she stared at me, and I felt that we had made contact.*) Marie, you are going to die and you are going to have a talk with God. Pete will play God. (MARIE *nodded assent. I turned to* PETE.) Now, your part is simple. You heard what Marie's problem is. She will have died and she will be coming to heaven for your judgment. That is all. Marie, sit here (*I moved a chair close to* PETE) and begin. Pete, talk as you think God will. Begin.

(MARIE *sat down dutifully. The group was quiet as they saw her expression.*)

PETE. My daughter, you have finally come here to me. What shall I do with you?

MARIE. There is nothing you can do.

PETE. What do you mean, there is nothing I can do? I am God. I can do anything.

MARIE. You have to condemn me.

PETE. I *have* to? I don't have to do anything except what *I* want. (*At this moment we felt rather than saw* MARIE *stiffen as the scene became real. Her voice changed.*)

MARIE. I mean, Father, I committed the unforgivable sin. (*Her voice lowered to a whisper as she was confessing to God.*)

PETE. *I* decide what is forgivable and unforgivable. You have suffered very much on earth, my daughter. You have suffered too much. Your hell has been on earth.

MARIE. But I married a priest. I seduced a priest. I took a priest out of the church. I must go to hell.

PETE. You will not go to hell. What kind of a God do you think I am that I would damn to hell a person because she loved? It is hate that I condemn, not love. No, my child, you will not go to hell.

At this point Marie burst into tears and fell on her knees. Her sudden action caused a moment of shock in the group. I took her by the arm, and lifted her, her thin body racked with cries, and led her out of the therapy room to another office and closed the door on her.

An hour later the session ended, and the various members having left, I opened the door of the office and let her out. She did not look at me and in a dream-like state walked out.

When Marie appeared the next week, one of the women in the group burst into tears at her sight. After she recovered she explained that the sight of Marie was too much—seeing her smiling and cheerful. And indeed, there was a new Marie, radiant, smiling, confident, happy. The other member stated that she had not been able to get Marie out of her mind and that she had been afraid that Marie might kill herself. When Marie was asked to tell what effect the prior session had on her, her remarks went somewhat as follows:

"Well, I was kind of confused about what happened last week, but I remembered just one sentence, and this sentence just kept hollering and yelling in my brain. I couldn't get that sentence out of my brain and I finally realized that it was right and that I was wrong, and when I finally accepted it I was in peace. And my husband thinks that it is true, too."

"What was the sentence?"

"God told me—I mean Pete—that he would not send me to hell because I loved Mike. I realized that I didn't really sin. We love each other, and as God is a God of love He can not condemn me because of love. I realized that I was too hard on myself, that I wanted to be a saint and when I wasn't a saint I felt that everything was lost. Well, nothing is lost, and I was just a foolish, dramatic, hysterical girl. I feel fine now, my appetite is coming back, and I am sorry that I have been upsetting my husband. Maybe I wanted to punish him, too, just because he is a man just like my father and my brother, both of whom I didn't really like too much I suppose."

Marie's further behavior in the group was unremarkable. Her participation was good. She became one of the most lively, witty, and active members of the group. She gained weight, and she left the group about two months later—well over one hundred pounds in weight. Six months later Marie had increased her weight to one hundred and twenty pounds, was working, and stated that she had completely overcome her driking problem.

JIM. The case of Jim is an example of immediate therapy with the use of the behind-the-back technique.

I had conducted a seminar on group psychotherapy for the staff of a prison. Three of the prison's staff members (two psychologists and one psychiatrist) agreed each to obtain two patients, so that the ten of us could form an experimental therapy group. We agreed the patients should be fairly aggressive and intelligent. I was to lead the group for three consecutive sessions. Following this, each of the other members would lead the group for three sessions.

At the first session I decided to start with an illustration of behind-the-back technique and asked for a volunteer. There were six inmates in the group, all in their thirties. One, a Negro, volunteered.

"You just tell us all about yourself next session. We will give you twenty minutes to tell us all about yourself, and then we shall discuss you behind your back," were the instructions given to him.

But when we met the following week: no Jim! I found out that he was in solitary confinement. I was told he had become involved in an argument with a guard at the school where he served as an English teacher, and that he had refused to accept another assignment. I called the deputy warden, a man I did not know very well, who had put Jim in solitary. I demanded Jim's attendance in our group—stating that we were treating Jim and that he (the deputy warden) had no right to deny a prisoner treatment. Ten minutes later Jim appeared with two guards flanking him; the guards insisted on coming into the therapy room. The prison custom was that any man taken out of solitary had to be in the continuous observation of two guards. Again I was on the phone with the deputy warden, who then told the guards to permit the patient to be without guard in the therapy room and to wait outside.

A half hour behind schedule we began with my curt request to Jim to "tell everything about yourself." Instead, he began a long and involved story about his present predicament, which he recited with precision. His story, in his own words but condensed to its essentials, went somewhat as follows:

"I got into a beef (argument) at the school, and this hack (guard) pointed (accused) me, and next I know I am up before the deputy. He doesn't listen to me which is par for the course, since a con is always in the wrong, and he puts me in the bing (solitary confinement) for three days. When my time is up he wants to change my assignment from the school to mopping up floors, and I told the man (the deputy) that this was double jeopardy, and that I'd rather do the book (all his time) rather than go on the mop."

The recital of his current grievance took about five of his allotted twenty minutes. When asked to tell all about himself, Jim stated that he had nothing else to say. This was all that was on his mind. The injustice of it was too much. I informed him that he had twenty minutes and we would wait the remaining fifteen minutes in silence if necessary, but we would not go on until he had used all his allotted time. He then recited two incidents. In the first, he described going into a town in the southern part of the United States. A banner over the main street announced that a local amusement park was open and on the banner the words, "Negroes permitted, but not invited," appeared. The other incident concerned a southern sergeant who had called him a "nigra" in front of a group. Both of these incidents were told with long intervals of silence. Finally, the twenty minutes were up, and Jim was asked to turn his back to the group. When he had done so, I said something to this effect: "Men, this session could help Jim a great deal, but only if we are all able to speak our feelings without witholding. Jim has told about himself. Apparently he is quite upset by the fact that two guards are waiting outside as well as other things. Let us now, in rotation, begin our comments." Feeling rather certain that Jim's present situation and his stories of his feelings of persecution would elicit sympathetic responses, I was almost shocked to hear, among the various statements, the following:

"There are people I call Negroes and some I call colored people. Jim is the kind of person I call a nigger."

"Jim is the kind of Negro who is always feeling sorry for himself and he is looking for reasons to get angry with others."

"I have noticed him. He is an agitator, a communist, a troublemaker."

"I have no reason to defend the deputy, but by Christ, he did just what I would of done. What the hell does Jim think he is anyway?"

"He has damn sure got a complex. That is a fact. Thinks everybody is against him. He is against others."

"I don't know him too well, but the little I have seen of him doesn't impress me at all. He is just a crybaby, uses the fact he is colored to justify everything."

The general tenor of the remarks was more or less in this vein from the convicts, but the remarks by the free people were considerably more restrained. Jim was asked to come into the group again after we finished our comments. I read off my notes to him about what had been said. (Part of the technique is to make believe that the person being talked about is really not in the room. In this way significant elements can be restated.) After I had finished, Jim was asked to comment on what had been said about him behind-his-back while he was "out of the room."

In a very reasonable manner he responded to most of the comments and stated that white people just did not understand how Negroes felt, and that those present had been privileged to hear the truth, and he felt sorry for all those who just didn't know the truth. He stated that he was representative of Negroes in general, that the various statements that had been made about him were completely wrong, and that he just felt sorry for their prejudice and ignorance. After he had finished, the rest of the group got into a discussion about the validity of Jim's point of view. The other prisoners insisted Jim was not representative of Negroes and that his problem was his own distorted personality. Jim did not participate. The session ended. Jim was taken back to solitary confinement by the two guards.

The following week when I showed up at the prison, I was asked to go to the deputy warden's office. The deputy began, "What did you ever do to Jim?" I was about to defend my treatment when he continued, "I have never seen anything like it. I have been thirty years in this business and I was positive he'd do the rest of his time in solitary, but the next morning after you got him he apologized and said he would do whatever I told him. Well, he is now on the mop gang, singing and carrying on like he didn't have a care in the world. I never saw such a change in a man in my life. I have been observing him carefully and have asked the guards to report to me, and it's no act. He is a different man. It really is a miracle."

Later in the afternoon when the therapy group reassembled, Jim recapitulated what happened to him. His story went somewhat as follows:

"After I left the group last week I was somewhat amused by the stupidity of the inmates. They just didn't know the Negro mind and they didn't really understand me. The whole thing didn't bother me too much. The whole silly behind-the-back thing didn't mean too much. So I had my dinner, listened to the radio, and went to sleep. It was about four in the morning when I woke up, sitting bolt upright in my bed. Somebody in the group had called me a "nigger." I had taken an oath—understand a vow—to kill anybody who ever called me that. I sat up on the bed, and my blood ran cold, and I felt I had to bust out immediately. My head was spinning and I thought I was dying. I tried to sleep, but I couldn't. Something was bugging me and I didn't know what it was. It wasn't what the fellows had called me. It was something else, like there was some monstrous truth that I couldn't accept. I felt like throwing up; sweat was pouring out of me, and then finally it came. You know what it was. Something one of you said. *It was not that you were prejudiced against me; I was prejudiced against you.* I had hatred in my heart for you. I suddenly realized that the deputy was right and that I was wrong. I suddenly realized that I had been operating with a great big black hard on against all whites, that I attributed all my problems to them. I knew a lot of them were prejudiced against Negroes, but I was prejudiced against whites. I saw the stupidity of my behavior. I realized I had been operating on the basis of a lot of false attitudes and so I accepted the whole mess and went to sleep. In the morning I apologized to the deputy and am now on the mop."

I happened to make a call several years later at that prison and found he had been promoted to the best job in the institution—running the telephone. In a little chat I asked him about the meaning of that session and he insisted that he had changed completely and that he had seen others with the same kinds of problems, but had been unable to convince them of their mistakes. Discussing him with several other people, including the deputy, brought forth the comments that he had been operating in a very satisfactory manner and that he was well liked by white and colored inmates and had earned this important job.

In this case, Jim did not show any climax of upset in the group but it did occur, some twelve hours later while he was asleep. The common and familiar symptoms of immediate therapy appeared: tension, inability to sleep, anger with self. This state changed when he finally found his answer. When he realized that he too was prejudiced he relaxed, went to sleep, and changed his behavior.

SUMMARY

Immediate therapy refers to a conversion-type phenomenon in which an individual, following a confrontation experience arranged by a therapist, undergoes a period of distress, but comes out of the situation with a new understanding of himself and the world, leading to changes in emotional tone and in behavior.

To produce such rapid ameliorative changes in behavior is quite difficult, and depends on the art of the therapist, but in general the following conditions are required: The patient must understand the whole process; he is to be understood in depth, that is to say, his history must be known and his general mode of dealing with life must be understood. When the period of therapy approaches, the patient must make a commitment to expose himself to the group in some manner, thus building anxiety. The situation employed depends on the suggestions made by the patient and the ingenuity of the therapist. A crisis-type, self-confrontation type of scene is developed, and when the patient appears to be upset, he is sent out of the therapy room to work out his own solution.

People who go through a confrontation experience, such as provided by the method of therapeutic role-playing (Corsini, 1965; Moreno, 1955) or by the behind-the-back technique (Corsini, 1953), but not exclusively by these methods, tend to demonstrate well-organized *new* personalities, *e.g.,* well thought-out cognitive systems, appropriate emotions, and successful behavior patterns. It is assumed that their prior personality was a fiction which could be discarded and that another personality is waiting in the wings, as it were, to take over.

My experience with attempts to induce immediate therapy is that it will occur in perhaps one out of three tries and that, like hypnosis, if the first attempt does not work, a second one may. Patients will fight attempts to achieve immediate therapy, and an approach-avoidance gradient will be found. The therapist who attempts to use this system must operate with much confidence, and must be steadfast in his lines of attack, but at the same time must be sympathetic but not directive.

To the best of my knowledge, no one else has reported using confrontation techniques with the intention of obtaining rapid personality changes. While the whole topic is inchoate as yet, it promises some hope for an inexpensive and simple method of attaining long-lasting, positive personality changes.

REFERENCES

Corsini, R. J.: Criminal conversion. *J. Clin. Psychopathol.*, 7: 139-146, 1945.

Corsini, R. J.: The method of psychodrama in prison. *Group Psychotherapy*, 3: 321-326, 1951. (a)

Corsini, R. J.: On the theory of change resulting from group therapy. *Group Psychotherapy*, 4: 179-180, 1951 (b)

Corsini, R. J.: Psychodramatic treatment of a pedophile. *Group Psychotherapy*, 4: 166-171, 1951. (c)

Corsini, R. J.: Immediate therapy. *Group Psychotherapy*, 4: 322-330, 1952.

Corsini, R. J.: The behind-the-back technique in group psychotherapy. *Group Psychotherapy*, 6: 102-109, 1953.

Corsini, R. J.: *Methods of Group Psychotherapy.* Chicago, James, 1957.

Corsini, R. J.: *Roleplaying in Psychotherapy.* Chicago, Aldine, 1965.

DREIKURS, R.: The psychological interview in medicine. *Indian Psychology,*
5: 59-71, 1963.

ELLIS, A.: *Reason and Emotion in Psychotherapy.* New York, Stuart, Lyle,
1963.

MORENO, J. L.: *Who Shall Survive?* New York, Beacon, 1955.

MOSAK, H. H.: Early recollections as a projective technique. *J. Project.
Techn.,* 22: 302-311, 1958.

MUNROE, RUTH: *Schools of Psychoanalytic Theory.* New York, Dryden,
1955.

III

MARATHON GROUP THERAPY

FREDERICK H. STOLLER

B Y rearranging important dimensions of the therapy group, the marathon approach has made a major breakthrough in altering the quality of the psychotherapeutic experience. Practitioners rarely appreciate all that is being conveyed by their way of conducting their practice and clients are rarely aware of alternatives. Therefore, few are able to testify what it is to have treatment given in carefully prearranged dosages designed to affect people in a limited way at a given time. What would happen if clients were given treatment in one massive dose? Since psychotherapists are giving interpersonal experiences rather than medication, the analogy with overdosage is really more semantic than actual. It is more accurate to differentiate between the effect of repeated warming and cooling as opposed to being placed in a pressure cooker. What actually happens to people under these two arrangements raises vital questions for those who profess to act as change agents.

Time is one of the basic dimensions of psychotherapeutic practice. The traditional temporal arrangements are largely a matter of customary procedure, often designed more for the convenience of therapists and institutions than for their maximum effectiveness. Marathon group therapy represents a basic challenge to conventional arrangements of time, in that its fundamental characteristic is that of the continuous session ranging over one or more days. Regularly scheduled meetings of one or two hours duration, stretching over many months or even years, have been customary.

The implications of the two basic approaches to people imply different views of man. Consideration of what is involved forces us to look at many features of the treatment model which are rarely considered. Questions arise as to what is actually taught within the therapeutic situation.

Entering a brief intensive therapeutic structure, such as the marathon, involves a very special set of expectations, constitutes a markedly unique experience, and calls upon distinct resources in the participant and group leader. Phenomena occur within the marathon which are rarely found in conventional treatment groups. Above all, its effects are often not predicted by current thinking about the development of change in people. Most exciting, it opens up new ways of conceptualizing the production of continuing growth in contrast to the heavy emphasis upon disability which has predominated.

THE ORIGINS OF THE MARATHON APPROACH

An appreciation of the position of marathon therapy among current conceptual developments is best obtained through an account of its early history. It will become apparent that the contributions of many are combined in varying degrees and that a variety of concepts are involved. Most important is the willingness to abandon a number of long-standing practices which have stood unchallenged in the therapeutic field.

In the summer of 1963, the author and a colleague, Dr. Ronald C. Waller, attended a sensitivity training laboratory conducted by Professor George F. Lehner of the University of California at Los Angeles. The participants were professionals and business executives and the session lasted from Thursday evening to Sunday afternoon. Within this time period, individual sessions ran for about three hours interspersed with breaks for meals and relaxation. Not only was this experience of tremendous personal value for those participating, but the psychologists immediately recognized that a number of important principles were involved which had implications for the mental-health area.

Continuous involvement without interruption was felt to be of prime importance leading to consequences different from intermittent routinized sessions. The powerful impact of an experience which emphasized intimacy and face-to-face encounter rather than emphasizing either the exploration or explanation of pathology led to unexpected possibilities of growth and change. In addition, it was recognized that a self-involving experience has considerable potential in any walk of life and for a wide range of life patterns.

Immediately, the technique was adapted to the population of the mental hospital where both psychologists were staff members. Dr. Waller worked with disturbed adolescents and the author met with chronic adult patients in continuous sessions that lasted two or three days. The results were very encouraging. A cooperative organization of group leaders was established with three other workers who had undergone similar sessions with Dr. Lehner.* In collaboration, an approach to group therapy was developed which was given the name of accelerated interaction (Stoller, 1966). The procedure was utilized, not only in a mental hospital setting, but in outpatient, private-practice situations utilizing weekends for the group meetings. Following closely its application to these settings the same approach was utilized with drug addicts, school dropouts, and staff development.

Early in the development of this innovation the author met with George R. Bach and told him what was being done. Dr. Bach immediately recognized the potential of continuous meetings—he had tried weekend retreats previously in which sessions were interspersed with recreational activities. These were not as successful as he had wished and he felt that introducing activities of a different order than group exploration might have dissipated what he had been seeking.

A number of marathon weekends were organized in which Dr. Bach and the author were co-therapists and these were enormously successful. Both Dr. Bach and the author have subsequently conducted over a hundred sessions. Out of this cumulation of experience, the conceptual framework of this approach has matured. Many therapists, particularly in southern California, have adapted this method.

---

* Other members of this circle, sharing in the developments of early concepts and fostering numerous innovative ideas, were Roger Wickland, Andrew Morrison, and George Lokie. Early products of their collaboration were reported by Wickland, Waller, and Stoller (1963) and Stoller, Lokie, Morrison, Waller, and Wickland (1964).

The major practitioners of this approach share most of the basic underlying assumptions. However, there are variations, both in ideas and practice,* as well as emphases which are individual. Because of the special importance of personal involvement on the part of the group leader, individual style takes on a heightened significance. The values, personal preferences, and especially the view of life and the world which are part of the group leader's individual system, color the proceedings of a marathon group: a marathon experience is qualitatively different because of the presence of a particular group leader. It is felt that such idiosyncrasies should be valued and utilized in the marathon to their fullest extent rather than diminished; the intensive group is much more a personal experience than a treatment.

Despite stylistic variations, there are important underlying principles within which marathon leaders operate and which appear to determine group development. These principles and concepts will be fully discussed, but the emphasis upon particular points represents, to a considerable degree, the author's personal style and framework. In order to appropriately discuss the concepts and assumptions inherent in marathon therapy, it is necessary to explore the organization of a typical marathon group.

THE ORGANIZATION OF A MARATHON GROUP

Setting

The most important consideration for arranging a marathon group is that of providing a substantial amount of time for continuous contact. Within this limitation there are numerous variations depending upon situation contingencies. Thus, the requirements of an institutional setting may have different demands than those of private practice. Given some flexibility on the part of an institution, one can adapt the marathon requirements to most circumstances. Marathons have been held in extremely bleak settings such as an abandoned prison dormitory as well as very luxu-

---

* Dr. Bach originated the term *marathon therapy* for the continuous, brief group, and it has become the generic term for it. Accelerated Interaction has as one of its major features a strict time limit (Stoller, 1966) and therefore should be considered to be a special application of the marathon approach.

rious resorts. The power of group involvement is such that it transcends minimal physical comfort and less than benign surroundings. All other things being equal, however, it is preferable to spend the many hours together comfortably with sufficient privacy to remain undisturbed by external interference.

Given a choice of settings, a private residence is preferable. Offices, no matter how well equipped, do not set the most appropriate tone. One of the major goals of a marathon is to create an intimate group in which all the participants, including the group leader, are as straightforward as possible. It is important that the approach of one human to another predominates over the roles of professional to client. The author prefers to hold as many sessions as he can in his home with his wife participating. Here the author feels he can be most open about himself and hide least behind the role of the professional therapist. It is as if he is saying, "This is where and how I live and this is how I cope with my family." An invitation is extended which is impossible under any other arrangements: "I would like you to share in an important aspect of my life as you are asking me to share in an important aspect of yours." Finally, the continued growth and renewed intimacy for the writer and his family reflect the mutuality which is an inherent part of the marathon group.

Marathon groups always have a definite starting and ending time. A preferred session begins at 8 P.M. Friday evening and ends at 6 P.M. Sunday. On the first evening the group will generally run until 2 A.M. It will reassemble at 10 A.M. Saturday morning and continue until 1 or 2 A.M. Sunday, reassembling at 10 A.M.* It is important that the group does not separate for meals but eat together, often continuing the session through a buffet serving. It is essential that meals be served by a nonparticipant to avoid withdrawal of a member, thereby diluting involvement.

---

* Groups which run continuously for twenty-four hours or more are preferred by Bach. The present arrangement permits people to separate for a few hours sleep during which important developments, initiated during the session itself, may continue within the individual participants. On the other hand, the continuous session builds up an unrelenting pressure. The author has conducted both types of sessions and feels that they are both equally effective. The choice will be made in terms of situational demands and stylistic preferences.

Contract

When someone makes a reservation for a group he is notified of all the relevant details: the fee, the dates, the time the session will begin, and the time it will end. As much as possible, the specific terms of the contract are made known to the participant to establish a tone of openness and honesty. The details are repeated in letters sent to the group members in which official notification of the session is given and their reservation is confirmed.

Ground Rules

The ground rules for a marathon are explicit. Remaining with the group is the major one; however, a group member may walk around, go to the bathroom, engage in some exercises in an adjoining room, or stretch on the floor while the session continues. Attempts to leave the group are considered violations of the basic ground rule, and is a breach of the commitment the participant made when he entered the session. In actuality, such violations are remarkably rare; when they do occur they invariably involve the individual's characteristic way of dealing with crises.

Other ground rules involve the style and content of interaction and are designed to define what is being attempted. Every group member is responsible for expressing his personal reactions to every other member as honestly and directly as he can. Understanding or having insight into others is less valued than the immediate mirroring of the impact others have on oneself. Therapeutic techniques with their routinized qualities are, for the most part, ruled out. Thus, psychodramatic role playing (Moreno, 1946) or game analysis (Berne, 1961), which may have considerable value in other settings, are discouraged as diluting the authentic encounter. Each individual is responsible for gaining and maintaining the attention of the group. In this sense, the group is not expected to develop an atmosphere of "fairness," but rather to reflect the world as it actually exists. Therefore, when a participant insists on engaging in long, detailed explanations for his conduct, the group may react by moving to another participant. It is the group's responsibility to explain its reaction and subsequent action, but the burden of altering this response rests with the individual. Psychological or psychiatric jargon of any school is ruled out because it constitutes a barrier to meaningful communication which reduces intimacy between people. Subgrouping also violates the ground rules: any comment worth making during the group should be for the entire group's benefit rather than for one or two individuals.

Leader's Responsibilities

As the group begins, the group leader repeats the details of the time arrangements, spells out the ground rules, and briefly states the goals and aims of the session. When everyone understands these details, the session begins. Warm-up routines, designed to avoid the awkwardness and pain of starting, are not utilized.

The group leader's position should be made clear and unmistakable. Although he interposes his own feelings and reactions as a group member as freely as possible, he is definitely the leader in setting the tone and making important decisions such as when to break, eat, and the like. The final termination time has been predetermined, but the group leader will announce the end of the session. Although considerable stress has been placed on the clarity of his leadership role, the group leader does not actually have to rule with a heavy hand. Most of these decisions develop out of the natural ebb and flow of the group movement, and a well-conducted group never feels it has been handled or manipulated in an arbitrary fashion.

Follow-up Sessions

Follow-up sessions are often included as part of a marathon group. How many will occur and when they will take place varies with the group leaders, but in all cases these will be part of the preliminary arrangements made when the group is first organized. The author prefers to have one follow-up session approximately six weeks following the marathon weekend. The follow-up will consist of an evening meeting. The specific date for the follow-up will be arranged with the group immediately after the close of the weekend session.

INDIVIDUAL PARTICIPATION IN THE MARATHON

In order to appropriately discuss the assumptions and theoretical contributions involved in the marathon approach, some comprehension of what occurs in a brief, intensive group must be gained. This section and the following are therefore included as appropriate background.

Within the boundaries of a marathon group a complex series of events take place. To an observer, it is fairly clear that changes occur in the conduct of individual participants. Any attempt to organize this crowded scene is essentially a falsification, to a degree, of what actually occurs. A special quality of the marathon is that participants enter a situation in which the unexpected awaits them: the group leader initiates a drama in which specific events cannot be predicted. Nevertheless, the broad outlines of the marathon have a repetitive quality which indicates that there are comprehensible processes in operation. The development of a marathon, both for the individual and for the group as a whole, can be described in a number of ways. One meaningful approach is in terms of the crises a participant faces within the marathon and their resolution.

Realizing that one of the central themes of a marathon group is the honest reaction of others to one's self-presentation, most participants are faced with a dilemma at the outset, *i.e.* how to give a good account of themselves. The earliest phase for each individual can be considered his introduction to the rest of the group, his initial revealing to others of aspects of himself, his life, and his current predicament. There is often an almost ritualistic quality to a participant's opening self-display, "I am here because. . . ." It is invariable that an individual will state a problem (or series of problems) which he considers to be most urgent in his current life situation. For the most part, such problems are presented as discrete segments of the person's life which have an entity separate from his own being. Such statements may take the form of complaints about loneliness, about a miserable marriage or a series of unhappy alliances, the inability to attain any joy or satisfaction in life, problems at work, or feelings of meaninglessness or depression. They can generally be reformulated succinctly, *i.e.* there is a part of an individual's life which he would like to be different from the way it appears to be.

Reactions to such self-presentations are usually different from those which the group member would like to receive and they present him with his first crisis within the marathon. Instead of an appreciation of his circumstances, the other group members are more likely to respond to his posture and to his person. The style with which he displays himself elicits feelings on the part of the others which, under the marathon ground rules, are stated explicitly and directly. His "problem" receives less attention than his manner of avoiding himself and concentrating on external aspects of his life. For some, the group may deal with their over-organized or over-rationalized way of talking about themselves. Rather than giving concrete solutions to predicaments, fellow participants may discuss the morass of confusing details expressed and find importance in the reluctance to share oneself in a meaningfully concrete manner. Still others may be confronted with the feelings they arouse: distrust, anger, or more disturbing, disinterest or boredom.

Thus, the most immediate crisis with which the individual has to deal in the marathon situation is the discrepancy between his perception of his situation and the response to his personal way of moving through the world. In order to reconcile such disparate emphases, he must either reject the view of others or force himself to look more closely at his own conduct. Where the participant's group involvement continuously grows in intensity and where each group member engages in reactions and responses similar to those he receives, rejection of consensus is an almost impossible posture to sustain indefinitely. At the same time it is equally impossible to feel completely understood by those who have reacted in such a discrepant fashion. No one can emerge from such a confrontation feeling that he has shown all there is to show of himself.

One of the most important features of a marathon group is that contact does not terminate following an individual's turn as the focus of the group. Immediately following his own attempt at self-justification and adjustment to unexpected responses on the part of others, a participant is frequently involved in another member's struggle with confused self-presentation. Even where he does not overtly respond, he is touched by the predicaments of others in situations very similar to his own. Not only do the quandaries of other group members reflect his own, but he can begin to sense in his own feelings the reactions that formal self-justification tends to arouse.

The initial crisis is not necessarily resolved, but subsequent experiences in the group begin to alter the group member's psychological state. Seemingly, no matter where they begin, whatever their overt situation or position in the world, regardless of the intellectual or material resources at their disposal, people face reactions to themselves which are incongruent with statements about their situations. Being repeatedly exposed to such infinite variations of personal crises cannot help but contribute to a cumulative effect upon the individual which begins to alter his perception of himself and the world.

A marathon participant is not a passive observer. He is an active reactor, becoming ever more adept at "reading" his own responses and bolder in stating them more directly with less fear of the consequences. Rejection in the marathon group is more likely to come from holding back and not carrying one's load of the contribution. But honest responsivity makes one a valuable member of the group, broadening the experience for all. By becoming increasingly more outspoken in his reactions, the individual becomes more aware of what is involved in his own relations with other people and deepens and changes the links he has with the others.

The second personal crisis for an individual participant develops when the group focus returns to him. It is now his turn to talk about himself once again. However, this time the relationship between himself and the others had changed considerably. Group response is now based not only upon the manner in which he presents himself, but also upon his contributions to the group members. He is seen not only in terms of his presented "problem" but also in terms of how he has dealt with others. The specific sets of feelings he has aroused in other individuals, the varying relationships he has established, enter into his current transactions. There are sides of himself of which he is now aware which he had previously neglected or which he had not had the opportunity to display in his initial self-presentation.

In talking about oneself under such circumstances, the individual is likely to be more thoughtful and less glib. He is now more concrete and specific and will deal with his internal conflicts less hesitatingly than when he had formerly stated his situation. In other words, he will move the focus of his concern more closely toward himself in contrast to the former more exclusive concentration upon external demands and situations. In the process of entering this type of dialogue, he will address himself to individual group members more directly. While he is still relating to the group as a whole it is less of an undifferentiated entity and is now composed of people who have become more individuated with an assortment of unique characteristics, attitudes, values, and stances toward the world.

By addressing himself to individual group members, the participant will often find himself in personal conflict. A personal crisis rises as others may respond to him with anger for particular interactions he had initiated. They may express puzzlement at his inconsistencies. His resources may be appreciated, contradicting the impoverished and powerless picture he paints of himself and his life. Others receive disgust at the repetitive quality with which they see themselves—the world for them has only one tone. Often, fellow participants sense a resemblance between the individual under consideration and other group members, sometimes themselves. The individual in focus may have contributed to the personification of the other group member with whom he is compared.

In any case, it is the person himself who is now under scrutiny, who receives a response which is somewhat unexpected. It is his way of dealing with others, of moving through the world, of sharing or holding back, or permitting himself intimate responses to individuals or his tendency to categorize people in terms of some outward quality. His range of responses, the flexibility with which he can shift under specific circumstances, and his capacity for engaging people on a variety of levels now form the basis for the reaction he is receiving. The disturbing nature of these responses may lie in the explicit manner in which they are expressed, rather than in their complete novelty; people often remark that they had been told similar things about themselves but never with the force and pointedness and with the emotional involvement of the current situation. Therefore, the individual is face-to-face with personal reactions which he can neither ignore nor evade. To a considerable degree he is forced to recognize that he has earned the feedback he is now receiving through his overall course within the marathon.

Regardless of the appropriateness of the personal challenge he is now confronting, it is only natural for the group member to react with injury and chagrin. He will attempt to retreat into silence or impersonal encounter, to reestablish the predominantly role-playing format with which he entered the group situation. He will often attempt to form an alliance with another group member and form a subgroup which will protect him from the onslaught with which he has to deal. Some form of protective maneuver is invariably resorted to, depending upon the typical style that is characteristic of him. However, under the marathon situation, particularly at this phase, the personal crisis will neither resolve itself nor dissipate through withdrawal or retreat. Literally, there is nowhere to go. If an individual is going to violate the basic ground rule and physically remove himself from the group, it is at this point that it will most probably occur.

The major characteristic of the marathon, its continuity of contact, effects the resolution of the personal crisis. Not only does the individual participant experience the personal crises of other members but he will also take an active role in precipitating them. At the same time that he is the recipient of personal reactions, he is engaging in similar responses himself. He begins to engage others in ways that are unlike his original manner of approaching people. His increasing boldness and honesty and his heightened empathy represent alternative ways of using himself, of digging deeper into his potential for intimacy. The accumulation of feelings which are invested in the other group members reaches a level which permits him to react with such openness that his former level of inhibition becomes increasingly apparent to himself. Because he begins exhibiting a much richer and fuller range of interpersonal responsiveness, the reactions which he, in turn, elicits from others begin to undergo a profound change. It is in this alteration that the resolution of the personal crisis can occur.

The final phase of the marathon for the individual participant is characterized by a readiness to respond differently from the way he had been aware of doing previously. He literally changes his behavior, exhibits different facets of himself, and in doing so, alters what occurs between himself and other people. The other group members now exhibit much more supportive and affirmative reactions; the personal crisis is no longer a pertinent factor. However, the responses he now receives are not necessarily the kinds of personal comments for which he was formerly searching. He, as well as others, is no longer primarily concerned with the solution to external "problems" nor in maintaining a particular front before others. They tell him things about himself which he now realizes he has a hunger to hear. Internal reactions of concern about the feelings of others and the effect of others upon his personal conduct are no longer warded off in the same manner as when he entered the marathon. His early approach to the group members now seems distant and foreign, belonging to another realm of behavior to which he is no longer as deeply committed.

The homestretch of a marathon group involves the individual participant in feelings of elation and excitement. He finds that intimate involvement with others and mutual concern can be a joy far exceeding situations in which deliberate attempts are made to create a light interpersonal flavor. Not only does he have a new sense of his capabilities and the possibilities of engaging in more satisfactory relationships, but he has attained a feeling of mutual accomplishment. Some of these feelings may well have their origin in relief over having emerged from an intense experience relatively unscathed. However, the predominant tone is a genuine friendship he feels toward the other members of the group. Whatever their origin, his elated emotions constitute a unique experience which he will always wish to recapture.

A group member summed up this feeling: "Immediately afterwards I felt great, very elated, energetic, and just happy. It seemed like I had a series of insights about my whole behavior. I was freer and more confident . . . other people at work noticed I was friendlier, but simply thought I 'warmed up' over time. And I do, but not that much. I just really began to enjoy not only my work, but the contacts with people."

Behavior has changed, and with it, a different response. The group member is now in a position to move through the world differently—with less fear of closeness and interdependence. He is now in a position to earn a different fate.

GROUP DEVELOPMENT IN THE MARATHON

The group development in the marathon is based upon cumulative individual experiences and follows a similar outline. What has just been described in terms of the individual participant, however, does not occur at the same time for different people. Some jump into the arena immediately and move swiftly through the various phases; others hold back and require the pull of the group to a greater extent. Resolution of crises is more difficult for some than for others. The precise way in which each individual member will move into his crises and the manner with which he will work them through is subject to infinite variations. However, the group undergoes phases which are quite orderly and predictable. When a sufficient number of individuals have moved from one phase to another, the tone of the group undergoes a decided change which, in turn, acts to pull the other members in a particular direction.

The early phase of the marathon is characterized by almost static and formalized styles of relating. Members tend to be given their "turn" and there is a concern with the individual's "story," his account of himself and particularly of his "problem." Members who have had psychotherapy previously often attempt to set the tone of the group through the conventional analyses and terminology of the psychologically sophisticated. This manner of entering a prolonged group experience tends to be exhausting and will often diminish even without counter-attempts on the part of the group leader. Receiving responses through a series of formulae, no matter how apt, tends to be exasperating when continued too long.

The second phase of the marathon involves a considerable amount of personal sharing. Rather than concentrating interest on matters external to the group, the behavior within the group becomes the main interest. Though important relationships that are not directly within the group itself are not ignored, the group relationships take on more meaning and immediacy. Clashes between individuals are more likely to occur as the general formality dissolves. Along with heated emotional storms, often alarming to those involved, humor emerges as a binding force rather than merely as a distancing maneuver as is so frequently the case. Each group develops private jokes which suggest the ludicrousness of the stances they attempt to sustain. Responsivity quickens while deadlocks become more serious.

As happens in most groups, there is much ebb and flow. Tension builds up as crises and logjams occur followed by a tendency to move into less loaded areas. However, the distance between moments of high tension tends to diminish as the group involvement deepens, so that, in the latter part of the session, crises sometimes follow one another in breathtaking succession.

The final phase of the marathon group has two major characteristics: urgency and elation. As the end of the session draws near, there is a growing realization on everyone's part (including the group leader) that there is only a limited time available to accomplish what is desired. As a consequence, the tempo of the group quickens: participants are able to respond more quickly and are willing to engage in more powerful struggles, both with themselves and with others. Bold forms of interaction which rarely take place under any other circumstance occur within this phase. A group member or the leader may challenge another participant in a fashion that would be considered too direct at any other time. In the final phase of the marathon, these confrontations will have positive consequences which surprise everyone, especially the one who initiated them. Sensing the limited time available, individuals tend to reduce their use of rationalizations and excuses.

As contradictory as it might seem, the final phase of the marathon not only has an urgency connected with it but an overall feeling of relaxation and informality. The very physical postures which people exhibit are more varied, suggestive of their lowered defensiveness and increased openness. This reflects the greater readiness to exhibit aspects of themselves which were formerly hidden and an inclination to reach out spontaneously which is rarely attained in our culture. Such a tendency is reflected in the outflow of enthusiasm and friendliness which occurs following the formal end of the session; people generally want to remain together in informal exchanges. During this phase, the participants are likely to express feelings of tremendous positiveness which would have formerly embarrassed them.

A final characteristic of this phase is found at the close of the session. As indicated earlier, a specific time has been set for termination. One of the more surprising phenomenon is the regularity with which a sense of closure is achieved at this point. In the words of one participant, "It seems just right. One moment more or less would have been either too much or too little." The author has often been struck by the elegance of such regularity.

A reaction to a group experience is most eloquently stated by a seventeen-year-old Negro youth from Mississippi: "The session to me is wonderful. It seemed to get you out of that fake shield that you been hiding behind practically all of your life, and man I must say it hurts at the moment when you are just about to break out of it, but after its all over you really feel good. . . . At times you really can get hung up in the session and then just at the right moment something happens and either hangs you up more or unhangs you. I've never known what love was until I went through a session. . . . Many nights I lay in my bed and think about myself being a priest and suddenly here comes some person screaming and crying for help and mercy and I feel pleased at knowing what to at least say to sort of calm them down and I say to myself 'Thanks to the session.' "*

THE BASIC ASSUMPTIONS OF THE MARATHON

The marathon approach was not originally developed from carefully predetermined theoretical principles. There are, however, built into it a number of assumptions concerning change and growth. Through accumulated experience and observation, a conception of the various forces at work has been emerging. It is

---

* The session referred to was conducted by a gifted young student based upon his own marathon experience. The Mississippi group has such profound implications for the flowering of potential in groups that have been the object of long-term prejudice and submission that it deserves a telling in its own right.

valuable to look at the principles which seem to be operating, both for their acknowledgement of human interdependence and for the illumination shed upon the effecting of interpersonal change.

The Massing of Tension and Involvement

Rearranging individual sessions into one prolonged unit produces effects which require consideration. The development of levels of tension and involvement represent an extremely important consequence. Under conventional practice, where intermittent sessions lasting an hour or two are spaced over a long, indefinite period of time, group involvement characteristically rises and falls. Every session has its warm-up period; the group takes time to get down to business. As the session progresses, the group members become increasingly involved and the particular struggle within that session creates tension among the participants. In a typical session, the tension rises to a peak just before its close. When the group reassembles, the tension and involvement have dissipated to a considerable degree and must be built up once again. Although there is a progressive growth in interpersonal involvement and commitment to the group's work, the rate of growth is limited by losses between sessions. Length of treatment may be, in part, a function of such inefficiency.

When the session is prolonged sufficiently, tension and involvement build up continuously and are maintained at an extremely high level throughout the life of the group. Very high intensity is frequently reached, but the increasing investment the group members have in one another permits people to tolerate a surprising amount of tension. Much of what can be considered an asset to the therapeutic process becomes intensified through prolonged sessions. Interaction becomes more specific and pointed as individuals develop the capacity for greater honesty and directness in their emotional interchanges. Greater intimacy has the effect of diminishing the need for defensive maneuver. Reduction in the loss of time concerned with warm-up periods means that more can be accomplished within the same number of hours.

While a high level of tension is of tremendous importance in sustaining effort and motivation, the essential contribution of involvement should not be underestimated. As the group remains together over many hours, the rest of the world seems to recede and the group members become very important to each other. They become concerned about each other's opinions; people attend, perhaps for the first time, to what they are conveying to others. Movement and gains far exceed what could be accomplished in a comparative number of hours under traditional arrangements.

A participant states it as follows: "Even in the first few hours, I could tell what was happening was going to be very different from the daily group I have been going to. This was the first time I felt that anyone has gotten to know me well enough to tell me more about myself than I already knew. I think everyone in the group got to know each other in a way that is impossible in normal day-to-day living and in the daily group. For myself, I found I have been giving other people an impression I don't like to give."

Development of a Group Career

Continuity of contact has another value of immediate importance. The reactions which an individual elicits within the group become the consequence of his own way of moving through that group. Both the other group members and, subsequently, the individual concerned come to realize that one's fate, one's career in the world, is the consequence of one's conduct and what it draws from the world. Most people can appreciate such a cause and effect from an intellectual standpoint. But being struck by their own concrete behavior is another story. In addition to the self-deception that everyone adopts as a ubiquitous characteristic, another quality of life contributes to the difficulty in being able to appreciate one's own contribution to one's own fate in a way that is useful. For the most part, the specific aspects of an individual's behavior, and the accumulated responses it gathers, are far removed in time. Not only are we limited in how we read our own responses, but our reactions are rarely verbalized under ordinary circumstances. The connection between these rarely can be made definitely and, in particular, the accumulated effects of such veiled reactions become almost impossible to specify. Thus, a specific interaction is not necessarily completely rooted in what has just transpired but has its origins, to a considerable degree, in what has taken place between the two people over a period of time.

When time is compressed as it is in the marathon, the consequences of one's behavior are placed in greater contiguity to the behavior itself. Both the individual and the others with whom he is involved have the opportunity to specify why he invites his particular fate. The assumption is made that the marathon group represents a sample of the world, and one's behavior within the group represents a sample of one's behavior in the world. The manner in which a person enters the group, his way of dealing with the others, elicits a set of responses from the very beginning which accumulate as the hours pile up and as he engages in interaction after interaction. It becomes crystal clear to the individual that he invites what happens to him, particularly when he is able to see others become involved in the same process. It becomes increasingly apparent that the responsibility lies with him and this is reflected in the diminishment of his turning outward for the sources of his dissatisfaction. He may realize that he is capable of achieving a much more satisfactory career for himself and decide to enrich his life through deliberate change. His view of himself and his world has undergone a considerable change with the realization of his own responsibility and the importance of his actions in distinction to his intentions.

The Primacy of Experience Over Treatment

It is important to understand that the marathon participant looks at his own behavior through the reactions of others *in situ*. Much of what takes place in most therapy situations involves considerable discussion of behavior external to the group. Events are frequently talked about rather than experienced firsthand by the group members. Marathons generally begin with a heavy reliance on this type of material, but events outside the group recede in importance as the reservoir of experiences shared by all the participants builds up. Increasingly, such group events contribute to the feedback which the participants are able to provide for each other.

Life situations which are talked about rather than experienced firsthand always run the risk of being dealt with in intellectualized fashion. Even though such events may have considerable importance for the individual with whom they are concerned, they become diluted in the reconstruction. Even within the marathon group itself, there will be an occasional attempt to reconstruct an event which occurred several hours earlier. Anyone who has attempted this can attest to the difficulty with which accuracy and agreement can be reached. Where such accuracy is possible, one is struck by the stilted quality such historical reconstructions (even though of very recent history) have for people who are involved in ongoing behavior. Invariably, such archeology is quickly abandoned as the lack of relevance to the current situation becomes apparent.

Because of the crowded series of events and the heavy investment in attending to these events, becoming involved in an intensive group has much more the characteristics of undergoing a profound experience than being the recipient of treatment. Technique, interpretations, and therapeutic maneuvers pale into insignificance beside the tremendous experience that a marathon group can become. No one who undergoes such an intense series of events and involvements can emerge quite the same as when he entered. Much happens which cannot be deliberately planned or effected by a therapist; many of the things that affect a participant are not necessarily specified within the situation nor do they become evident at the time. Much of significance that occurs to a group member becomes apparent only after events subsequent to the marathon accumulate. It is as if the internal structure of a participant, the way in which he organizes his perceptions of himself and the world and the manner in which he tends to conduct himself, becomes stirred up as he is involved in a complex experience. The elation which frequently occurs at the end of a marathon and which lasts for a week or so, may well be, in part, a reflection of this sudden change. When the internal structure settles down once again, it is never exactly the same as it was originally.

The significance of becoming a participant with others in a growth-inducing experience is profound. Entering the patient role involves a shift in responsibility for a practitioner. According to Haley (1963), the therapist always defines the situation and much that goes on is at his option. Although the therapist gains initial strength from establishing the rules, much effort must ultimately go toward counteracting the dependency this fosters. When someone places himself in the hands of another with the implication that this practitioner posesses superior knowledge about his behavior and has access to techniques to which he will submit himself, he does not necessarily expand his awareness of his own capacities. Entering a situation with other participants in which he involves himself in mutual give and take and which concentrates upon his own conduct within the situation itself, puts the individual into a different relationship.

The group leader plays an extremely important role in the marathon and this will be dealt with in more detail in a subsequent section. However, it should be noted that, in the marathon situation, the group leader deliberately avoids gathering case history material. Instead of arming himself with privileged information about the individual, often of a one-sided and distorted nature as suggested by Goffman (1961), the group leader builds up his impressions of the participants as he encounters them within the marathon situation. Benefits of the marathon are maximized when the group leader shares the total impact of a participant along with everyone else. Knowledge about a person which does not emerge from the group experience, is not necessarily as helpful as might be believed and may even dilute the impact that the individual makes within the situation. The author has had the experience of consulting with a coleader about a group member whose conduct was confusing and difficult to grasp. In discussing this person outside the group, considerable clarification was attained. Because this insight had not developed within the shared experience of the group, it turned out to be less helpful to the participant than to the leader. In retrospect, it is likely that the total impact of confusion that this individual generated would have been more important feedback to him than was the heightened understanding on the part of the leader. The essence of the marathon is that a person is not necessarily understood but is reacted to. Being understood may or may not be a comfort, but it can represent a diminishment of responsible adulthood; the work of understanding must be done by someone else and does not represent the actual operations of the world. Reaction, on the other hand, does represent an ever-recurring feature of the world; it is the direct verbalization which differs from other social interactions.

Many features of the clinical approach to helping people appear to be out of place in the marathon. Diagnostic labeling, for example, whether of people or their behavior stands out as being highly irrelevant and not particularly helpful to the person toward whom it is directed. In fact, if brought into the group too often by a participant, it is likely to be reflected in terms of annoyance and an evaluation of his style of behavior. Professional therapists and veterans of therapy often find themselves in an alien environment as the marathon goes into its midphase, unless they are able to shift their way of functioning. Any highly structured or stylized manner of engaging people elicits similar pained reactions; the distancing effect they have is a barrier to genuine encounter and they ultimately place the user of the system in a superior position to the ones placed in the "patient" role. Ultimately, however, systematized ways of looking at people inhibit growth through freezing the individual into a structure.

Dissolving Role Addiction

The facility with which we learn to adopt appropriate roles and the practice we have in filtering our behavior to create a specific personification can frequently act as deterrents to growth and realization of capacities. Under ordinary circumstances, the roles create practically no strain for the one adopting them. The adaptive features of role-playing are not in question; they are a necessary part of the social machinery within which everyone is embroiled. It is the flexibility with which an individual can shift from strict role-playing and mannered dealings with others to less studied, more spontaneous responses, that is important. In this sense, role-playing can become adaptive to many kinds of functioning, particularly those concerned with mastery. At the same time, it can become a counter force to the development of intimacy and self-knowledge. Exclusive encounters determined mainly by the maintenance of status relationships to others result in losing touch with an important aspect of oneself and result in cutting off a substantial part of the spectrum of interpersonal relationships.

Sustaining role-playing under prolonged contact where leveling and honesty are highly valued becomes a tremendous strain. The extent of this strain can scarcely be appreciated without having entered such a situation. Conventional therapeutic arrangements simply do not last long enough to reveal the ultimate fatigue that intensive investment in role-playing causes. People have no difficulty at all remaining within ascendency-oriented interactions within limited time periods; they rarely are aware that there is any other way for them to be. Through the marathon, the strain of maintaining such poses and the manner in which roles get between people and prevent them from developing emotional contact become increasingly apparent. Those who can shift, who can drop their masks, find themselves undergoing a renewed surge of movement at the point where fatigue should be slowing them down. Those who must hold on to their roles most rigidly find themselves in a position of increasing exhaustion and dissatisfaction. It has been the author's experience that professionals who have a great deal invested in their roles, such as psychotherapists, ministers, and school principals, often have more difficulty in the marathon group than others. A unique feature of the marathon is the tremendous release that can occur when people learn to shift from exclusive reliance on roles; the toll of such rigidity may be comprehended for the first time.

The Fulfillment of Potential

A weekend group can last thirty or more hours with very little sleep. Fatigue unquestionably is an important element in facilitating mask-dropping. Invariably, those who enter into the marathon most unstintingly and who participate most freely end with the most exhilaration. On the other hand, those who hold back the most and are least active show the most effects of fatigue. The marathon calls for involvement, participation, and contribution. Those who give of themselves find the greatest rewards. It is holding back which requires the greatest amount of effort, not giving of one's self. This is a lesson which has profound implications for the individual and how he manages his life. Many understand this on an intellectual level and find no difficulty in mouthing it as a cliché. It is another matter to experience this as a personal fact—the difference between being preached at and personal experience.

Many enter the marathon with fear of their ability to sustain the expected strain of so many continuous hours of effort. An extremely important self-discovery is one's capacity to become more involved and more energetic with the passage of time. A participant will generally emerge from the marathon with a different concept of his capacities than when he entered. It is no longer possible for him to conceive of himself as being limited as he had formerly been. In the future, he is likely to show more readiness to extend himself than he had in the past. Such a discovery, made within the confines of a weekend, has a positive value far exceeding many of the specific discoveries a participant will make about himself. It cannot be given to an individual; it cannot be taught. It must be experienced firsthand.*

The Break With History

Concentration upon the here-and-now is almost inevitable in the marathon. In the first place, there is only a limited amount of time available and lengthy investigations of the past are out of the question. Such a condition is immediately recognized by most participants and there is little insistence on historical exploration. Invariably, the similarity of explanation as various individuals take their turns at rationalizing becomes quite evident. For example, as complaints about mothers begin to mount, there is a humorous realization on the part of the group members that they could spend their whole weekend in such a fruitless search and top each other with horrendous accounts of their earlier difficulties. It becomes clear that explanation all too often becomes a search for a scapegoat, a reason for one's difficulties

---

* The author has been told by a participant that the intense and crowded experience of the marathon made her realize how she conducted her life at a carefully measured and low level. She now exhibits much more readiness to reach out for a richer way of life.

which lightens the responsibility of the individual for his own fate. While such a goal is rarely the one sought by the therapist, it becomes obvious that many people are only too ready to use historical exploration for this purpose. The final reason for the growing disinterest in the past arises out of the increasing intensity of the moment. Too much is happening too fast with growing involvement creating a pull which is hard to resist.

As people begin to evidence new aspects of themselves in the group, and as their altered participation begins to elicit different responses from others, the group member develops a sense of the degree to which he can choose his path. Movement forward seems to go along with lessened interest in the past. Many marathon participants have previously benefited from traditional psychotherapy. They often spontaneously recognize that much effort had been spent in searching for elusive insights which, when found, do not necessarily result in significant change. It is just as feasible to conceptualize changes as following altered conduct: if one acts differently, one will become different. Self-understanding, in this respect, may be irrelevant.

A long-term habitué of therapy, following a marathon experience, summed it up as follows: "I also feel the closeness experienced, especially during the last few hours, was another extremely important aspect. In short, I felt as if I knew everybody for a long time by the end of the session. I somehow feel a little bit better prepared to love. . . . There were many personal items clarified because of the 'honest reactions' and the 'we' feeling with group members. I think I would like to attend a marathon about once a year. In the meantime, I'm going to exchange therapy for living."

The Value of Sharing

Interest in the past is not completely missing in the marathon. Misconceptions sometimes develop in participants that any such historical delving violates the ground rules. Such a misunderstanding is often the result of the zeal with which the existential moment is stressed. But it is actually the quality with which the past is invested that is important. A completely detailed history, well organized and filling in all the details, presented to all the other group members will likely create a feeling of discomfort on the part of the audience. It smacks of a "contribution" for which the group should be thankful and, in gratitude, leave the individual alone. Or it may represent a decoy, a garden path replete with interesting corners and byways, which leads the interested by-stander away from the person of the individual. On the other hand, knowing a person means knowing something about him. In particular, it means having shared something of that person's life. Some participants would be content to allow themselves to be blank outlines, completely without any specifications concerning their siblings, their economic status in childhood, their father's occupation. Such a person has not really let himself be known.

Frequently, an important turning point for an individual in the marathon occurs when he is given the opportunity to share something of the past with the group. The key word is "share": permitting the others to feel intensely an important aspect of the participant's life or feelings. Under such circumstances, the quality with which the past history is dealt differs markedly from an archeological account. It causes the others to be moved and permits true empathy to occur. The shared past is rarely used in terms of explanation. Rather, the other group members tend to react to the different aspect they sense in the individual when he permits them to participate in his life, when he ceases to hold them off.*

A sense of the consequences of sharing is stated by a group member as follows: "The feeling that a person has nothing to hide either from himself or the other people involved was one that I had throughout the two days we were together. It sort of gives a person more confidence in himself, and I imagine this was felt by others. Not only that but it seemed like after it was over, the ten people involved felt more close to each other. I have noticed this since then, we seem to be more in closer contact and more amiable towards each other. I also notice that we seem to want to get involved in our group more often. To summarize all this, I can

---

* Although it may represent part of a similar movement, sharing is not the same as confession as emphasized by Mowrer (1964); it does not necessarily involve revelation of some guilt-inducing conduct. There is more affinity with Jourard's (1964) openness, though the element of letting others be touched by one's own experience is more fundamental to sharing.

sincerely say I sort of felt clean and elated, like a person who has finally relieved himself of a lot of pressure. Maybe I didn't, but I felt like it."

The Immediacy of Change

Behavioral breakthroughs are frequent occurrences within the marathon group. Sometimes the changes are quite marked and dramatic, almost to the point of being difficult to believe. At other times they are subtle and only perceptible long after they have taken place. But an important goal of the marathon is immediate change: a different way of dealing with people. The expectation is not that a participant will talk about how he will be different, how he will work on himself, but that he will evidence differences at the time he is confronted. Such immediate changes are much more possible than is frequently conceptualized. The requirement for a long, difficult struggle, an idea that has been bought by most of the population, should be reappraised. Participants frequently bridle at the group leader's insistence that he is tired of hearing people talk in the same old manner. It is apparent that the concept of gradual change serves the purpose of putting off new behavior to some indefinite time in the future. The idea of the need for prolonged treatment as a necessary correlate of change has taken on some of the aspects of a self-fulfilling prophecy. It has created an image of man which is only partially correct and the changes that frequently occur before the group members' eyes are often corrective experiences for such a concept.

New Ways of Resolving Crises

Participants are in a situation which they cannot leave. This is only partly due to the basic ground rule. It is also a function of the pull which the increasing group involvement develops. Group members finds themselves personally deeply entrenched in a series of dramas to which they must see the ending. Not being able to leave forces them to deal with their crises within the group in a manner that is distinctly different than is customary.

For the most part, we have all learned to pull away from the individual with whom we are in critical confrontation. This is accomplished through actual separation, through increased role playing, through deliberate maneuver for advantage. Whatever the manner an individual may characteristically adopt, it involves withdrawal from intimacy. However, the marathon situation provides no room for this. Consequently, the participant is forced to deal with his crises in a different manner. Instead of retreating, he is forced to step closer to the person with whom he is in conflict. Frequently this takes the form of engaging this individual in a manner that differs from what has transpired previously. He may find himself talking to him on a different level. He may become more open and share his inner bruises. Other times he may admit to similar crises with other individuals in his life situations. A personal crisis of this nature generally involves a challenge to an individual's self-image and he may resolve the crisis by surrendering aspects of this image he had formerly valued and protected. Whatever the means, he stays with the crisis and changes it rather than relieving the situation; withdrawal alters nothing.

One of the most exciting aftermaths of the marathon can be found in what occurs when participants find themselves in personal crises in the future. There are many suggestions that there is an increased readiness to move into critical situations, to resolve them by changing the terms of the relationship which is causing the conflict. Such growth seems to emerge far beyond the marathon experience, suggesting that internal processes have been set in motion.

The Value of the Special Event

The marathon is a special circumstance in a participant's life. It stands apart from the rest of his life and requires a rearrangement of his routine in order for him to be able to attend it. The accelerated pace of the marathon differs markedly from any other social situation. His anticipations are generally of a mixed nature—fear of what might occur and high hopes for a turning point in his life. Because it is not routine, the factors which enter into it can often be differentiated from other life situations. His expectations are high and he will attempt to meet them. Routinized participation tends to be avoided. Accommodation to the other group members is not as likely to take place because of the limited time. He retains a memory of the experience to which he can frequently return; participants often recall aspects of the group long after it is over. This permits the participant to use the experience in a fashion that is relatively rare for sessions that occur repeatedly in his life.

Above all, the marathon gives participants a sense of what is possible. There is little question that some of the effects of the experience fade, with a certain residue remaining, just as occurs in any therapeutic situation. An important part of that residue is the realization that one can no longer think of his own limitations in quite the same way. Equally important, one can no longer feel the same sense of distrust in others that formerly guided much of his life. He has now had an experience of tremendous openness and sharing, of placing himself in the hands of others without being trampled. He has felt a tremendous joy and elation which is almost unique in his experiences with people. Much of what he has gone through bears startling resemblances to Maslow's (1962) description of the peak experience. He now knows that both he and others are capable of engaging in such experiences and his sense of what is possible is never quite the same again.

THE MARATHON GROUP AS A CHANGE AGENT

Insight, in terms of relating the past to the present or of determining complex motivations, is less a factor in the marathon than in other therapeutic modalities. However, learning does take place and is translated into behavioral change at an impressive rate. Many of the changes which occur are the results of specific interventions on the part of the group leader and group members. Many of the very important alterations cannot be engineered so precisely, but are a consequence of certain features of the marathon itself. In this sense, the marathon can become a singular agent of change.

As in any form of group psychotherapy, the participant learns specific things about himself. Marathons should be conducted with this aim in mind: to highlight the conduct of the group members in as concise and concrete a fashion as possible. The effect his behavior produces is made explicit with the stimulus and response being relatively close together in time. When behavior is changed, the response is changed so that the group member has a chance to explore a variety of actions—those which are characteristic of him, in general, and those that are comparatively new. In doing this, he is in a position to realize that he does not necessarily have to learn completely new ways of being, but to make available to himself that which is already within his capabilities. The individual has more options than he generally considers to be the case; at any given moment he is capable of a richer variety of behavior than he thinks.

The marathon differs from traditional group therapy in its greater compression and intensity. This means that what occurs is in the context of very heightened feelings, both of anxiety and involvement. The intensity of the marathon is extremely important; learning under such conditions does not necessarily take as long or require the continual trial and error, as well as practice, which is generally considered necessary. Learning about oneself is not unique to the marathon, but the rapidity of learning and the adaptation to new patterns within a very brief span of time occurs with this approach in a way that is not likely under traditional arrangements. In a sense, one-trial learning becomes much more feasible.

Not only does the participant develop new ways of looking at concrete facets of himself, but he learns much about his career or life style. Although the marathon, with its twenty-four to thirty hours, constitutes a complex of events, it is, nevertheless, a unitary affair. There is a clearly defined beginning and end along with a very definite development, both for the individual participant and for the group as a whole. A group member can see his own experience, within that unit of time, as a career. What happens to the individual in the marathon is largely his own doing, a consequence of his own way of entering the clearly defined world of the intensive group. The parallel between one's career in the marathon and one's career in the world is made explicit. Thus, the group member is able to develop a sense of his own fate and his contribution to this fate. What happens to him in the marathon reflects what happens to him in the world, particularly in terms of his intimate relationships. The short, intense nature of the marathon experience forces upon the individual in a very dramatic fashion a sense of his own movement through the world.

The combination of concentration upon specific ways of communication or of engaging others and the overall course of one's life pattern are powerful change agents for the participant. People change in ways that are often immediately noticeable and which can be acknowledged by those who knew them before and after the marathon. Ways of talking, reluctance to deal with certain areas in conversation, physical gestures, lability and directness, are all specific ways in which people show differences. Making important decisions about the course of their life and establishing new levels of honesty and closeness are ways in which people reveal their new concepts about their life styles. Sometimes a participant must give up old relationships that cannot enter into the styles of involvement that the marathon participant now seeks, and he finds he must change the intimate circles he has formerly had. Change is both immediate and long-term.

A marathon group constitutes an island during its existence. It is a world stripped of many of the irrelevancies which enable us to escape the essence of how we move among people. By concentrating on the social matrix, the marathon highlights what is often most significant about our fears, our dishonesties, and our disguises. Activity and busyness, as well as many of the details of living, are often used to avoid intimate contact. The significant portion of the world is seen in terms of the give and take that occurs with people. One gets out of the marathon what one puts into it; the world is seen as operating in the same manner. The individual's responsibility for reaching into that world, for looking at it in terms of what it has to offer, to attend to one's own contribution, are all important consequences of particpating in marathon experiences. Not only is the world seen as a complicated combination of possibilities, but the individual comes to see himself in terms of unused potentialities. Once having reached beyond himself in the group, while experiencing a powerfully exciting expansion of self, he is less likely to be satisfied to hold himself back as much as he formerly did. Risk-taking assumes a different value. This capacity to sense the world differently is a special function of the marathon and can only be developed where intensity of experience is fostered.

It would be misleading to give the impression that all changes become a permanent part of a person's equipment. Many of the gains fade with time. Others become overlaid with new difficulties that everyone accumulates as they move through life. Nevertheless, there is a surprising amount that does remain with the participant. Informal reports suggest that many of the changes are still apparent a year or more after the group experience. One of the features of the marathon is that it is a special event to which the individual can return in memory and which he can often point to as a turning point in his life. Many enter new marathons and their gains are evidenced in the different manner in which they move through the new group.

Formal research on the permanence of the gains attained in the marathon has not yet been made. There is a decided need for such research and programs for just such investigations are now in the planning stage. For the most part, research of the marathon has been conducted only in an exploratory fashion. The following are, however, suggestive of some of the directions such research will be taking.

Among the preliminary data which have been collected are a series of questionnaire reports obtained by Bach. On the whole, these attempts to gather personal reports on the experience have indicated that about 80 per cent of the reactions are characterized by the description of a profound and meaningful experience which has been extremely helpful, while about 20 per cent express some doubt and reservations about its ultimate value (Bach, Stoller, and Wolpin, 1964).

The author and his associates have used a series of questions directed at descriptions of self and of difficulties as seen before and after the group experience. Preliminary data are highly suggestive of much more conciseness in these descriptions following the marathon with a definite movement of the locus of difficulty toward the individual and away from the external world.

The marathon is considered to have a group development which is qualitatively different from the conventional group as well as an effusion of feeling which is unique. Serious attempts to evaluate such differences between the marathon and the intermittent group session have been undertaken by H. L. Myerhoff.* Group interaction is being investigated through the use of the Hill Interaction Matrix (Hill, 1965) correlated with emotional development as measured by an adjective checklist. Analysis of one group suggests that a marathon quickly moves into high-risk interaction which is sustained at a higher rate than in an intermittent group. Much more affect is generated with a greater amount of variation. With a hospitalized population, more negative affect is produced in the marathon. Such finds are very tentative, since many technical problems have to be resolved and the question of group composition with a hospital population leaves many unanswered questions.

Measurements of outcome raise the most difficult problems as it is obvious that most traditional instruments which have been utilized in the past do not adequately strike at what is most likely to change (Pattison, 1965). For example, Kruschke and Stoller (1967) conducted a group for drug addicts in which marked changes were evident over a period of many months. However, none of these was detected by a Leary Interpersonal Checklist.

It is safe to say that marathon therapy will be the subject of more study, particularly as its use becomes more widespread. Its short duration makes it more attractive to investigators than the thorny problem involved in researching conventional length therapies.

GOALS OF MARATHON THERAPY

Although there is considerable overlap between the aims of a marathon group and other approaches to psychotherapy, there are some very distinct differences. For example, understanding, in the sense of explaining away one's characteristics in terms of dynamics rooted in the past, is not one of the purposes of the marathon. Such insights may occur in the course of an intensive group experience, but more as a serendipitous finding than a deliberate-

---

* Personal communication. Myerhoff and the author have worked closely to develop Myerhoff's initial studies conducted at Camarillo State Hospital, Camarillo, California.

ly sought after one. Neither is symptom relief necessarily a purposefully sought after goal. It frequently does occur that individuals drop seriously incapacitating symptomatology, but symptoms are rarely treated as such within the group. Sensitivity toward others is not necessarily considered a deliberate aim of the marathon, though this is frequently a byproduct of participants' attention to communication in interpersonal transactions, both on their own part and on the part of others. The goals of the marathon, which frequently determine the kinds of interventions the group leader will attempt, are stated in specific fashion below.

Responsibility for One's Actions

There is a consistent pressure, within the marathon group, for group members to change their ways of behaving toward others. Promises to change in the future or to "work on one's self" are not accepted at face value; only when the participants can see differences in the individual through his actions within the group is there any acknowledgment of change. Much is made of the difference between a person's intentions and what he actually does. The individual is responsible, in large part, for his own fate because his acts determine so much of it. By focusing interest on the here-and-now rather than on the distant past, the participant is not permitted to be satisfied by the delegation of responsibility to someone else. Whatever the accumulated reaction to a participant may be, it is clearly a consensus based upon his own contribution; it is very difficult to avoid such a realization for very long.

Precise Personal Goals

Over and over again, group members are asked what they want. When answers are stated in imprecisions such as "I want to be happy" or "I would like to be successful," the group tends to be dissatisfied. In place of this, the individual is forced to restate his aims until they bear some relation to his behavior. In addition to his own struggles in searching for his real goals, the group member is witness to the struggles of others. In doing so, he is in a position to see the difference between cliché-ridden goals and goals that are actually closely related to the individual's stance in the world. As a consequence, a person will likely emerge from the intensive group experience capable of specifying his goals and monitoring his behavior to be more in line with them. In particular, inconsistencies between goals become very clear; such contradictions generally are reflected in verbalizations and behavior. Verbalizations are more likely to reflect what is socially safe while behavior reflects one's true intention. The marathon makes such a distinction very clear and forces an alteration in the conflicting intentions. Very often a participant can state more specifically what he does not want, but the real aim of the marathon is to help him specify what he does want and direct his conduct along those lines.

Leveling

The early phases of a marathon group are marked by maneuvering and misunderstanding between the participants. It is rare for people to be able to talk directly to one another, and there is generally a hidden agenda in most of the communication. Even when such indirection is not present, people are so accustomed to searching for it that they rarely are in a position to hear what is being said. One of the major characteristics of the marathon is that the participants learn to deal with each other as equals, because they are all in predicaments which give them little superiority over each other. The shift from strict role playing for the purpose of maintaining an advantage over the other can be detected when the characteristics of communication change. What a person says has the feel of being honest and evidences some inner struggle on his part, rather than glib parrying. Thus, the manner in which the individual talks to others communicates more than what is actually being said. It signals that the person is not merely trying to create an effect upon others, to handle them, but is trying to tell them something that comes out of his internal structure and is willing to let them see this hidden part of himself. It is obvious that this form of transaction is extremely rare and difficult to achieve. It can only be attained when everyone levels with everyone else. Leveling suggests both honesty and equality of status.

Trust

Because the marathon consists of a group of strangers who, in a relatively short period of time, become intimates, the question of trust in the world becomes important. It is inconceivable that those who enter a marathon would not fear the reactions of the others and anticipate being hurt. These expectations are generally fulfilled since feedback is not gentle. One of the important developments is that negatively laden responses tend to come predominantly in the early phases of the session. Following the initial injuries, other sentiments are expressed, generally because the participant has made himself known to the others in a different manner. Thus, the more positive comments tend to come when there is a general air of increased honesty in the group and also in the context of having been earned through behavior. Trust in people* almost invariably grows because an individual can learn that injury from others is not necessarily devastating nor is it all that one can expect. Perhaps, most important of all is the discovery that people hunger for intimacy and it is their fear of it which ordinarily prevents it from emerging.

The Expression of Aggression

Above all, honesty is valued in the marathon. Under the prolonged pressure of the continual contact, dishonesty, in whatever form, becomes extremely tiring. The one who consistently attempts to avoid the possibly disturbing connotation of directness, even where it means condoning another's childishness or weakness, begins to receive irritated comments himself. Therefore, much of the learning which takes place in this type of group concerns itself with the expression of aggression. Since there is opportunity to live with consequences, the participant can learn what will be the ultimate effect of permitting this side of himself to be exposed. He will certainly learn that showing only a narrow range of himself can have a less than satisfactory result. When there is an honest expression of aggressive affect, there is a clearing of the clouded atmosphere between individuals; it is often the most helpful act the person can commit.† Some of the more thrilling events in the marathon often follow explosions on the part of

---

* Jack R. Gibb has worked most intensively with the concept of trust formation and has applied it to the development of the marathon.

† George R. Bach has developed the concept of the relationship between intimacy and aggression. He has emphasized procedures to foster open, rather than underground conflict; only with honest aggression can true intimacy be expressed.

some of the participants and the most heartening changes will often follow them. A subtle distinction with other therapeutic groups should be made. It is not so much the repression of anger that is important in an interdependent situation but the specificity of the feeling. A participant has an obligation to attempt to spell out what in the other person causes him to feel the way he does. It is not enough to express the anger just because "it is a good thing to do." In making explicit what it is that elicits this response, the individual not only clarifies his own feelings to himself but permits his interpersonal conflict to be open to change. In the long run, it is one's willingness to permit movement in a deadlock with an intimate which determines whether one is merely "expressing feeling" or engaging in an adult encounter. The marathon will ultimately force the individual to use his aggression in this fashion if he is to move with the group's growing intimacy. Learning the close relationship between the open expression of aggression and the development of intimacy is an important part of the marathon. Learning to use one's aggression to further a relationship rather than blocking it is an extremely important part of life.

The Production of Opportunities

Aggression within the marathon has a connotation other than the expression of angry feelings. The intensive group is an arena in which many individuals take their turns to hold the group's attention. It is not infrequent for some to hold back until it becomes apparent that they are in danger of being overlooked and, thereby, letting an extremely important opportunity pass by. The group reflects the world, and one's participation reflects one's movement through the world. If group members would let the marathon opportunity go by, they are likely to do this in the world at large. They must learn, then, their own responsibility to reach for what is available to them.

Seeing the group in terms of opportunities can be extremely valuable in its parallel to the world; if someone wants attention, he must draw it to himself, rather than wait for the good will of others. How he goes about this will determine the kind of attention he will receive. Once having drawn attention to himself, he must keep it, since it is not uncommon to relate to people in such a tiresome fashion that they soon want to move on. Because the responsibility rests with the individual rather than with the group or with a therapist, the participant can learn firsthand how he utilizes the opportunities which lie all about him but which are often disregarded or used without regard to the consequences for himself. Marathons are no fairer than the world; they are merely more explicit.

A Fuller Use of One's Self

As indicated earlier, the marathon is an experience which raises people's doubts about their capabilities. The long hours, the grueling confrontation, and the ordeal of the unknown are all features about which there are many self-doubts. Discovering that one not only survives but also finds genuine enjoyment in such participation can be a revelation about one's potential. This is partly a consequence of facing up to crises rather than retreating; people find what they are capable of facing once they have been hurt. However, there is another aspect to the release of potential in the individual which can be an extremely important goal of the marathon. Being less afraid to be open means dropping a portion of one's armor, the part which watches both oneself and others and which holds back spontaneous action. Dropping such defenses means a release of energy since holding back uses more of one's self than it is possible to realize. The newfound energy can be applied to goals that are more precise. In this manner, a participant can discover specific potentials that lie unused within himself and gain a sense of the general pool of talent and ability that is always available. He may even learn that a good portion of his discontent is related to his diminished use of himself, a discontent which is generalized and difficult to specify since it is based less on action than on lack of action. In a very real way, the marathon points to the future and to a fuller use of oneself: the ultimate consequence of increased self-trust.

UNIQUE CONTRIBUTIONS OF THE THEORY

While continuity of group interaction is the feature which is most characteristic of the marathon, there are many implications which are built into this approach and into the underlying assumptions. Many of these points have been suggested in the preceding discussion, but they require highlighting because they stand in direct opposition to traditional practice. To the degree that they are stated here, they are considered to be a deliberate, rather than an accidental part of the marathon approach.

The Value of Direct Experience

Most therapeutic approaches value the immediate experience over secondhand discussions of what occurs outside the therapeutic arena. However, the marathon goes further in providing an intense and full experience which, in itself, has a profound impact upon the group member. Not only are there the interactions which directly affect the participant, but there are also a wealth of incidents to which he is witness. Such crowded events impinging on the individual are very important elements in the marathon; it is not infrequent that the critical breakthrough for a group member occurs when the group is focusing on someone else. Almost invariably, participants comment upon the experience itself as something they value beyond the specific things they learned about themselves. What is gained from such participation cannot be directly engineered by any conceivable technique.

The Discovery of Consequences

Because of its concentration, the marathon group enables a participant to sense the aftermath of his own behavior; he does not come and go, permitting many events to intervene between his acts and their accumulated effect upon others. Resurrection of behavior which is remote in time fosters both distortion and dilution. The accumulated impact of an individual upon others, and the resultant behavior on their part, constitutes a most important element of this approach. Bringing these together in a relatively short time sequence which, nevertheless, provides ample opportunity for a significant sample of behavior to emerge, leads to realization rather than explanation—immediate recognition as opposed to drowning in long involved sentences. The focus in a marathon always returns to the individual's responsibility, and nothing is permitted to dilute his sense of this. If nothing else is gained except the gut-level realization of one's own responsibility for one's fate, a considerable change in an individual's stance will have been effected. Sensing the consequences of one's conduct brings this home in a way that repeated comments can never do.

The Development of Change

Since most patterns of behavior which affect our lives in any significant manner tend to be long-term possessions, it is generally conceptualized that change takes a long time to develop. This has been one of the most widely accepted concepts clinical practice has passed on to the general public; whatever its validity, it is clear that such a concept relieves the pressure for immediate change in the minds of many. In the traditional historical approach to psychotherapy the initial role given to the development of insight fostered the long-term approach to change, but in the marathon insight as a goal is minimized. Instead, changed behavior in the immediate situation and actions in the group of a different order which elicit a different quality of response are fostered. Such an approach toward change encompasses within it a basic picture of man. Instead of seeing only fixed patterns of behavior requiring extensive removal operations because of their almost life-long characteristics, man is seen as having many capabilities within him at any given moment. By sensing his own capacities and trying them out, he is in a position to establish different kinds of outcomes. Therefore, the marathon has a tendency to insist upon changed behavior immediately within the situation rather than accept the individual's resolution that he will "work on his problem." Instead of seeing change as a long, hard struggle, it is seen as a short, hard one.

The Difference Between Intimacy and Accommodation

Berne (1961) has made the avoidance of intimacy the basic focal point around which most of his system of transactional analysis is built. The marathon develops intimacy in a powerful manner, and the experience of intense intimacy with those who are relative strangers is an important goal. Once having experienced the intimate relationship of the group, the individual is likely to be more ready to reach for intimacy in life situations, since he has been in the situation where openness and closeness to others developed in the context of a peak experience. Those who have experienced the difference between the usual diffidence of most social intercourse and the free and honest commerce which takes place under conditions of high trust and clear communication realize the amount of armor which is necessary in order to maintain distance. The marathon deliberately attempts to foster an atmosphere of intimacy without long preparation. Contact with others without hesitancy is like its subsidiary form sex—better experienced than talked about.

Most important relationships are relatively long-term and people get to know each other quite well. Marriage and prolonged group therapy are two examples of "knowing" about another without necessarily developing intimacy. Accommodation and avoidance of unpleasant situations are forms of learned behavior which are sometimes substituted for intimacy. There is a very important distinction between what happens between people who have known each other a long time and those who have shared in profound experiences. A light manner which lacks candidness is adopted by the former; whereas, the latter are ready to engage one another on any of a variety of levels—shifting in appropriate fashion is the essential feature rather than a grim insistence on constant honesty. Once having tasted intimacy, the group member will be less hesitant to reach for it in the future.

The Limitations of Treatment

When the marathon is seen as a treatment, in which a practitioner engages in a series of techniques or applies a specialized body of knowledge, it loses its most important quality—the shared experience. Where case histories are assessed, processes evaluated, and techniques applied for particular effects, people's humanity may be diminished. A variety of learnings are involved in such manipulations: the locus is moved away from self to problem, help is seen as forthcoming exclusively from specialists rather than from intimate relationships, and the individual sees himself more incapacitated than he actually is. The marathon is an exercise in pushing people closer to the limits of their capabilities rather than an attempt to guard them from their apparent weaknesses. In this manner, the marathon represents a true application of the value of growth in contrast to the frequent "first aid" approach to reparation fostered by the clinical model.

The Axioms of Traditional Practice

A marathon experience, and especially repeated marathon experiences, suggests that much of the standard practice of traditional group therapy should undergo questioning. It is obvious that considerable doubt is already being generated by such influential figures as Masserman (1965) and Alexander (1965). However, the attempt to alter the basic dimensions of the traditional approach to practice and to question the basic assumptions of treatment procedures is only in its infancy. Marathons clearly indicate that what is often considered axiomatic in psychotherapy is really a set of long-standing assumptions. By defining the requirements for change, therapists engineer people's expectations (Frank, 1961) and find themselves in a position of having to struggle with these expectations. It may not be necessary to completely wipe away traditional assumptions, but it is essential to destroy definitions since they are difficult to question. The marathon can be seen as an attempt to experiment with preconceived assumptions, evidence of an emerging era of vigorous change.

MODIFICATIONS OF THE MARATHON

It is still too early to speak meaningfully of variations of the marathon, but rather of continuing exploration. A form of continuous contact for a substantial period of time is the essence of the marathon. How long an appropriate marathon should last and whether there should be any interruptions for sleep are questions which are still open to investigation. There is reason to belive that arrangements of this nature are effective in terms of the group leader's style and the requirements of the situation.

Marathons have been attempted in a variety of institutional settings such as mental hospitals, juvenile job centers, and drug-addict facilities. Their utility in such settings is very high when their purposes are in line with the overall goals of the institution. Given the framework in which most institutions operate, the marathon approach is best seen as an aid in promoting the participation of the inmate in the program rather than in producing changes that could not be supported by the institutional environment. An exploratory attempt to institute the marathon group in a weekend hospital program has been made at Camarillo State Hospital. A basic concept is to provide a possible alternative to hospitalization. Because of the importance of crisis within this type of group, it has natural application for people who are undergoing intense emotional storms. In the light of the current trend toward community psychiatry, the marathon has important implications for new developments in working with those under overwhelming stress. As an approach to crisis intervention, it has tremendous possibilities.

Organizational marathons, in which the significant members of an operating organization attempt to promote their capacity for working together, for improving communication, for trust formation, and for constructive aggression, are becoming increasing phenomena. Bach and Gibb have developed the concept of the "intimate organization" and feel that it represents an advance in both concept and technique. The author has adapted the marathon approach to supervisory groups, concentrating on the attitude and personal styles such personnel give to their work situations and attempting to aid them in being more open to creative possibilities. Though there are obvious parallels to sensitivity training, such groups have basic differences.

Family and marital groups are also a natural development. Other practitioners have adapted the marathon approach to psychodrama and still others to nonverbal communication. These are applications of the marathon concept which have validity in themselves. The author and his colleagues have incorporated video tape within the marathon structure (see chapter on focused feedback) and it is likely that this represents the next major development. The technical problems of such an undertaking are enormous and have not yet been completely solved.

Some practitioners hold marathons as integral parts of an ongoing group. It may be used either to initiate a group or to interpose at some phase in the group's life. An important question concerns the value of a continued group. Should an individual enter marathons with those in his working group and with whom there is some accommodation or should he encounter new people? Both Bach and the writer have had the experience of participants making breakthroughs in marathons with group leaders other than the usual one. In one case, a woman who had been thrown out of an ongoing group because of her disruptive behavior held forth in a marathon until the last half hour when she began to deal with the group in a completely different fashion. Afterwards, she commented that she had learned she never listened, something that she had been told repeatedly.

GROUP LEADER ROLES

The group leader plays an extremely important role in the marathon group and his presence is, of necessity, of a different order than in other therapeutic approaches. Both from a physical and emotional standpoint, the demands upon a marathon group leader are considerable. How he enters the group will determine to a large degree the nature of that group and will define how rewarding an experience it will be for him. Because it is such a subjective experience, yielding continuing personal rewards, it is most appropriate to describe how I see myself as a group leader. Undoubtedly, I often veer away from the following description, but it does encompass my vision of the group leader's participation in the marathon.

Since it is the experience which determines the kinds of gains that are made by group members, my primary responsibility is to lead the way in promoting a succession of events which will culminate with profound impact upon the participants. One of the very serious errors a group leader can make is to consider that the most meaningful kinds of learning emanate from his actions or his technique. Rather, one of the most gratifying aspects of the marathon is that events occur that could never be deliberately brought about; they emerge out of the admixture of interactions, emotional arousal, and heightened involvement on the part of all the participants.

The immediate goal in the initial phase of the marathon is to help the group members react as honestly and directly as they can to each other. In order to do this they must be able to read their own reactions rather than engage in the more tempting roads of delving into problems or speculating about each other's dynamics. The major responsibility for developing this personal way of dealing with the other group members is mine and it is inevitable that the group members will take their cue from me. If I interpret, they will attempt to do the same. If I interview for facts about external problems, the group members will follow. Also, if I make explicit my own personal reactions to group members, the others will quickly follow suit.

Therefore, it is essential that I be able to read my own responses to others and to express these as directly as I can. Rather than taking the role of the expert, I am a group member, but the one who is more courageous, and therefore I can generate my reactions more quickly. The group situation provides an appropriate setting for this manner of interposing myself; if my personal reactions to a particular group member reflect my own biases or difficulties rather than being representative of the world, the rest of the group will not echo my feelings. But where my reactions do have validity in terms of a general pattern of responses from the world, I am merely leading the way.

The most significant factor to keep in mind is that I can only shape the group's manner of dealing with each other by what I put into it. If I feel it important that the group members share intimate aspects of themselves and be open and level in their interactions, I must be this way myself. Maintaining myself in the therapist role, keeping my own personal concerns and difficulties away from the group does not foster what I myself might want for the others. Keeping myself strictly as a commentator upon the group members—allowing myself to be a blank figure without juices of my own or a life of my own outside the professional role —engenders distancing and diffidence rather than intimacy and openness. As the manner of dealing with each other begins to shift through the various phases of the marathon, I am forced to go along or stand even more apart. The strain of maintaining a therapist role becomes very clear under these circumstances; it is only by being real that I can sustain the vigor and zest I require for conducting a marathon.

Because I enter as a real person rather than a carefully drawn outline, responses which I elicit from the group should be considered to be a consequence of my personal involvement, rather than strictly as transference phenomena. Under such circumstances, it is not the irrational elements of these feelings which are important but the manner in which I handle direct responses to myself. Unless I try to handle them openly, no matter how disturbing they may be, I give off a message of evasiveness. Letting the group see me as being vulnerable does not jeopardize my relationship with them but rather draws them closer into a mutual endeavor. In fact, my most exciting experiences took place when I opened myself for personal growth within the experience. It is most gratifying when I permit myself to share with the others my own difficulties which their struggles touch in me, and I attempt to work them through together with the group members. Not every group will touch on my current predicaments, but I try to carry myself so as to be open to them when I can sense my own problems emerging through the struggles of the others. When I hold the group in my house with my wife participating,* such openness is more likely to occur. I am literally sharing an important, and generally hidden, side of my life with the group members, and strains and difficulties within my own family life are always in the wings waiting to enter the stage. Instead of looking at this as a danger, I view it as an excellent opportunity for growth in my own life and the most valuable part of myself I have to offer: my own willingness to grow and my trust in the group members.

The clinical stance generally stands in the way of developing trust in the participants of a marathon. A leader's willingness to encounter the group members without preconceived information based upon case history material is extremely important. Reserving the tendency to label or categorize the participants is an absolute necessity. Such an attitude takes considerable discipline on the part of someone like myself who has learned the clinical

---

* George R. Bach and the writer have led the way in including their spouses in the marathons to the degree where it has become almost standard practice. Universally, group members respond with warmth and respect and express their preference for this type of setting. It seems to have several advantages for groups in which couples are involved.

approach, but it enables me to view participants in terms of what they could be rather than their limitations. It is easy to state that one views people in a positive light, since very few will admit to any other kind of attitude. But in actual practice this is rarely done and is only accomplished through the courage of the group leader to suspend clinical judgment. When this is actually done, the ability of people to grow beyond their apparent psychopathology can be very surprising. Clinical experience can become an asset when it permits one to fearlessly engage an individual who appears to be undergoing marked disorganization; such fear, when present, more than any other single factor, cripples a true growth-producing experience.

Personal style is an important component of how the leader enters the group. Because he is truly a person, each leader will conduct himself somewhat differently. It is important for the leader to have some awareness of his own tendencies and to turn his idiosyncrasies to assets rather than to deny them. I tend to be impatient with weakness and have difficulty generating sympathy when it appears. As a consequence, I will likely encounter a participant in such a way as to almost force him to express other sides of himself. Yet I realize that such an unwavering attitude can sometimes produce an overly harsh and grim atmosphere; sharing this with the group helps soften it to a degree. At times I have had the experience of almost rejecting a participant because of the accumulated responses he elicits in me. Such a predicament may place a group leader in his most difficult situation and he must use the group freeely to turn this to the advantage of the particular participant.

While style is extremely important, stylized manners have a way of backfiring. It has been my experience that a certain kind of interaction has led to meaningful growth on the part of a group member. When this interaction is repeated in another group, the same outcome rarely results. One of the most dramatic breakthroughs I have had resulted from my angry confrontation of a participant whose rigid religious attitudes constantly interposed themselves in his dealings with others. Upon meeting a similar individual, my attempt to repeat the same situation did not have as happy a result. This has taught me to watch myself when I am tempted to see an individual in terms of someone else because of superficial similarities. A rehearsed self-presentation on the part of a group member diminishes the value of the experience, and the same holds true for the group leader who comes to the group with well-practiced and well-rehearsed techniques.

Entering marathons without a planned presentation can be highly threatening since the usual protection of the therapist's posture cannot be used. As much as the group members are responsible for their fate in the intensive group, so is the group leader. Since I am not strictly an observer, I find myself frequently involved in conflicting relationships which threaten me. One of the most disturbing situations occurred when I found myself growing increasingly irritated at a group member who kept repeating, "I am not mad at anyone." By Saturday night she said it once too often and I exploded, threatening to strike her physically. This resulted in a confused altercation, culminating in the woman and another participant's walking out. I was extremely upset and let the group know the depths of my disturbance despite the insistence of some members that I was deliberately trying to effect a change in the woman. Both women returned the next morning and concluded the marathon in very satisfactory fashion. For many members, my own struggle with the consequences of my own behavior was an important experience. My open attitude was one of the most valuable parts of the group. I have never regretted risking myself in the marathon, since I find that caution invariably diminishes the experience—both for myself and the group members.

The rewards that come to a group leader in the marathon are important considerations. He enters a grueling and risky situation in which he is forced to give more of himself than under any other circumstance. Why should he want to do this? The financial rewards are not necessarily equal to his contribution of time and energy. Altruistic motives concerning the help being given others are insufficient to sustain such an endeavor for very long. It has become clear that my own personal rewards come from what I get from group members and from extending myself. When a marathon group catches fire it is one of the most exhilarating experiences I can have. The enthusiasm and joy of the participants encompasses me and I am usually more energetic, enthusiastic, and happy for days following the group—despite physical fatigue. I have no question that I have become stronger, more enterprising, and more aware of myself and my capacities because of the fifty marathons I have led.

QUALIFICATIONS OF THE GROUP LEADER

It should already be clear that the leader of a marathon must be prepared to enter a group of this sort with openness, with an awareness of his own responses, and with a total commitment to the experience. In order to attain this he should have been a participant in a number of marathons himself. Professionals in a marathon face considerable difficulty since it is so hard for them to relinquish their roles. Yet, it is just such a breakthrough which is required if one is to give of himself in the required manner.

Two almost contradictory requirements should be considered. With an adequate clinical background, particularly with extensive experience facing disturbed and disorganized individuals, a group leader can gain the necessary courage to face almost anything that could occur. Judgment is particularly important since he has no opportunity, within the marathon, to consult with anyone when a difficult situation arises. On the other hand, it is absolutely essential that the group leader does not become so enamored of the clinical approach that he cannot relegate it to the background where it belongs.

The marathon leader should, in addition to his own personal experiences as a participant, undergo a series of groups in which he is a coleader with an experienced person. Not only will he be in a position to absorb the approach of another but it should also necessitate his having to deal with his inevitable conflicts with his coleader within the group rather than privately. This forces him to take on a new attitude toward his own openness and an ability to put himself in the group arena.

Consultation or training with a practiced marathon leader is strongly recommended if the approach described here is to be followed, since a different concept of human conflict and the requirements of behavioral change are required than most group therapists have. This cannot be stressed too much, since it is very easy to echo and mouth one's positive view of man without realizing that he is continually seeing people in terms of their limitations.

COMPOSITION OF THE MARATHON GROUP

Preselection is rarely practiced in marathons since there is little attempt to screen participants. Therefore, there is no particular composition that is favored for a group beyond random selection. There is, however, a problem that occurs when part of the group does know each other from another situation and another part of the group does not share these experiences. It is difficult to keep the ingroup from talking about their mutual experiences, and when this is done the others in the group have to contend with much material outside their immediate experience. Breaking up the conversation of those who know each other becomes a group problem, and the writer knows of no way in which this can be done in a completely satisfactory manner.

In contrast to many other approaches, married couples are encouraged to enter the marathon together. This enables them to share in a very important experience which can be of great value. In the author's estimation, the marathon approach is particularly effective as a corrective for marital difficulties and for strengthening marriages. In the words of one couple, the experience "ended our cold war." Marriage relationships that cannot endure the heightened intimacy of the marathon are not likely to sustain themselves for any period of time; the marathon has a way of establishing people's commitment to the goals they really have. However, there have been some excellent results when partners have gone into different marathon groups; one can become too identified as a husband or a wife and deny his own individuality. For the most part, those who are considering a marathon can generally make this decision for themselves once the possibilities are explained to them. Another rewarding circumstance has been the participation of couples contemplating marriage.

Groups tend to number between ten and fourteen in size. Fourteen seems to be the maximum number above which the desired intimacy is difficult to develop, and in larger groups some of the participants tend to escape the attention of the group's focus. If fewer than eight, there are not enough people to constitute an adequate sample of the world: too little variety in feedback is generated to make the group as meaningful as it might be.

LIMITATIONS OF THE APPROACH

Surprisingly few participants have adverse reactions from a marathon experience; although all do not gain in equal fashion. The author's experience has shown that individuals who have undergone hospitalization in the past have made tremendous gains in the marathon. However, some of these individuals are so disorganized that they cannot sustain any kind of meaningful communication with the remainder of the group. It is more important to consider how disorganized and scattered the individual is rather than how rigid or frightened or depressed he might be. Despite considerable marathon experience, it is difficult to predict how a particular individual might fare.

The greatest limitation on the effectiveness of the marathon concerns itself with the opportunity which an individual has available to him to put into action what he has gained from the experience. If he is too overwhelmed with financial problems, for example, the press of his immediate needs may be such that he has no room to maneuver and he falls back into his situation too deeply before any change he may want to put into action has any chance to take effect. Those who lead isolated lives must reach out immediately for others or their gains may dissipate; often their first move is to share their intense experience with someone else.

As with any other approach, individuals should not be coerced into a marathon. It is not infrequent that the group forces a reluctant member to become involved; these individuals are generally ambivalent rather than clearly opposed to the intensive group. The marathon is clearly not brainwashing; it cannot force the individual to do something that he is not, in some way, prepared to do. While group pressure builds up to an impressive degree, it should never be used to batter an individual into submission. Not only are there moral and ethical considerations in such an approach, but the changes engendered under such circumstances are not likely to be of any lasting value to the individual.

OTHER READINGS

Bach (1966) presented his initial view of the marathon and has since followed up with a series of papers recording the results of questionnaires given to marathon participants. All of these papers can be found in the same journal, *Psychological Reports*. A paper on Accelerated Interaction (Stoller, 1966) presents a brief account of this approach, stressing the implications of time-limited programs. Kruschke and Stoller (1967) have described an accelerated interaction group in a correctional facility for drug addicts and discuss the potential of this approach for this particular population as well as its promise and limitations within institutions. Less scientific but nevertheless authentic within its framework is a novelist's description of a marathon weekend, *The Lemon Eaters* (Sohl, 1967).

SAMPLE PROTOCOLS

It was felt that there was inadequate room to include the extensive sample protocols that would be required to convey the sense of a marathon experience. However, an example from a marathon group conducted with video tape is included in the chapter on focused feedback. These protocols are a very limited example of what can occur in an intensive group. Attention is particularly directed toward the latter part of these protocols, in which an example of what has been referred to as "sharing" is shown; a participant permits himself to affect the other group members in a fashion that is distinctly different than his previous behavior.

SUMMARY

Marathon group therapy involves a rearrangement of time in that a group meets continuously for twenty-four to thirty or more hours. As opposed to the traditional arrangements, the marathon group heightens the experiential nature of what occurs, producing singular effects. Intense levels of emotion and involvement are attained which permit much more rapid learning about oneself than generally occurs. The continuity of contact permits individuals to learn more readily about the cause and effect in their own behavior as opposed to looking for understanding in their past history or in their situational problems.

The significant amount of time spent together gives participants the opportunity to sense their course through the world which tends to parallel their career in the marathon. Above all, the intense experience of such groups provides a concept of potentials, both within the participants themselves and within the world at large. By placing the individual within a situation which makes extraordinary demands upon him, the realization of one's potential is possible; the marathon leans more heavily upon the future use of oneself than it does upon past shortcomings.

Rather than technical manipulation on the part of the group leader, the marathon is conceived as an experiment in intimacy, with honesty, directness, and immediacy of response, and the demand for change within the situation being deliberately fostered. Because a specific time limit is built into the arrangements, an urgency is developed which forces the participants and group leader to reach further than they are likely to do under ordinary circumstances.

While clinical experience is necessary, adherence to the clinical approach is minimized and participants are seen purely in terms of how they enter the marathon situation and what they elicit in the other group members. Leveling, honesty, trust, and the constructive expression of aggression are all considered to be essential elements of the marathon experience which promote the utilization of these characteristics in the participant's life.

The marathon can be seen in terms of developing crises through threats to the individual's self-image and the necessity to resolve these crises in alternate ways to the usual withdrawal and increased role playing, because of the impossibility of pulling out of the marathon situation.

REFERENCES

ALEXANDER, F.: Psychoanalytic contributions to short-term psychotherapy. In L. M. Wolberg (Ed.), *Short-term Psychotherapy*. New York, Grune, 1965, pp. 84-126.

BACH, G. R.: The marathon group: intensive practice of intimate interaction. *Psychol. Rep., 18*: 995-1002, 1966.

BACH, G. R.; STOLLER, F. H., and WOLPIN, M.: Symposium on Marathon

Groups. California State Psychological Assn Meeting, Los Angeles, 1964.

BERNE, E.: *Transactional Analysis in Psychotherapy*. New York, Grove, 1961.

FRANK, J. D.: *Persuasion and Healing*. Baltimore, Johns Hopkins, 1961.

GOFFMAN, E.: *Asylums*. New York, Doubleday, 1961.

HALEY, J.: *Strategies of Psychotherapy*. New York, Grune, 1963.

HILL, W. F.: *Hill Interaction Matrix*. Los Angeles, Youth Studies Center, Univ Southern Calif, 1965.

JOURARD, S. M.: *The Transparent Self*. Princeton, N.J., Van Nostrand, 1964.

KRUSCHKE, D., and STOLLER, F. H.: Face to face with the drug addict: An account of an intensive group experience. *Federal Probation, 31(2)*: 47-52, 1967.

MASLOW, A. H.: *Toward a Psychology of Being*. Princeton, N.J., Van Nostrand, 1962.

MASSERMAN, J. J.: Historical-comparative and experimental roots of short-term therapy. In L. M. Wolberg (Ed.), *Short-term Psychotherapy*. New York, Grune, 1965, pp. 23-50.

MORENO, J. L.: *Psychodrama*. New York, Beacon, 1946.

MOWRER, O. H.: *The New Group Therapy*. Princeton, N.J., Van Nostrand, 1964.

PATTISON, E. M.: Evaluating studies of group psychotherapy. *Int J Group Psychother, 15*: 382-397, 1965.

SOHL, J.: *The Lemon Eaters*. New York, Simon and Schuster, 1967.

STOLLER, F. H.; LOKIE, G.; MORRISON, A.; WALLER, R., and WICKLAND, R.: Accelerated Interaction: A collective presentation by members of "Swing," a professional cooperative of group psychotherapists. Paper read at the Group Psychotherapy Assn. of Southern Calif Annual Conference, Los Angeles, 1964.

STOLLER, F. H.: Accelerated Interaction: A time-limited approach based on the brief, intensive group. Dept of Mental Hygiene, State of Calif. Bureau of Research. No. 352. 1966.

WICKLAND, R.; WALLER, R., and STOLLER, F. H.: Innovations in Group Therapy. Symposium at the Calif State Psychological Assn. Meeting, San Francisco, 1963.

IV

EMERGENCE THERAPY

The TORI Process in an Emergent Group

JACK R. GIBB AND LORRAINE M. GIBB

THERAPY is the process of restoration of the growth processes. Health is growth—both in the person and in the group.
This growth viewpoint toward therapy is central to what the authors have called "emergence therapy" the basic propositions of
which will be summarized in the first section of this chapter.

During all social interaction, four modal concerns arise in the
person and in the group: concerns about acceptance, data flow,
goal formation, and social control. In normal interaction there is
movement, in individuals and in groups, toward trust and away
from fear, toward open and away from closed behavior, toward
self-realization and away from imposition, toward interdependence
and away from dependence. For communicative ease these processes of growth have been called the TORI processes, representing movement toward trust, openness, realization, and interdependence (see Table I). These processes are therapeutic—
define therapy—are independent of the presence of a therapist,
regenerative in character, and intrinsic to all normal life processes
in human organisms.

Persons as they grow are continually confronted with four life
issues which parallel these modal concerns: How much can I
trust? How intimate can I be? What do I want out of life? How
do I influence my world? Life is a process of continual confrontation and resolution of these issues. They are never in a sense finally resolved in the person or in the group.

Growth is facilitated by nondefensive inner conditions and
high trust interpersonal relationships. The authors distinguish between growth relationships (Table II) and defensive or counter-
growth (Table III) relationships. Growth occurs inevitably in re-

lationships that are genuinely trusting, open, reciprocally fulfilling, and interdependent. Growth is inevitably inhibited in defensive relationships— relationships initiated and sustained to ward off perceived or anticipated threat. Defensive relationships are characterized by high fear, masking, reciprocal persuasion, and dependency.

Life is a blending of growth experiences and defensive experiences. During the process of building memberships, making decisions, developing goals, and evolving social controls the person develops a life style that can be described on these four critical dimensions: from trust through fear, from intimacy through withdrawal, from self-determination through duty motivation, and from interdependence through dependence. This life style is rationalized and buttressed by a more or less implicit life theory which is to a large degree consonant with the expressive life and which services the self, justifies one's actions, reduces one's guilt, and lends a self-perceived consistency to one's actions.

The life theory becomes more or less articulated, representing one's implicit assumptions about his trust, intimacy, identity, and influence. This set of assumptions is continually being confirmed or disconfirmed in social interaction. Because of the self-fulfilling quality of the perceptual defense system, the theories tend to be confirmed by experience and difficult to dislodge. The life theory becomes a theory of management. Whenever a person is placed in a position of responsibility, he is predisposed to be trusting, open, integrative or interdepending, or to be distrusting, strategic, persuasive-coercive, or controlling. All of his "managing" behavior can be described as having some degree of each component. This managerial theory is consonant with his need system and tends to guide and motivate his actions in all interpersonal situations and particularly in situations in which he assumed responsibility as a parent, leader, manager, teacher, or therapist.

Two need systems are hypothecated which become differentially activated with the relationship (Table V). A defensive-need system becomes activated with defensive relationships. A growth-supportive need system becomes activated in growth relationships.

Therapy takes place in growth relationships. Therapy is a relationship, a social process. All relationships which are growth-producing and defense-reductive are therapeutic. All relationships which are trust-reductive and defense-producing are contratherapeutic. It is the writers' thesis that all group relationships can become "growthful" and thus therapeutic. Under certain conditions all groups become regenerative. The TORI processes occur inevitably—growth toward trust, openness, realization, and interdependence—unless special and sustained fear is present. These processes occur independent of the presence of a special therapist. Because of the nature of these growth processes, continued membership in a strong healthy group is more therapeutic or growth-producing than in special dyadic therapy or special group therapy, unless the special therapy does in effect produce a "strong" group in the sense herein described. The TORI processes are therapeutic in themselves. As healthy social groups occur in families and in volunteer and work groups, special therapy becomes less and less necessary in our culture. Social engineering or social reorganization is a process of inventing the conditions under which strong groups can occur.

The therapist can participate in the therapeutic processes by facilitating these TORI processes. He does this by becoming as trusting-personal, open-intimate, realizing-integrative, and interdepending as he can become—by entering into growth relationships with clients, either in dyads or in larger groups.

In the present frame of reference change in the person comes about through changing one's experiences and changing one's life theory. The therapist, in order to intrude into the life process of the person, must act in such a way as to facilitate the TORI processes. The TORI processes tend to predispose the person to seek and to some extent to create growth experiences for himself. A person produces his own experiences. These experiences may gradually or suddenly change the TORI life theory of the person.

In certain cases experiences must be compelling and intense enough to disconfirm the life theory of the person and hence change his life theme and life style, thus predisposing him to new growth experiences. Experience has shown that enduring and sustaining life in intimate groups produces these special and intense experiences which the authors have called the *TORI experiences* of caring, consensus, commitment, and interdependence (Table

IV). These special depth experiences are rare and occur only after sustained supportive life in intensive, role-free groups which relate for a period of from fifty to two-hundred hours or thereabouts. These TORI experiences have special significance in accelerating growth and in increasing the predispositions and skills which enable persons to enter and sustain growth relationships in the marriage, the family, the job, and all other relevant and potentially intimate groups.

Therapy is of little significance to the person if it does not (1) change his TORI theory in a significant way and (2) predispose him to change significantly his behavior in his home, his job, and his relevant life groups.

It is the aim of this chapter to discuss in detail the above theory, particularly the growth relationships, the defensive relationships, the TORI processes, the TORI life theories, the TORI experiences, and the therapist's role.

BASIC MODAL CONCERNS

Largely as a by-product of a decade of research sponsored by the Office of Naval Research, the authors have analyzed developmental sequences in several hundred therapy, sensitivity, and natural groups of varying size and duration (Gibb, 1964a). The theory of growth outlined above is derived from these studies. Basic to the theory is the assumption that the following four basic modal concerns are characteristic of the growth and development of persons and groups subject to internal and environmental forces inducing change.

One set of concerns has to do with *acceptance and membership*. Persons and groups are concerned about the acceptance of self, the acceptance of others, the development of trust, the reduction of fear, and the achievement of satisfying membership in relevant groups. This acceptance concern is antecedent to the other three concerns. It is represented by such questions as the following: Whom can I trust? How much do I love myself? Whom need I fear? How fearful am I? Which of my fears are legitimate? Am I basically loved and lovable? Can I accept all that I see in myself? How can I get love and caring from relevant others? How do I learn to love and trust? How do I learn to give and receive love? How do I attain membership in social groups which are important to me? Is nature trustworthy, neutral, or to be feared?

A second set of concerns has to do with *intimacy and decision making*. These concerns are about communication with self and others, intimacy and psychological distance, role and personness, authenticity, understanding and being understood, and the processing of these data into group decisions. This concern is intimately intertwined with the membership concern and can be satisfyingly dealt with only when some genuine processing of the membership concern has occurred. This concern is represented by such questions as the following: How do I get in touch with myself? Can I open myself even to me? What are my real feelings? How much do I have to deceive myself? How much person and how much role am I? Where am I in my various role prescriptions? How lonely need I be? How do I reveal the genuine me to others? How open can I or need I be? How do I communicate my real self and my own feelings to others in ways that will not hurt me, be misunderstood, or hurt others? How close can I come to others? How do I learn to give and receive intimacy? How can I process all the relevant data into my own decisions and into decisions that I must make with others? How much need I be concerned with image and facade and impression? How well can I feel into another person's world, or he into mine?

A third set of concerns has to do with *motivation and productivity*. These concerns relate to motivation, purpose, personal identity, self-actualization, group goal setting, and the influencing of the goals of others. This concern is best dealt with after some progress has been made on the membership and intimacy concerns. It is represented by such questions as the following: Who am I? What do I want to become? How do I find myself? How do I translate my impulses into sustained action? How can I find goals that are deeply mine and that will bring meaning and significance to my life? What should I seek for, work for? How do I find realization? How can I get help from others in my own quest? How can I mesh my goal life with the goal lives of relevant others? How can I create with others goals that are more than a compromise? How do we mesh seemingly irreconcilable goals? What should I do about group or organizational goals that are incompatible with mine? How can I change these goals? How can I contribute to group life around me?

A fourth set of concerns has to do with *control and organization.* This concern relates to authority, freedom, control, interdependence, rebellion, and cooperation. This concern is clearly contingent upon development among the three other major concerns. This concern often disappears when the other three are adequately resolved. This concern is represented by such questions as the following: How do I relate to authority? How do I influence others? How do I achieve freedom? How adequate am I? How important am I to myself and to others? How do I express and handle my rebellious feelings? How can I rebel in a way that is satisfying to me and influential on others? How can I get significant and satisfying power and influence? How do I work with others in getting work done? How do I give and receive freedom? How do I enter into organizations and groups? How much do I need to control others and how do I manage these feelings? How do I handle others' needs to control me?

Although the modal concerns may be camouflaged in various ways under imposition of goal or control structure, the authors' data suggest the hypothesis that the concerns are present in all groups and all persons, regardless of leadership, task, structure, or social context. These concerns become life issues. Growth is a continual process of confrontation and partial resolution of these issues. Optimal growth occurs as a concurrent and interdependent development on each of the four factors with the four factors "leading" each other in optimal sequence: climate, data flow, goal formation, and control. Growth on each factor is contingent upon growth in each of the preceding factors in the contingency hierarchy.

TORI PROCESSES AND DEFENSIVE PROCESSES

Persons grow. Groups grow. With normal interaction, persons and groups move toward increasing trust, openness, self-realization, and interdependence and away from the antithetical states of fear, closed behavior, impositional motivation, and dependency. It is assumed that these growth (TORI) processes flow naturally from all human relationships, and emerge from all normal social interaction. Table I portrays how the personal and group TORI processes parallel the modal concerns and the basic life issues. Growth is seen as a natural, healthy state of social systems. Growth is essentially an inner process, the rate and direction of which can be influenced by the environment of the system. The authors are in the process of doing extensive research on the determiners of differential rates of growth (Gibb, 1963). We assume that a direct route to improvement of the effectiveness of therapy is to make progress in determining how the rate of growth may be altered and accelerated.

Under certain conditions a person develops a trusting orientation toward the world, makes trust assumptions about people, is predisposed to take TORI attitudes and build the growth relationships described in Table II. Under other conditions a person develops a fear orientation towards the world, makes fear-distrust assumptions about people, is predisposed to defend himself, takes countergrowth attitudes, and builds the defensive relationships described in Table III.

In the system described herein, trust and fear are antonyms representing polar ends of the central life processes. As a person grows, his trusts become more enduring, more reality based, and more intertwined with his life theme and life theory. He learns to trust more and to fear less. With increasing trust the person learns to be more caring, more intimate, more search-oriented, and more interdepending.

Growth is a movement toward greater acceptance of self and others. The trusting person comes to accept more parts of himself. He comes to trust his impulses and other manifestations of his unconscious urges. He learns to trust his body and its messages. He accepts and lives with his feelings, urges, and fears. As he experiences more of what he really is, he is able to be more personal, remove his protective masks, depart from prescribed roles, and contact other persons in depth. With greater trust the world becomes a friendlier place. He allows himself to come closer to other persons. With increasing intimacy, others become more predictable and less frightening. For the trusting person the

TABLE I

THE TORI GROWTH PROCESSES IN PERSONS AND IN GROUPS

Basic Modal Concerns	Derivative Personal and Interpersonal Problems	Directions of Personal Growth	Directions of Group Growth
Climate	Membership (How do I learn to trust myself and others, and gain satisfying membership in significant groups?)	Trust (Toward trust and acceptance of self and others: more trust and less fear of persons and of nature)	Trust (Toward a climate of trust and support, low defense and low fear)
Data Flow	Decision Making (How do I reveal me, and how do we process feeling and perception data into valid decisions?)	Openness (Toward greater awareness and reception, and more valid output, open spontaneity)	Openness (Toward a more valid feedback system and consensual decision making)
Goal Formation	Productivity (How do I find out who I am and what I want, and how do we find out what to seek, produce, and work for?)	Realization (Toward self-fulfillment and actualization; goal integration; self-determination and self-assessment)	Realization (Toward an integration of group goals, group determination, and group assessment and progress)
Control	Organization (How do I find an inner, emergent control and value system, and how do we achieve a functional interdependence?)	Interdependence (Toward an emergent integration of values and ability to take a "with" relation)	Interdependence (Toward an emergent norm and control system, a participative interdependence)

TABLE II

THE GROWTH (THERAPEUTIC) RELATIONSHIPS

Basic Modal Concerns	Growth Relationships	Typical Behaviors and Attitudes	Typical Feelings
Climate	Trust-acceptance (Reciprocal state of deep trust, caring and affection)	Acceptance (Confidence, trust, personal and nonrole relationship, nonjudgmental attitude)	Warmth (Affection, love, esteem, sympathy, caring)
Data Flow	Openness-intimacy (Two-way communication in depth, reciprocal empathy and receptivity)	Empathy-listening (Rapport, communion, impulse, spontaneity, intimacy)	Intimacy (Serenity, warmth, freedom, comfort, safety, coziness)
Goal Formation	Realization-search (Reciprocally fulfilling and shared problem solving and search)	Quest (Searching, actualizing, fulfillment, achievement, exploring)	Zest (Eagerness, exhilaration, fervency, satisfaction, well being)
Control	Interdependence-emergence (Participative, emergent and rule-free state of interdependent cooperation)	Integration (Participation, interaction, freedom, spontaneity, cooperation, working with)	Freedom (Power, importance, worth, adequacy, potency, sense of being needed)

risks of loving and caring seem small. He enjoys expressive love and affection.

Growth is a movement both toward intimacy and away from social distance. As one trusts the world he allows himself to come close to it. Being more in touch with his own person he can bring his person in closer touch with other persons. As he comes in deeper touch with more parts of himself he can understand and empathize with more parts of another person. He can find within himself all representations of psychological reality. All of reality is in him. With greater communication with self and others he sees and feels his deep kinship with all other persons. He can fight, love, hate, share—show all of himself—confident that this process will bring greater intimacy and reciprocal empathy. The trusting person hears better, with less distortion. He filters less, judges less, and evaluates less. There is also less distortion in his output system. He becomes more impulsive and spontaneous. He worries less about facade, politeness, caution, masking, public relations, and image-making. He feels more comfortable and safe in intimacy.

Growth is movement toward greater realization and fulfillment. As the trusting person becomes more in touch with himself he develops more confidence in his own abilities. He comes to trust the unknown, and thus be more venturesome, exploratory, creative, curious, and open to new experiences. He is predisposed toward shared searching and joint inquiry. He is less conserving of the world that was and more oriented toward the world that might be. The trusting person comes to look at new experience with zest and eagerness. Life becomes more fulfilling—either alone or with others. When with others, life is more often shared fulfillment and less often competitive striving.

Growth is movement toward feelings of freedom, power, and interdependence. As one trusts others he finds them less threatening. As one learns to like himself he sees himself as having worth and value. He makes positive assumptions about others' attitudes and motivations. He assumes that others will find him of worth, value, and importance. Early experiences with authority tend to create fear, psychological distance, and closed communication. With trust the person is able to break away from domi-

TABLE III
THE DEFENSIVE (COUNTER-GROWTH) RELATIONSHIPS

Basic Modal Concerns	Defensive Relationships	Typical Behaviors and Attitudes	Typical Feelings
Climate	Fear-distrust (Reciprocal state of fear, distrust, high defense)	Punishment (Evaluation, judgment, moralizing, coldness, fear, distrust)	Alienation (Hostility, envy, suspicion, fear, cynicism)
Data Flow	Distance-facade (Reciprocal masking, strategic distancing, superficial communication)	Strategy (Circumvention, masking, distortion, deception, politeness, ambiguity, formality)	Loneliness (Estrangement, withdrawal, depression, sadness)
Goal Formation	Persuasion-competition (Reciprocal imposition, polemic, counterforce, and dissonant locomotion)	Persuasion (Coercion, guidance, manipulation, passivity, resistance)	Indifference (Apathy, disinterest, resentment, latent hostility)
Control	Dependence-dominance (Differential status and power, dominance countered by submission or rebellion)	Control (Management, dependency, counterdependency, rebellion, submission)	Impotence (Inadequacy, tension, latent or manifest hostility)

nant-submissive relationships with others, to free himself from his
early authority attitudes, and to build more interdependent and
cooperative relationships with others.

Table III summarizes the counter-growth processes, behaviors,
and feelings that arise when fear becomes the prepotent factor in
the momentary or enduring relationship. Fear predisposes the
person to defend his behavior, attitudes, life theory, and perception of the world. He becomes less trusting of others and of himself. He tries to manage his own communications, his impulses,
his motivations, and his relationships with others. The threatening world must be managed and controlled. His impulse is to
change others rather than to change himself. The world is seen as
impassively neutral, as unfriendly, perhaps as hostile. Behavior
tends to be defensive, distancing, impositional, and controlling.
Bred in fear, defensive climates breed new fears and distrusts.
Fearful people underperceive their own adequacy. When people
are confronted with situations in which they see themselves as
having no adequate response they respond with some degree of
apprehension and anxiety. The affect life is a mixture of fears and
trusts. New situations call forth a mixture of curiosity and apprehension. In defensive climates fears become ascendent and well
differentiated. Persons develop fears of being seen as inadequate,
unimportant, unskilled, or uninformed. They fear being misunderstood, hurt, embarrassed, alone, or disliked. Latent fear becomes the dominant emotional theme of the defensive climate.

Fear predisposes a person to build fear-distrust relationships
which inhibit growth. The fearful person is more disposed to
make judgments than to observe and describe, to be cold or neutral rather than warm and personal, and to be suspicious rather
than trusting. The projections of the fearful person contain the
punishing, distancing, coercive, and controlling elements in himself. He therefore sees the world as increasingly unfriendly and
full of the elements that corroborate his fears. His fears are thus
exacerbated.

The fearful person manages, filters, and distorts his communications with himself and with others. He has difficulty coming
into direct and deep communication with himself. He finds it
difficult to determine how he feels, what he wants, whom he

trusts, and even what he fears. He masks and camouflages himself to himself and to others. He often finds it especially difficult to recognize his fears. Fears are fearful. Facades emerge or are deliberately fostered in the process of image making, public relations, and communications management. Much energy, conscious and unconscious, goes into making of masks and the taking of depersonalizing roles. Depending upon the life style, facades emerge which involve mixtures of caution, deception, ambiguity, politeness, strategy, humor, game playing, and role taking (Gibb, 1961).

Fear predisposes a person toward impositional motivation. The fearful person looks outside himself for legitimation of his behavior, sanction for his goals, and validation of his life. He is not comfortable with his inner motives, nor trusting of his impulses and spontaneous desires. He is predisposed to look for what he ought to do. His motivations are likely to come from authority, role, custom, a sense of obligation and duty, and role prescriptions of others. He feels strongly the restraints of social control. His motives can often be managed by others. He can be manipulated by extrinsic rewards—competition, approval, grades, money, and kudos. He can be programmed by friends, groups, and authorities. The fearful person, requiring programming himself, attempts to program and manage the motivations of others. He guides, persuades, argues, teaches, manipulates, counsels, protects, and disciplines. His reactions to the controls of others range from frenetic compliance to resentful passivity.

Fear predisposes a person to overperceive and overreact to the significance of authority figures and to the importance of management and control. In a world perceived as unfriendly or hostile, powerful figures are most dangerous of all. His respect for status, hierarchy, and power is tinged with fear. The presence of people in authority may increase his feelings of inadequacy and insignificance, or he may derive his feelings of adequacy from identification with the authority figures. When in a position of power he is apt to dominate, protect, manage, or overcontrol. Depending on his life style, he will be fatherly, protective, domineering, or coercive. He becomes dependent or counterdependent, both states being dynamically similar and accompanied by latent hostility.

LIFE STYLES AND LIFE THEORIES

Life is a blending of growth experiences and defensive experiences predisposing persons to some mixture of fear and trust. Out of the basic modal experiences in building memberships, making choices, developing goals, influencing and being influenced, the person develops a life style. This style becomes more or less stabilized and enduring. The person's life style, management style, implicit life theory, management theory, defense level, and perceptual system tend to stabilize, accommodate, and develop into a constellation that becomes predictable to self and to others.

Many phenomena serve to perpetuate and confirm this stable system. Projective perception helps the person to see the world of people and things as he wishes to see it, as he *must* see it to rationalize or justify his trusts or his fears. If he presents a seemingly warm and open self, his partner in the perceptual relationship, if predominantly fearful-defensive, can see his presenting behavior as a facade confirming his cynical perceptual predisposition. If the perceiver is more trusting-accepting, he can see the presenting behavior as general confirmation of his trust-oriented view and theory of people and things. The person tends to overperceive confirming and underperceive disconfirming data. A person thus produces his own experience—at least to a significant degree.

One tends to act out his fear or trust tendencies and attitudes. The fearful person acts fearful and breeds fear and distrust. The trusting person acts trusting and breeds trust. In positions of responsibility, the fearful person acts to some degree punishing, strategic, persuasive, and controlling and produces the behavior, attitudes, and feelings that confirm his fear-determined expectations. People *are* less trustworthy, more circumventive, more resistant-apathetic, and more rebellious or submissive. This is exactly what his "high fear-low trust" theory would predict and what he has come to expect from those who need his managing and for whom he is responsible. The process, again, has a self-fulfilling quality. The people in the system for whom he is responsible become less responsible, more resistant, more dependent and more circumventive; that is, less trustworthy.

The converse, of course, is also true. In positions of responsibility, the trusting person acts to some degree accepting, empathic, reciprocally fulfilling, and interdepending and produces the attitudes, feelings, and behavior that confirm his high-trust hypotheses. People *are* more trustworthy, more intimate-spontaneous, more creative-realizing, and more interdependent. This result tends to confirm his high-trust theory and what he has come to expect from people for whom he has been given responsibility. The process is, again, self-fulfilling.

Thus a person develops a set of rationalizations and implicit assumptions that become a relatively stable life theory. This life theory is highly consonant with his prepotent need system and his stablilized life style. The theory is supported by the need system at many levels. It is confirmed by his projective perceptions and his self-created experiences. It enables the person to feel rational and consistent. Even to the sophisticated person this theory is relatively nonpermeable to disconfirming data. A person is continually performing little informal experiments with his world. The experiments confirm the theory. In each informal and fragmentary experiment the person sets up his own hypotheses, determines his own levels of confidence, selects and tabulates his own data, and makes his own conclusions. The idiosyncratic nature of the experiment makes it highly likely that it will come out in the predicted direction. Thus the life theory comes to be remarkably persistent.

In interpersonal relations one's management-theory aspect of his life theory is of particular importance. When people are in positions of responsibility—as parent, teacher, therapist, manager, friend—their informal management theory emerges. One's management style and management theory emerge from his fear and trust assumptions and needs (Gibb, 1966). In high trust, persons in positions of responsibility tend to be more accepting, empathic-listening, reciprocal-actualizing, and freedom-giving. In greater fear, persons in positions of responsibility tend to be more impersonal, strategic, persuasive-coercive, and controlling.

Behavior and motivation are complex. The person who is predisposed to be trusting always sees some amount of love with the hate, some approach with the withdrawal, some seeking with the avoidance, some permitting with the coercion, and some searching with the persuasion. Conversely, for the person predisposed to fear there is some withdrawal in the approach, some hostility in the affection, some manipulation in the sharing, and some deception in the openness. There are always both fear and trust components in the action and its motive. Fear predisposes us to react to the fear component and trust predisposes us to react to the trust component. Trusting people tend to attribute good intentions and motivations to others. The more we distrust, the more we tend to attribute negative motivations or ill will to others. Motivations are always invisible and inferred, and thus the perception of another's motivations is full of projective distortion. Inasmuch as motives always have both fear and trust components, there is always some reality to the fear or trust projections. People normally have mixed needs and intentions, which are never completely clear either to the actor or to the perceiver. The apparent presence of conflicting motivations within the person leads us to the hypothesis that there are two need systems.

CONTRAPUNTAL AND DYADIC NEED SYSTEMS

Man acts as if he is under the energizing and directing influence of two contrapuntal need systems. Growth is a constant polyphonic process of counterbalancing within the organism the needs to love and to punish, to be intimate and to withdraw, to fulfill others and to manipulate them, to interdepend and to control. Most social actions have an ambivalent, complex, and polar quality. When we withdraw to sulk, we wish that someone, somehow, would find us and invite us to intimacy. When we hate, it is because someone is important enough to matter. When we punish, it is with guilt. We give freedom with some implicit, perhaps unconscious contingency. When we rejoice in another's good fortune, there is an accompanying tinge of jealousy. Punishment and coercion are motivated in part by concern for the other's welfare.

Under high trust man acts as if he has four dominant needs: to give and receive love, to give and receive intimacy, to give and receive fulfillment, and to give and receive freedom (Table V).

TABLE IV
THE TORI DEPTH EXPERIENCES

Basic Modal Concerns	The TORI Personal-enrichment Experiences	The TORI Group-enrichment Experiences
Climate	Trust-love (I feel loved and trusted now and am a lovable person, fully deserving of love and trust.)	Caring (All group members have a deep sustained feeling of trust and love for all members of the group.)
Data Flow	Intimacy (I feel at this moment completely understood at all levels and feel that I can be again; am relating as a role-free person.)	Consensus (Complete group understanding and agreement on a course of action after full exploration of all relevant alternatives in personal, role-free interaction)
Goal Formation	Zest (I have found a goal that is deeply mine and gives full meaning and becoming to my life at this moment.)	Commitment (Sustained and genuinely zestful search by all members for an enduring, consensual goal)
Control	Freedom-power (I feel exhilaratingly free and powerful and am not anxious about anyone abridging either my freedom or my power.)	Emergence (The emergence of a true constraint-free group interdependence with no rules or status-role hierarchy)

Under high-fear defense he acts as if he has four prepotent needs: to give and receive punishment, to give and receive distance, to give and receive persuasion, and to give and receive control.

There is a high degree of interrelationship in the cluster of high-trust motivations and behaviors and also within the cluster of high-fear motivations and behaviors. An angry, hostile person is likely to attempt to control and to manipulate. Punishment and control are especially related, both in motivation and in manifestation. The defense systems are triggered as a constellation. Manifest and phenotypical behaviors are diverse and complex, depending upon the life style. The authors are assuming that the need system is mobilized in a genotypically unitary way. This is true of both the fear system and the trust system. Phenotypical diversity masks the underlying unity of the two need systems.

When the fear-defense system becomes mobilized, the manifest behavior is inimical to the long-range growth needs of the person. Fear-defensive need-behavior systems are functional in the sense that they meet temporary system needs, *i.e.* to punish, withdraw, control, or manipulate. They are dysfunctional, neurotic, and self-defeating in the sense that they do not meet the long-range system needs, which are in this sense more fundamental, basic, and intrinsic to the enduring nature of the organism, *i.e.* to trust, open, realize, and interdepend.

When the fear-defense needs are low, when man is not threatened, and when growth needs are prepotent, man's presenting behavior is predominantly loving, intimate, fulfilling, and interdependent. A diet of experiences over a long period or in significant depth with man in this state leads to a life style and a life theory which are significantly loaded with trust components. It then seems to the self and to observers that man's nature is basically trusting, that he is "essentially good," that he is possessed by a Holy Spirit, that human nature can be changed, that society can progress, or that group therapy can be more than temporarily remedial.

When fear-defense needs are high, when man is threatened, when growth needs are immobilized, man's presenting behavior becomes predominantly punishing, distancing, competitive, and controlling. A heavy diet of experiences over a long period or in some depth with self or with others in this state leads to a low-trust high-fear life style and life theory. It seems to self and to observers that man's nature is basically distrusting, that he is "essentially evil," that he is possessed by the Devil, that human nature cannot be changed, that society can make only ephemeral progress, or that therapy can at best be remedial, expedient, and like the fighting of recurring fires.

Significant experiences in depth are required to make enduring changes in life styles and life theories.

THE TORI DEPTH EXPERIENCES

During the process of growth, persons in groups create the conditions which maximize social learning. Elsewhere the writers have described what their research has indicated to be the essential conditions for a learning climate (Gibb, 1958). These conditions are norms which permit (1) *exposure* of a person's behavior, life style, and life theory to himself and to others, (2) utilizable *feedback* to the person of the effects upon himself and upon others of his behavior, life style, and life theory, (3) a *high-trust climate* which permits processing of the relevant data, and (4) *provisional behavior* directed toward gradual, emergent, or sudden modification of the behavior, style, or theory.

Research by the authors has indicated that these conditions occur in a wide variety of settings: some therapy groups, sensitivity groups, programmed groups, natural groups, and leaderless groups. The conditions are most powerful in groups that are leaderless and that come together for the special purpose and expectation of personal learning, in what the authors have called emergent groups. The TORI processes occur inevitably in sustained periods in such groups.

As trust and intimacy increase, members inevitably share a wide variety of feelings and perceptions, including one or more of the typical feelings associated with defensive relationships: alienation, loneliness, indifference, and impotence (see Table III). These feelings are usually reported as parallel with and accompanying the defensive relationships.

The feelings of *alienation* are reported as associated with a deep and persisting experience of being unloved, of being an unlovable person, or perhaps of never having *really* been loved. These feelings are often associated with a prolonged and/or intense period of being distrusted or punished.

The feelings of *loneliness* are associated with deep and/or continuing feelings of being misunderstood, of never having been really understood, or of never being in communication with a person who understood one enough to care what one was really like. These feelings are reported as associated with a prolonged and/or intense period of deceptive distancing, often when others seemed to feel or pretended to feel intimacy.

The feelings of *indifference* are reported as associated with sustained periods during which one has failed to find a goal of sufficient importance to create meaning or zest in one's life. The feelings are often associated with periods in which central-authority figures have tried to guide or manipulate the person toward impositional goals.

The feelings of *impotence* are reported as associated with prolonged and/or intense periods when the person has not felt free, has felt dominated by authority figures, usually parents, or has felt that others seemed to feel he was inadequate or unimportant. These feelings are usually associated with feeling dominated by authority.

The story of the group as a learning climate is essentially a description of continuing exposure, feedback, trust, and provisional behavior. This sequence repeats itself in continuing cycles of increasing depth and significance. The therapeutic TORI processes continue to develop in persons and in the group. Of particular significance and special potency as therapeutic media are four depth experiences which both emerge from and disconfirm the four defensive feelings mentioned above. These TORI experiences are described in Table V. There are, of course, all shades, varieties, and complexities of experience in a depth group. These four experiences have a global and dramatic quality that makes the experience immediately recognizable to one who has undergone the experience.

The *caring experience* is a powerful experience in which all members achieve a deep and sustained feeling of some high degree of trust and love for all members of the group. The experi-

TABLE V

CONTRAPUNTAL NEED SYSTEMS IN THE PERSON

Basic Modal Concerns	Growth Needs (Those ascendent during high-trust, low-fear states)	Defense Needs (Those ascendent during low-trust, high-fear states)
Climate	Love (To give and receive love and trust)	Punishment (To give and receive punishment, to manage warmth)
Data Flow	Intimacy (To give and receive communication in depth, to be intimate)	Distance (To give and receive social distance, to withdraw, to manage intimacy)
Goal Formation	Realization (To give and receive personal fulfillment)	Persuasion (To give and receive persuasion-imposition, to manage goals)
Control	Freedom (To give and receive freedom)	Control (To give and receive controls; to be dominant or dependent)

ence is definitely an unprecedented and unpredicted one for almost all members. During or following the experience, individuals may report a special personal experience of being lovable and deserving of love and trust, perhaps experienced for the first time in such depth. A significant element in the experience is a growing trust for persons, particularly for this group of special persons, but also a feeling that people are potentially more lovable than they had previously seemed. Members report many learnings: the relationship between love and trust, the finding that one can deeply care for a person of the same sex, the fact that loving a person in a trusting way makes it easier to love others, the feeling that every person can be loved. The authors' impression is that this experience of feeling truly loved and trusted and lovable is the one indispensable requirement for personal growth.

The *consensus experience* makes it possible for persons to get a specific image of what group decision making can be after group growth. Most people have experienced action decisions where group members have expressed no verbal dissent, but very few have experienced a convincing and meaningful consensus. A *full* consensus involves complete group understanding and agreement on a course of action after full exploration of all creative and relevant alternatives in working on a significant problem that confronts the group. A *deep* consensus means that group members have expressed feelings and perceptions in an open, spontaneous, and creative way. Such a consensus implies that a state of deep trust exists, and, may even be a good measure of trust. The consensus implies involvement, intimacy, and effective communication on relevant issues. A deep consensus typically occurs only after forty or fifty hours of very effective group learning. Achieving the consensus is very satisfying to group members. The achievement is accompanied by real feelings of euphoria and a sense of personal and group effectiveness.

The *commitment experience* is a sustained and genuinely zestful search by all members for an enduring, consensual goal. The group must have reached a consensus on a goal after deep sharing of personal goals. The commitment experience implies sustained intimacy and trust. It means that the group has created a goal that is highly satisfying to all members, that is considerably more than a compromise, that is a creation of the group out of deep sharing of individual goals, and to which members feel unequivocal commitment. Members feel that they have created something new. They feel a sense of power. They feel they could change the goal if they so wished. They feel they have overcome the early feelings of cynicism and impotency that arise inevitably when the common-goal question first arises in unstructured groups. Members learn, perhaps for the first time, what a group goal can be, and what the potential for effective group action can be.

The *emergence experience* is a feeling on the part of all group members of freedom from constraints at the same time they feel a deep sense of power. They experience a feeling of getting much from the group without having to give up anything to get it. Each member has contributed a great deal to the group but feels no deprivation. The true interdependence experience is different from either an experience of dependence or an experience of independence. Members feel fully dependent upon other members of the group—for resource help, for emotional support, for information, for contributions to the shared task. The feeling of absence of restraint is significant. Members do not feel conformity pressures.

Early in the life of the group, the members fear commitment, conformity, dependence, and group involvement. Groups are normally fearful objects to members who first come into therapy or training. The significance of the emergence experience is that groups become objects of trust. Once the member has a true experience of freedom and power in genuine interdependence, he has a depth experience that groups *can* be unfrightening and power-giving rather than power-taking.

The emergence experience is more rare than any of the other three TORI experiences and requires that the group have gone through the other three experiences in order to achieve interdependence. This experience, more than any other, gives members a feeling of hope and potential for their own lives and for their own natural groups. This experience opens up to members the possibilities for interdependent action in government, community, and business groups. Most members report that it has most relevance for the home and family. It opens up the real possibility for depth and meaning to family living.

These TORI experiences are seen by members as special, unique, and of *central significance* to personal life. There is usually a feeling of being lucky to be in this special group. "I'm glad that I am in this group and not the other groups I might have been assigned to" is a typical comment. Persons are seen as important. Thus, a member often says something like "I don't see how we could have felt this way if any single person had not been here." The experience is seen as unique. Sometimes doubts are expressed as to whether it would be possible to do this with another group. Generalized trust builds slowly. It is easy for members to comment in letters to each other that "this was the most meaningful experience of my life" or that "never before had I known what it was to love another person."

The experiences are usually seen as having *intrinsic validity.* Members do not doubt the existential authenticity of the experience. Members do not doubt each other's commitment, honesty, or ardor, once the experience is in full flower or even in retrospect. Other persons, hearing about the experience, may be incredulous or demand evidence or doubt the honesty of members' reports of feelings. The group members themselves do not feel that evidence is necessary and are sometimes confused by the suspicions of others. Members develop a new sense of confidence in their own diagnostic abilities.

The experiences are deeply *personal* and deeply *satisfying.* They seem to meet deep personal organismic needs that have not been met before. Variations of the following are reactions to these experiences: "I now *know* that there is a God"; "I now *know* what it means to feel understood"; "I have never before gone to bed feeling so serene and genuinely happy"; "I feel that I can now go home and change my life"; and "I want to hurry home and tell my wife that I *really* love her, because I was never sure before." The experiences are genuinely enriching and reveal new potential to the person. They clearly go beyond early expectations of remedial effects. These experiences convince the authors that an experience which is viewed as remedial is not genuinely therapeutic. Only as the experience is seen as enriching and growth-renewing is it truly remedial or curative! We are not cured until we see new vistas of personal potential. True growth opens up new positive motivations to the person. Life is filled with zest and feelings of importance and power. A growing person feels more than simply not feeling bad. Emotions take on new importance. It feels good to have spontaneous and free emotions, without embarrassment or guilt.

The experiences are felt as being *emergent,* as growing out of the group experience, as intrinsic to the growth of the group, as natural and integrated. The experience seems to grow from the needs of the persons and of the group. It does not seem imposed, contrived, taught, or produced. It has flowed and flowered.

The experiences are felt as being an *achievement,* as coming from effort, as not accidental. Although members report the experiences as seeming to emerge, they also see the experiences as something that was attained and that can be replicated by effort in the same group. Sometimes doubt is expressed about the ability of members to create such an experience in other groups of which he is a member.

The experiences are felt as *group experiences.* Although each of the TORI experiences has personal elements, each is experienced by members as a genuine group effort, group product, and group experience. The group *qua* group is important; it is seen as a living organism. There are deep feelings that the group should live and not die. The authors, from many such experiences, are convinced that the deepest and richest of human experiences are social and group experiences. The intimate and trusting experience is necessary for the deepest human moments. Man is a social organism. Groups have potential of which we are only dimly aware.

THE PROCESS OF CHANGE

In order to grow and change a person must be in the process of reducing his fears and increasing his trusts. This is the central process of growth. The central process of therapy is the restoration of growth. As growth is restored the person is better able to (1) move toward becoming more personal and loving, more open and intimate, more zestful and self-realizing, and more interdependent, thus increasing his capacity to make growth relationships with others and (2) move toward a life theory and a management theory that are more consonant with the above behavior.

The critical conditions that facilitate these processes are as follows:

1. The personal TORI enrichment experiences: The person must experience himself as deservingly lovable, deeply understood, intrinsically dedicated, and free-powerful. He must genuinely experience love and trust, role-free intimacy, sustained goal orientation, and constraint-free interdependence.

2. Confrontation of his life theory and management theory with experiential reality: He must develop some awareness of his theory, understand its energizing and directing functions, and confront his assumption world with social reality.

3. The group TORI enrichment experiences: The person must have some experience in depth with what the potential of enriched interdependent living can be like. His growth is greatly facilitated when he has experienced sustained caring, genuine consensus, enduring commitment, and constraint-free and emergent interdependence.

4. Continuing experiences in natural groups that are to some significant degree interdependent: Growth is a continuing interaction between inner states and environmental conditions. The person's capacity to create his own growth environments in his family, job, and social life must continue to grow.

Goals of The Treatment

In the traditional sense there are no goals of treatment. The assumption is that presence in a leaderless group, under the minimal conditions of joint commitment to work together in a personal-learning group, will inevitably lead to the TORI growth processes, which are therapeutic in nature. The therapist does not have conscious goals which he hopes his therapy will accomplish. He does have trust and confidence that group therapy will lead to growth among the participants. His own goals are the same as the goals of other participants: his own personal growth and learning.

Special Contributions of the Theory and Treatment

There are several special strengths of this systematic way of looking at growth and therapy.

First, there is no transfer problem of relating learnings in the therapy group to behavior in natural groups. People can learn to live in the same integrated way as patients, therapists, teachers, parents, children, administrators, and any other social role. On the four critical dimensions of social behavior, effective living has the same essentials in all social situations.

Secondly, the treatment is based upon a single integrated theory of social behavior which is consistent, practical, simple to understand, susceptible to empirical test, and related to all normal interpersonal behavior as well as to abnormal behavior.

In the third place, the treatment has the potential of meeting the social problem of social and psychological illness in our culture. The magnitude of the problem of mental illness is so great that even with the great acceleration in group therapy at present, there is little likelihood that current methods can make an appreciable inroad on the problem. This advantage is of no significance if emergence therapy is not effective, but if significant personal growth does occur with such therapy then it is a significant social invention. We have had dramatic success with the method used with over 6,000 executives, teachers, and organization leaders in a variety of personal-growth programs. Our data (Gibb, 1964b) suggest strongly that therapy and personal growth occur during emergent group interaction under a variety of specified conditions, that the presence of a therapist or leader is not a necessary ingredient in this growth process, that certain therapist behaviors inhibit significant growth, and that under certain conditions, which we are coming to understand and predict, the growth of the person is more greatly enhanced in an emergent group in which no therapist is present.

A growing body of evidence indicates that the physical presence of a therapist is not necessary for group and personal growth. The work of the authors and their associates at the Human Relations Laboratory at the University of Colorado (Gibb, 1963, 1964a) indicated that significant personal and group changes occurred when data collection instruments were used to replace the therapist-trainer in a training group. A significant and inventive program of research centered around work at the Veterans Administration Hospital at Houston indicates that significant therapeutic change occurs in hospitalized mental patients when they are members of groups in which instruments serve as facilitating factors and in which therapists are not present (Johnson, Hanson, Rothaus, Morton, Lyle and Moyer, 1965; Morton 1965a; 1965b; Rothaus, Johnson, Hanson, and Lyle, 1966). Berlin and his associates at the Human Development Institute have demonstrated that it is not necessary to have a therapist present in order for significant change to occur in management-improvement programs or in marriage counseling (Berlin, 1964; 1966). Work at the Western Behavioral Sciences Institute has demonstrated that therapeutic change is often more the result of group interaction than of the presence of a therapist (Berzon, Pious, and Farson, 1963).

Research by the authors has indicated that instruments often serve as therapist-surrogates and deprive the participants from certain kinds of personal growth that apparently come as a direct function of working through the membership, decision making, goal setting, and steering functions without the presence of the therapist or the therapist-surrogates (Gibb, 1963; 1964a; 1966). It is increasingly clear that the therapist is not the relevant factor in the therapeutic or growth process. The evidence is growing that the *critical* element in growth is the *emergent interdependence* of persons. Emergent interdependence is therapeutic, per se, and is the *sine qua non* of enduring personal growth.

Finally, the theory and treatment are oriented toward personal growth rather than toward remedial processes. Treatment is best when it is aimed at enduring growth of the person rather than toward symptom removal, extirpation of an illness, exculpatory help, or even at preventive treatment. Though there are encouraging signs of change, at present therapy is largely oriented toward removing or preventing illness, rather than toward development of the potential for new, unpredictable, and perhaps infinite growth.

Modifications of the Theory and Treatment

The emergence groups have been used in a variety of settings: executive development, organizational team training, hospital wards, YMCA management training, training of religious leaders, and youth groups. Variations have consisted of using different ways of preceding the groups with orienting experiences: group touching, body movement, dance therapy, presentations of TORI theory, microlabs, nonverbal communication, and various kinds of experiences within the organization before the training is held. Because emergence theory has so much stressed natural group life, the authors have increasingly worked within the organization setting. Emergent groups with natural teams and living units seem far more powerful and relevant than do groups composed for special training and therapy.

The experiences before and after the emergence groups are probably critical in personal and organizational growth. Of particular importance have been the following: consulting with the person in the natural setting (family, work group, social organization); varying the number of meetings of emergence groups, duration, time interval between groups, size of groups, and composition; and the use of touching, body awareness, and body image experiences.

To the extent that they work with groups in which no leader is physically present, the following are variations of emergence groups: the "instrumented" groups used by Blake, Hanson, Morton and others (Johnson *et al.*, 1965; Morton, 1965a); the "programmed" groups used by Berlin and his associates (Berlin, 1964; 1966); and the "self-directed", instrumented groups used by Berzon, Solomon, and their co-workers (Berzon *et al.*, 1963). In each of these settings the groups are programmed by leaders, and the leaders are in some ways more present and less able to be dealt with than in other situations where the therapist is present. The emergent processes of the groups are thus muted and truncated, and the growth potential of emergence in a more imposition-free and role-free ecological field is lessened.

The Therapist Role

Since 1949 when the writers first began experimenting with leaderless groups of various kinds, they have observed and analyzed many different therapists and group trainers in a series of studies (Gibb, 1963). The writers have each personally tried many styles of relating to a training group and to a therapy group. At present they are committed to entering the group as persons, being as "role free" as possible, and attempting to work as persons in interdependent membership. In the emergent groups no therapists have been used, so there is in this sense no "therapist role." Taking a therapist role or stance interfers with the development of interdependence and group strength. The data show (Gibb, 1963) that in many significant respects the events and processes in emergent groups are similar to therapeutically-relevant processes that occur in many groups where therapists and trainers are present.

When a therapist or counselor is present in a true emergent group, he can be therapeutically effective by being as effective a person as he can be. That is, he can be as personally open, self-realizing, and interdependent as it is possible for him to be. He can work his way into the group as a member in exactly the same way as any other member. Because of differential expectations, the therapist may have more difficulty gaining membership than do other members. Any "member" who attempts a "role" entrance has similar difficulty. The therapist can be helpful in the group just as any other open, warm, trusting, interdependent, listening, role-free person can be helpful.

For the authors, the therapeutic agent is the emergent group. As the group becomes stronger and more truly interdependent, it becomes a more effective therapeutic agent.

Special Qualifications of the Therapist

A therapist who is going to join an emergent group must have a deep trust in the emergent group processes. He must understand his fears and their effects upon his behavior, and particularly their effects upon his trust of the internal growth processes. If he is known to be a therapist, the group may make special role demands which make it difficult for the therapist to be a member and a person. In order to resist the role demands he must be especially clear about his own attitudes. He must be able to deal openly with his feelings and attitudes, particularly those that relate to dependency and counter-dependency.

Composition of the Group

The authors have tried a variety of solutions to the composition question. The best solution arrived at is to completely randomize the composition of the group if it is started with a large number of people who wish training or therapy. High-trust theory guides the authors in this situation; the continuing assumption is made that a group of people placed in a personal, confronting, emergent group will have a growth experience. The impulse to compose the groups on the basis of a fear-distrust assumption that certain categories of people will not respond well to the group situation is resisted. Another high-trust method of composition used is to have people select their own groups, beginning with a larger population of people requesting the experience.

Group size makes less difference than originally thought. Groups have been tried that ranged in size from 5 to 174. Large groups make surprisingly good progress if they feel confident that they can. In the usual situation, groups of nine to twelve give people an opportunity to experience diversity, difficulty in goal setting, difficulty with a wide range of control needs, and other advantages of problem confrontation. Groups this small give members sufficient time to verbalize individual feelings and attitudes, a process which is difficult in larger groups unless the larger groups last for long periods.

The authors have experimented with natural groups (families, work teams, boards, management groups) which meet for relatively long periods of time and which have the potential of being enduring intimate groups. It is helpful to work with the total population of a team unit—all those who make decisions together or who could potentially make decisions together. For the authors, interdependence is such a significant aspect of mental health that the building of genuine interdependent groups is of prime importance. Thus, they have worked with total teams which ranged in size from 5 to 174.

Limitations of the Theory and Treatment

There are many limitations of both the theory and the treatment. There are probably some psychotics who are, for various reasons, too far out of verbal and nonverbal communication with others to be available to an emergent group. At the same time the authors agree to this limitation they are aware of the many encouraging demonstrations that indicate the accessibility of a great many persons who were previously thought to be not accessible. The history of the development of leaderless methods in teaching, training, and therapy is a history of overcoming relatively stable and impermeable distrust-fear attitudes toward what people can do on their own. Given people who have some confidence that persons can be cured by emergent groups, and who can communicate this confidence to the patients, there are unforseeable limits to what can be done with emergent groups. In a sense there are no limits except in the expectations of the members.

Lack of trust and high timidity are barriers. So many people who work in the helping field have had fear-producing experiences that they communicate the fears and distrusts to group members. These fears communicate in a self-fulfilling way described earlier in the chapter. For the authors, their groups have become increasingly more effective as they have deepened their trust of the emergence processes.

The lack of convincing demonstrations of the effectiveness of emergence groups is a limitation. Adequate measures of trust, intimacy, realization, and interdependence, the critical variables in the theory, are lacking. The writers are continuing to develop measures, get more data on what happens during group sessions, try out groups with an increasingly wider range of persons and situations, and develop other ways of preceding and following emergent groups with supportive and integrative experiences.

SUMMARY

A theory of group therapy has been proposed which assumes that therapeutic processes of personal and group growth emerge inevitably as persons interact in small groups that meet for agreed-upon purposes of personal learning. There are four (TORI) growth processes: movement toward (1) trust, (2) openness, (3) realization, and (4) interdependence, and movement away from fear, closed behavior, imposition, and dependence. These processes are intrinsic to the nature of persons and of groups, are independent of the therapist, and are regenerative in character. Growth is accelerated in high-trust relationships and is inhibited in defensive or high-fear relationships. In the process of growth, each person develops an implicit life style and life theory which are consonant with the particular balance of defensive and growth-need systems of the person.

In order for therapy to take place the TORI processes must be restored if placed in imbalance by sustained high fear, and the life theory must be confronted by social reality in an environment where the person can use relevant data gradually to modify his life theory and bring it into line with his fear-trust state.

Of particular significance in therapeutic growth are four TORI personal-depth experiences and four TORI group-depth experiences which occur inevitably in emergent groups. The personal experiences are trust-love, intimacy, zest, and freedom-power. The group experiences are caring, consensus, commitment, and emergence.

In order for therapy or growth to occur the person must both change his depth experiences and change his life theory in ways that predispose him to change his behavior in his home, his job, and his relevant life groups.

The presentation in this chapter is the most nearly complete description of emergence therapy that is currently available in the literature. The chapter authors are revising a book-length manuscript tentatively titled, The Emergent Group: A Study of Trust and Freedom, which presents in detail the theory described in this chapter.

REFERENCES

Berlin, J. I.: Program learning for personal and interpersonal improvement. *Acta Psychologica, 13*: 321-335, 1964.

Berlin, J. I.: *Management Improvement Program,* 2nd ed. Atlanta, Human Development Institute, 1966.

Berzon, Betty; Pious, Constance, and Farson, R. E.: The therapeutic event in group psychotherapy: A study of subjective reports by group members. *J Individ Psychol, 19*: 204-212, 1963.

Gibb, J. R.: A climate for learning. *Adult Education, 9*: 19-21, 1958.

Gibb, J. R.: Defensive communication. *J Commun, 11*: 141-148, 1961.

Gibb, J. R.: *Factors Producing Defensive Behavior within Groups, VII.* Final Technical Report, Office of Naval Research, Contract Nonr-3088(00), 1963.

Gibb, J. R.: Climate for trust formation. In L. P. Bradford, J. R. Gibb, and K. D. Benne (Eds.): *T-Group Theory and Laboratory Method.* New York, Wiley, 1964, pp. 279-309. (a)

GIBB, J. R.: Communication and productivity. *Personnel Administration,* 27: 8-13, 1964. (b)

GIBB, J. R.: Fear and facade: Defensive management. In R. E. Farson (Ed.), *Science and Human Affairs.* Palo Alto, Science and Behavior, 1966, pp. 197-214.

JOHNSON, D. L.; HANSON, P. G.; ROTHAUS, P.; MORTON, R. B.; LYLE, F. A., and MOYER, R.: Human relations training for psychiatric patients: A follow-up study. *Int J Soc Psychiat, 11:* 188-196, 1965.

MORTON, R. B.: The patient training laboratory, an adaptation of the instrumented training laboratory. In E. H. Schein, and W. G. Bennis (Eds.), *Personal and Organizational Change through Group Methods.* New York, Wiley, 1965, pp. 141-151. (a)

MORTON, R. B.: The organization training laboratory: Some individual and organizational effects. *J Adv Management, 30:* 58-67, 1965. (b)

ROTHAUS, P.; JOHNSON, D. L.; HANSON, P. G., and LYLE, F. A.: Participation and sociometry in autonomous and trainer-led patient groups. *J Counsel Psychol, 13:* 68-76, 1966.

V

LOSS AND RECOVERY OF COMMUNITY

A Guide to the Theory and Practice
of Integrity Therapy

O. HOBART MOWRER

IN a number of reviews of my book, *The New Group Therapy* (1964), which were otherwise favorable, the criticism was made that it was not sufficiently "descriptive" and "prescriptive" (Frank, 1965; Kantor, 1965; Lakin, 1965). I had not, the reviewers thought, given a clear picture of the specific nature of the groups denoted by the title and also had not provided adequate instruction on "how to do" the pertinent operations. In light of this criticism, I welcomed the opportunity here afforded to try to be more explicit, and to push forward another step in the elaboration of a general point of view and set of procedures which have recently become known as integrity therapy (*cf* Anderson, 1965; Belgum, 1963; Dabrowski, 1964; Drakeford, 1967; Glasser, 1965; Jourard, 1964; Kline, 1964; London, 1964, Parlour, Cole, and Van Vorst, 1967; Pratt and Tooley, 1964; Tkacik, 1964).

In the summer of 1966, I was asked to write an article for a newspaper series *Illini Horizons* (Mowrer, 1966c), and I used the occasion to set forth, as clearly and compactly as possible, the assumptions which seem to me most justified concerning the nature of psychopathology. The basic supposition is that the states known as *neurosis* and *functional psychosis* arise, not from repression of *instincts* (as Freud believed), but from the suppression, in the sense of denial, of the simple (but painful) behavioral

A portion of this chapter has been reproduced from Mowrer, O. H.: Integrity therapy: A self-help approach. *Psychotherapy, Theory, Research, and Practice* 3(3): 114-119, 1966. Courtesy of *Psychotherapy, Theory, Research, and Practice*.

truth about oneself, *i.e.* from moral failure which has been compounded by secrecy, alienation, and the inevitable tendency toward social withdrawal. This short article is reproduced as the first section, Social Alienation and Reintegration: Historical Perspective, and will hopefully provide a conceptual backdrop for the chapter as a whole.

As the second section, Psychotherapy as Self-authentication: An Interpersonal Process, I reproduce a paper published under the title of "Integrity Therapy: A Self-help Approach" (Mowrer, 1966e). If psychopathology arises less from what others have done to us than from what we ourselves have done and then hidden, the task of "therapy" or "recovery" is not so much a matter of receiving "treatment" from others as of actively taking steps to set the record straight, authenticating ourselves, and "leveling" with the "significant others" in our lives (Sullivan, 1947). If neurosis, or Erickson's (1958) preferred term, "identity crisis," is something which human beings get themselves into, by the same token they must take most of the responsibility for getting themselves *out*. Others may point the way and offer encouragement, but most of the effort must be exerted, most of the actual "work" done by the individual himself. Thus integrity therapy is basically a self-help approach; and the best therapist, the best helper, in this context, is one who helps others to *help themselves*, instead of persuading them of their helplessness and endless dependency upon professional assistance. (Here, incidentally, may be the long-sought key to a vigorous and effective program of community mental health—*cf* Albee, 1965; Jarvis and Nelson, 1966; Reiff, 1966; Smith and Hobbs, 1966. But this is a matter for later and independent consideration).

The main body of the section called Integrity Therapy In Action: An Illustrative Interview is the transcription of a tape-recorded interview (conducted in May, 1965) with a then recently hospitalized forty-five-year-old female patient. It may strike some readers as singular that a chapter in a book on *group* therapy should devote so much space to an individual, or personal interview. According to the tenets of integrity therapy, the initial interview, if properly conducted, *is group therapy* of the purest and most intensive kind. By group therapy I shall not in this chapter mean a situation in which a specialized therapist "treats" a group of other persons, or "patients." Group therapy, as it is here conceived and exemplified, is the process whereby two or more persons become deeply and *mutually acquainted.* And a situation, if it meets this requirement, is no less *group* therapy if it involves only two persons than if it involves ten. The important consideration is the nature, the pattern, the *quality* of the interaction, not the absolute number of persons present. Once an individual has developed with one other person a relationship of deep mutual openness, movement into a larger group usually presents no problem. The process which has been started in the two-person group is thus extended and gradually consolidated, but the difference between a two-person and multi-person group is not a categorical one. However, the two-person interview, while an essential first step, is just the beginning and must be pursued into a larger circle of persons with similar intent and purpose. Thus, the basic pattern is much more on the model of Alcoholics Anonymous than of conventional professional group therapy. In fact, integrity therapy has recently been dubbed, not unfairly, "AA for civilians." But it should be added that this approach is considerably more humanistic, less theistic, than the AA program.

I have, of course, many recordings of group-therapy sessions involving several persons and might easily have reproduced one of them here for illustrative purposes. But the interplay between a group of persons who already know one another well is often not immediately intelligible to others, and the amount of background material which would thus have to accompany such a transcription seemed prohibitive in the present context. Therefore, I have decided to limit the protocol used here to a two-person "transaction," with most of the pertinent information immediately and fully available in the recording itself.

Some group-therapy leaders, I may say, like to start groups as groups, with everyone coming in at the beginning. But my observation is that things move faster if an experienced person spends about two hours with a newcomer and then "sponsors" him into an ongoing group; or if he starts with one or two such persons and by this procedure *builds* a group, if one is not already in existence. It is a great incentive as well as support for a newcomer to feel already well acquainted, in the sense described, with at least one member of a group; and the group as a whole functions on a considerably deeper level if everyone has had an initial interview of the kind described and exemplified in the section Integrity Therapy in Action: An Illustrative Interview. The practice of having each new person interviewed in depth prior to joining the larger group also permits a certain amount of screening, *i.e.* persons who thus appear unmotivated, uncooperative, and insincere in the face of deep openness and sincerity may not be immediately admitted into the larger group. Such persons (whose personality crisis has usually advanced from the acute stage to chronicity, or whose character development has been seriously deficient) commonly require rehabilitation of a thoroughgoing and *total* nature. (For an indication of what can be achieved with persons of this sort under an intensive and properly designed program, see Shelly and Bassin, 1965.)

The fourth and final section of this chapter, Explanations, Interpretations, and Comments, consists of a series of comments on various aspects of the recorded interview and on the adjustment which Mrs. Saunders (as the woman in question will be called) made in the group which she immediately entered and in her family and home community when she was released (relatively soon) from the hospital.

For the interested reader there is, in addition to the works already cited, a series of other publications which will be found relevant (Mowrer, 1961; 1965; 1966a; 1966b; 1967a; 1967b). But it is hoped that this chapter can stand alone as an introduction to integrity therapy as a group method, and that what is said here will be intelligible, in at least a preliminary way, without further recourse to other sources.

SOCIAL ALIENATION AND REINTEGRATION: HISTORICAL PERSPECTIVE

Some twenty years ago I recall having heard the psychologist Kurt Lewin make the statement that a man cannot today understand his own personality or the world around him unless he knows two thousand years of history. At the time, I confess that this remark did not have much meaning for me. I knew very little history, and most of my fellow psychologists seemed to be about as uninformed and uninterested in this area as I. However, during the intervening years I have become increasingly concerned with a problem which is indeed intelligible only if one approaches it historically.

My own decision to enter psychology as a profession dates back to high school and came, in considerable measure, from the fact that I was then suffering from certain personality problems which I did not at all understand. For a number of years after I completed my formal training in psychology, I worked in quite unrelated areas, namely, physiological psychology and learning theory. But during World War II, I was in a branch of Government service which required that I function as a clinical psychologist. Since that time, I have been increasingly concerned with the urgent and baffling problem of so-called "mental illness" and mental health. And it is here, specifically, that I have found the historical dimension so essential and illuminating.

Today it is widely recognized that in former times the problems of psychiatry (which literally means the care or cure of souls) were handled largely within the sphere of religion. And the indications are that during the first few centuries of the Christian era, the church was extraordinarily competent in this regard. Religious congregations were then not the large and relatively impersonal masses of people which today make up the membership of so many of our churches. Instead, they were little bands or groups (sometimes called house churches) whose members knew each other intimately and who deeply shared their life experiences.

Today we are finding that the essence of psychopathology lies in the fact that the afflicted person is socially alienated, out of community, estranged. Characteristically, and quite understandably, he is uncomfortable with, and afraid of people, and the tendency to withdraw from human contact is an almost universal symptom. In early Christian times, such wayward or lost souls were encouraged to join a little community or group of persons who called themselves, not Christians, but simply People of the Way. And this "way" was specifically designed to lead the lost and estranged back into authentic, fulfilling human existence. This was the essence of salvation, healing.

And how, exactly, was this end accomplished? First of all, there was a theory, an assumption as to what was wrong with the soul-sick persons. They had *sinned* and then *hidden* their sins. As a result they were afraid that other persons would see through them, fathom their guilty secrets, and punish them; hence, the tendency to withdraw from human contact. But in such a retreat, a man carries a piece of the community with him in the form of conscience; and this "inner voice" continues to bother him, not because it hates and wants to hurt him, but because it loves him and wants to bring him back to community—motivate him to rise up and return to his father's house, as the story of the prodigal son puts it.

The Early Christians understood all this well. And the first step in the restoration of the wayward was a procedure known as *exomologesis*, namely, a deep, thoroughgoing, unreserved form of self-disclosure, perhaps first to one or two individuals and then to a small group. After this, the individual placed himself "under the judgment" of the group. The group responded to his confession of past wrongdoing with love and compassion, and rejoiced at his new-found honesty and courage. But "forgiveness" was not automatic. The individual, depending upon the nature and extent of his misdeeds, was expected to make restitution, do penance. And when this was accomplished, the person's self-respect returned, his apprehension and fear vanished, and he was restored to the community healed.

But this powerful and effective form of "psychiatry" was to undergo a strange fate. In 325 the Roman Emperor, Constantine, called the Council of Nicaea, and there made the Christians a remarkable offer. If they would give him a consistent, monolithic description of their faith and functions, he would not only end the persecution in which he and his predecessors had engaged but he would also make Christianity the state religion (and thus, hopefully, stop the impending disintegration of the Roman Empire). Understandably, the Church Fathers who assembled at Nicaea accepted this proposal. But this action was disastrous. The church now had to be popular, had to have a universal appeal, with the result that "salvation" became progressively easier—and less and less genuinely effective. By the twelfth century, confession was no longer made to a congregation or group, but to a priest, in secret; and penance also became trivial and irrelevant.

By the sixteenth century the church had, in this way, so far lost its original power and purpose that a revolution took place—the so-called Protestant Reformation. But instead of restoring the highly effective psychological and social practices of the early church, the Reformers "sealed" the confession still further. The one remaining representative of the human community, the priest, was eliminated; and the faithful were admonished to take their sins directly to God in silent prayer. The result was that the church now became even less effective in dealing with sick souls than it had previously been. The "insane" were said to be possessed of the Devil, and were frequently beaten, thrown into prison, and otherwise abused.

What is sometimes called the "first psychiatric revolution" involved a reclassification of the psychically disabled. No longer were they regarded as evil, but ill. Their abode changed from dungeons to hospitals; and instead of being punished, they were to be helped, treated. Despite abundant good intentions, this movement was not successful. There was no very explicit theory of "mental illness," and treatment was accordingly diffuse and ineffective. People went to mental hospitals, and stayed there. They did not recover. And the belief grew that "insanity" was essentially incurable, untreatable.

The "second psychiatric revolution" was introduced, around the turn of the present century, by Sigmund Freud. He, at long last, gave psychiatry a theory, and the attendant method of treatment he called psychoanalysis. The "sick" person, he thought, had repressed some of his "instincts," notably those of sex and aggression. And the cure consisted of helping him undo these repressions and learn to be freer, more expressive. But now, after half a century of energetic application of this approach, the situation is still critical; and many believe that we are today caught up in a third revolution. This is variously called social psychiatry, community mental health, or group therapy. But, in any case, the underlying assumption is that people get into emotional difficulties because they have been deviant and dishonest, *i.e.* out of community. And therapy calls for a return to community through improved communication with significant others and commitment to a more responsible and mature style of life.

The language which is thus being used is obviously different from that of the early Christians (who spoke of having been lost and then found, dead and brought to life), but the underlying principles and operations are strikingly similar. And if the church, by proceeding along these lines, was once effective, there is reason to believe that modern psychology and psychiatry can also be. Here, interestingly, science and religion seem to be coalescing. The term "religion" comes from the Latin word *ligare*, which is also the root of our words "ligament" and "ligature." Thus religion means, literally, a reunion, rebinding, reintegration. And when conceived in this way, the objectives of religion become virtually identical with those of social psychiatry and group therapy. Seen in historical perspective, the problem of personality disorder, which for a long time has been dogged by confusion and failure, is once again being approached in a way which justifies at least guarded optimism and hope.

PSYCHOTHERAPY AS SELF-AUTHENTICATION: AN INTERPERSONAL PROCESS

Somehow the notion has gotten about that if one is emotionally disturbed, the only thing one can do is seek professional help. This view, I believe, rests on a misunderstanding of the origin and nature of the condition in question. Sometimes it is called a *neurosis*, with the implication that one's nerves are "bad" and need treating, most logically perhaps by a physician. Sometimes it is assumed that the difficulty lies deep in an "unconscious" part of the mind which only a psychologist or psychoanalyst knows how to "reach." And sometimes the difficulty is interpreted as a sin against God, in which event the services of a theologian might seem indicated. Still another possibility is that the chronic state of tension and apprehension with which we are here concerned arises from a "bad conscience," *i.e.* from some unworthy act or acts we have committed and concealed or some obligation we have slighted and then had too little courage and too much conceit to confess and rectify.

What is most clearly needed, if the latter understanding of the situation is valid, is the determination and strength to *admit*, to the "significant others" in our lives, the exact nature of our wrongs—and then get about the business of correcting them. For this there is no need of an expert or specialist. And when we have recourse to one, is it not frequently with the motivation of finding an "out" which will avoid the necessity of coming to grips with the problem on its own terms?

For those who wish to take a more responsible, self-directed approach to such matters, I have a few suggestions to offer. The most frequent objection I hear to the notion that it is useful to talk about one's emotional problems to relatives and friends is that "they aren't interested in hearing about your problems— they just don't have the time or the patience to listen to you." We are likely to be lulled into disastrous inaction by this half truth, for it provides an excuse for not doing something which, although radically effective, is temporarily painful. And the professional "listeners," in both psychiatry and religion, are also loath to encourage us in such a venture, lest it be discovered that we can perhaps get along without them. "That's right!" they say. "Others *aren't* interested in listening to your difficulties. Nor will they really understand or know how to 'treat' you. So, consult us instead!"

If secret confession to priests and psychiatrists had a really good record of accomplishment, we should be glad enough to be spared the embarrassment of having the "ordinary" people in our lives know who we are. But that record is *not* good; thus, reluctantly, many people are today experimenting with *open* confession of one kind or another. When you stop to think of it, *secret* confession is a contradiction in terms—secrecy is what makes confession necessary. And it is not surprising that the attempt to cope with unresolved personal guilt by means of continued furtiveness does not work out very well. Should we actually expect much to come of letting a priest, minister, psychiatrist, psychologist, social worker, or some other "specialist" hear our sins if we continue to live the Big Lie with the people who really matter to us? As a result of my ongoing experience with group therapy, both in mental hospitals and in ordinary community settings, I am persuaded that healing and redemption depend much more upon what we say about ourselves *to others, significant others,* than upon what others (no matter how highly trained or untrained, ordained or unordained) say *to us*. It is the truth we ourselves speak rather than the treatment we receive that heals us.

This paper is an attempt to help those who wish to help themselves, *i.e.* persons who would like to make the most of the opportunities for change and restoration which constantly surround us all. By this, I mean opportunities for improving the quality of our relationship with members of our families, friends, working associates, and the "strangers" we meet in those groups which are specially designed to provide practice in "getting honest"—and "getting well." Some suggestions will also be made about how we can best serve others when they try to be candid and tell us who *they* are.

If one talks about one's troubles in the sense of merely *complaining* about how bad one feels, then others are indeed likely to get bored and withdraw. Why shouldn't they? We are not giving them any information about the real source of our difficulties; and there is not much they *can* do to help us, in a basic or lasting way. They may try reassurance, suggest a "drink" (or some more modern type of tranquilizer), or recommend a "good psychiatrist." None of these alternatives is likely to be permanently effective, so our friends, understandably, get discouraged and disappear—physically if they can or if this is not possible, they simply stop "hearing" us. Thus it is easy to blame others if nothing comes of our "talking" to them. Can it be that the fault is more nearly ours, in that we haven't talked about the right thing, in the right way?

It has been my consistent observation that if, instead of complaining, one tries *confessing*, others do not get impatient, and genuinely useful things start happening. When we stop talking about how much we hurt and get down to the good and sufficient *reasons* for our discomfort, the effect is dramatically different. In the first place, it permits us to be brief, to get to the point quickly. We can go on forever about how bad we *feel*, but even the most wicked of us can, if we choose, be fairly concise about how bad we have *been*. Others are rarely bored with a sincere confession, because they intuitively recognize its importance; and they do not feel helpless, either. When we let them know what is really "bugging" us, they can begin responding relevantly. We do not have to talk endlessly, now. The truth is out, and others have something to "work on"—and so do we! Although there will be a time of shame and sorrow, peace and strength will ultimately follow if, after confession, we *act* as we should.

How often, when we are presenting a shell of pretense and hypocrisy to the world, we come to feel that people in general are dull, uninteresting, and uninterested. Life itself, our very existence and experience of self, ceases to be meaningful or even tolerable. How *can* others interact authentically, validly, meaningfully with us when we are giving them only limited and perhaps systematically distorted data? It is a never-ending delight to see how warmly, intelligently, and helpfully people respond to a previously inauthentic, "neurotic" person when he begins to "come out of his shell." Then others know what his problem is and can become specifically helpful. As long as we let others know only what our "symptoms" are, all they can do in return is "symptom therapy." But when they hear what we have *done*, and perhaps are *still* doing to cause and deserve our symptoms, others—even the most ordinary others—can give us real support and help.

So, if we want basic, enduring change in our lives, let us stop complaining about how much we *hurt* and try admitting who we *are*.

My next suggestion is, Don't blame *others* for your problems. If you bore people by complaining about how you feel and want to get a more lively reaction, one way to do this is to try holding them responsible for your problems. If you really want to "lose friends and alienate people," start complaining *about them*.

There are, it seems, two ways of "confessing," of being honest— honest about ourselves and honest about others. When someone says, "I'm going to be frank with you," duck! He means he is going to be frank, "honest" *about you*. He is displeased about something (probably his own shortcomings) and is going to "take it out" on whoever happens to be available at the moment.

Others undoubtedly have had an influence upon all our lives; but if we are now adults, its hard to improve our situation by changing others. Fortunately, there is a better way if we will but take it. Small children are, to be sure, often disorganized because their parents are; and if the parents will straighten out their lives, the children's difficulties tend to disappear. But any adult who continues to act as if he were still a helpless, irresponsible child who is at the mercy of others is asking for trouble—and usually gets it!

At the hospital where I am associated with a group-therapy project, we recruit new members for our groups on the admissions ward; and not long ago one newly admitted patient spoke at length about how she had been "railroaded" into the hospital, how everyone was "against" her, and what a blameless life she herself had led. When we eventually asked the next woman how she happened to be in the hospital, she replied, simply, "I goofed." It is not difficult to predict which of these two women is going to leave the hospital first. There is, in fact, a real possibility that the first woman may *never* leave it. She has destroyed whatever place she may once have had in other people's affections; and as long as she retains her present set of attitudes, she will not regain it.

As a result of the incident just reported, I continued to think for several days about what a fateful difference there is between "the shamers" and "the blamers." Those who can say, "I am to blame and am ashamed" have a far brighter prospect not only of leaving a mental hospital but of remaining out of one than do those who think the way to "salvation" is to use others as scapegoats. Not many years ago there was a widespread tendency in mental hospitals for the professional staff to lead the patients to believe that their difficulties had arisen primarily as a result of the way they had been treated by others, and to encourage relatives and friends of patients to try to be *nicer* to them when they "came out." Our observation is that it is *the patient* who needs to learn to be nicer, more self-critical, responsible, and open, and that as this change comes about, the response he gets from those about him improves automatically.

This is not to say, of course, that others are perfect or have no faults themselves. The point we are making is simply that the best way to get others to "improve" is to work on ourselves. One can pick and nag and criticize until doomsday, and about the only result is that others respond in kind. But if one thinks and acts responsibly with respect to *his* shortcomings, he makes it very difficult for others to continue to be inconsiderate or abusive. One sure way to get others with whom we have been strenuously disagreeing to start agreeing with us is to acknowledge and do something constructive about their criticism *of us*. Try *thanking* someone for a criticism, and show your sincerity by appropriate action. That will "take the wind out of their sails." And the reason for this is that when others see us being self-critical and responsible, they can stop being so concerned, angry, fearful about *our* behavior and have a little time to think about their own!

In our groups, people quickly come to appreciate all this, and when someone makes a painful but liberating self-disclosure, there is no attempt either to condemn or forgive that person. Instead the emphasis is upon what the person is doing, here and now, by way of trying to become more honest and authentic. But sometimes people who are new to this philosophy follow a less helpful practice. Not long ago a small group of people were meeting in my home, and in the course of one man's account of his life, he related an incident about which he felt deep guilt and shame. At this point one or two newcomers to the group tried to reassure this man with such comments as "Oh, that wasn't so bad. Lots of people have done worse things than that. Forget it!" The man rightly refused to take comfort from these well-intentioned but idle reassurances. He said that he had been saying much the same sort of thing to himself for years, and it had not helped. Now he wished to speak candidly, take full responsibility for his life, and have the transforming power that can come in no other way.

Our earlier point was, Do not complain; confess. But as we now see, there are two ways of confessing: one can confess others' sins, *or* one's own. Only the latter procedure is likely to be truly helpful. If one is honestly self-critical the chances are that others will respond with very similar behavior. Paradoxically, the best way to "change" other persons is to change oneself.

"But if I let others know me as I know myself, won't they reject, criticize, gossip about, or otherwise punish me?" someone will ask. "That is, if I let others know my sins and shortcomings, won't they just 'throw them up' to me and make me feel worse, rather than better?"

Perhaps the first thing to note here is that if we have been behaving badly, one of the strongest incentives for *change* is to have the eyes of others upon us, to bring ourselves, so to say, under criticism. With striking regularity, persons who become deeply open with a group find that their "willpower" is mysteriously strengthened. (Not only do they change with respect to the problems which brought them into the group; they also, for example, often stop smoking and make alterations in other areas of their lives which they originally did not know they *could* change. Smoking, drinking, and pill taking are rendered considerably less attractive when we deal with the guilt in our lives in other, more basic ways.) Through secrecy we shield ourselves from group sanctions, so it should not surprise us that while practicing secrecy we are often helpless in the face of temptation. We are "weak" because we do not allow the strength, concern, *and discipline* of others to operate to our advantage. By confession we indicate our willingness to live "under the judgment" of our fellows, and it would seriously defeat the purpose of this whole procedure if we asked and received "forgiveness" and "acceptance" in the sense of no questions asked and nothing expected of us, nothing demanded.

Of course, if we attempt to become honest in the presence of persons who have a similar need but no intention of doing anything about it, they may react in some not very helpful ways. They may give us bogus reassurance, they may make fun of us, or they may become contemptuous and angry. But other, more experienced members of a group will effectively offset such reactions, and even the worst that persons who are still "in hiding" can do to us when we become honest is not nearly as bad as what is almost certain to happen if we, ourselves, persevere in deceit and scapegoating. Besides, there is always the possibility that our honesty will make others less satisfied with their dishonesty. Often the best way to "help" others is simply to be honest about ourselves. This encourages *them* to be honest in return.

Gossip is, of course, a calculated risk. But if the members of a group follow the policy of telling only their own story, the risk is minimal. Gossip, in general, represents an attempt to explain and understand otherwise unintelligible situations. If we are making a deliberate attempt to "get by" with something, others have a right to form their own conjectures—and, incidentally, to set up indirect social controls. Thus, the surest way to avoid gossip is to make our lives so open that there *is* no mystery, nothing for anyone to conjecture or be concerned about.

One of the arguments for "professional help" is that a doctor or priest can be relied upon not to reveal our secrets. That is true. Unfortunately, such persons can also be "relied upon" to discourage *us* from revealing our secrets to anyone but them. Today it is a common practice for physicians when consulted by persons in deep distress of soul to say, "Here, take a pill and keep still. No one else should know anything about this." And priests likewise commonly fail to encourage confession and full honesty with the people in our everyday lives. Implying that the sacrament of penance alone will "do the trick," they often lead penitents to believe that no other action is necessary. There is steadily mounting evidence that nothing is so radically redemptive—and so relaxing—as having no secrets, at least no shameful ones, *from anybody* (Smith, 1966).

The next objection one is likely to encounter is this: "Granted that you may be safe in making an intimate disclosure to the ordinary people in your life, do you have any *right* to do this? Although the disclosure may make *you* feel better, isn't there the possibility that, in the process, you will hurt other persons quite unnecessarily?"

In September, 1964, one of our popular magazines carried an article entitled "The Limits of Intimacy," in which a great deal was made of this point. The author of this article had consulted a number of psychiatrists, clinical psychologists, and marriage counselors, and they all agreed that if one has done something reprehensible, it is better to "talk it out" with a detached, objective professional person than to bother members of one's family or close friends.

Where did we get the idea that merely talking to anyone was sufficient resitution for bad behavior? Even the professional listener asks for repayment, although it is rationalized as a fee for professional services rendered and not as atonement. And in the matter of "objectivity," would we expect to find it in persons who make their living by thus hearing what may be termed "misplaced confessions"? The notion that "significant others" can appropriately receive our deepest and most painful confidences threatens the livelihood and status of the members of various professions, and the prospect of growing unemployment, if nothing else, might be expected to arouse opposition. By the very nature of their economic involvement, we would hardly expect the experts to be impartial judges in the matter.

There are, admittedly, sometimes complications when we try to deal with our mistakes and the ensuing guilt in the context of our ordinary interpersonal relations. If, for example, a man confesses infidelity to his wife, it will almost certainly be the occasion for her to do some systematic soul-searching. And if the man deliberately tries to evade responsibility for his conduct by blaming his wife, much of the benefit of the confession is, of course, lost. In this event it becomes less a confession than an accusation, an attack. And, until the man can approach his wife in a different frame of mind, he will probably do well to keep his silence. But even when such a disclosure is made in all sincerity, consideration, and humility, it will put pressure upon the wife to ask herself what contributions, if any, *she* has made to the estrangement, loss of communication and trust, and the final infidelity. If she can honestly say that she is blameless (and, for all practical purposes, she may indeed be), then the husband's admission of wrongdoing can be no staggering blow to her. In fact, she should be grateful to know that he cares enough about her and their marriage to try to reconstitute it on an authentic basis. And in the event that the wife does find upon reflection some cause to be critical of herself, would she ask to be spared this measure of self-scrutiny and awareness of her own need to change? The chances are, of course, that the wife already knows there is something wrong with the marriage, and the husband's avowal makes it possible for her, at long last, to begin thinking, talking, and acting relevantly. One woman's reaction to her husband's confession of infidelity was more or less typical. She said, "What a mess! But at least now I know the truth." And on this truth she and her husband started making a new life for themselves.

Are we not admonished somewhere in Holy Writ to "bear one another's burdens"? Why have the professionals so conveniently overlooked this and started urging us *not* to reveal ourselves humbly and honestly to the people who really matter to us?

There are, of course, some circumstances in which one cannot confess without "hurting" others—although, even here, the effect may in the end be salutary. Consider, for example, the case of an adolescent girl who accepts the advances of a lecherous father and is then overcome by her guilt. Confession of the wrong she has committed obviously cannot be made without implicating "the other person." But the question is, Does he, in this instance, have any right to "sanctuary," any basis for really expecting the daughter to "protect" him? He has already betrayed *her* and forfeited any claim to loyalty on her part. And surely no one would seriously censure the girl for exposing both herself and her father under the circumstances. Even if the daughter has been somewhat provocative, the father still has little ground for expecting her to shield him. He manifestly should have known better than to enter into such a relationship, and even though there was an element of seductiveness on the girl's part (motivated perhaps by the wish to neutralize her father as a moral authority and source of control in her life), the father can claim little consideration. If we were more prepared to be "hurt" by others when we behave in an unworthy manner with respect to them, it might have a decidedly helpful effect on our conduct.

But, in general, it is probably true that we ought to tell our own story and not take anyone else's "inventory." For example, when a husband confesses infidelity to his wife, she will harm herself far more than she harms her husband if, out of resentment, she extends the "confession" for him. There are very likely other persons *he* needs to tell, but as long as he accepts the responsibility for what he has done and does not try to place the blame upon his wife, the problem is his, and he should be allowed to handle it as such.

"But," someone is almost certain to interject, "isn't confession likely to be psychologically dangerous? Regardless of how others react, isn't there a question of what the individual himself may do? What about the possibility of suicide or psychosis?"

This question gains substance from the fact that many psychiatrists, even general practitioners, can cite instances in which someone has admitted serious misbehavior more or less openly, to relatives or friends, and then become so disturbed that hospitalization was necessary. On the face of it, such confession, far from being "good for the soul," has just the reverse effect. Much depends, it seems, upon the expectation of the person making the confession and of the persons receiving it. If there is a naive belief that confession itself is enough, there is almost certain to be trouble, perhaps very serious trouble. And those who hear the confessions of others and hasten forthwith to assure them of forgiveness and acceptance, either human or divine, are performing a very doubtful service. Confession is not enough! It is a beginning, an essential first step, but it is not the last one. Voluntary penance, restitution, and amendment of life are also necessary. And anyone who believes or is led to believe that confession alone will suffice is likely to undergo "unconscious," *i.e.* conscience-inflicted, involuntary penance of one type or another.

Suppose it were true that we could do anything, no matter how despicable and base, eventually confess it, and go scot-free. What deterrence would there be for *any* form of immorality or crime? In recent times, both psychology and theology have given us very bad advice in this connection which society, through the agency of law and law enforcement, is today having to repudiate and correct. For example, the April (1964) issue of *Reader's Digest* carried an account of marked reduction in juvenile delinquency and traffic violations which a judge in Helena, Montana, has achieved by the simple expedient of *not* following the common psychological and psychiatric dictum that it is "therapeutic" to be "warm, accepting, permissive, and protective" in dealing with those who commit such offenses. And *Time Magazine,* for July 17, 1964, bluntly observes, "To lawyers, divine code is too vague for the earthly task of preserving peace and good order here and now. Were all men free to act out their individual 'consciences,' *i.e.* without external restraint or compulsion, victory would simply go to those with the most power, the most guns. By contrast, the rule of law provides enforceable standards—and machinery to change them" (p. 63).

In order to encourage confession in wayward, alienated persons, a social system ought to show some tendency toward mercy and clemency in the event of confession and usually it does, but the notion that one can be suddenly delivered from responsibility for his misdeeds by merely *talking* about them, either in a religious, psychological, or legal context, is a grave misconception and the source of much confusion and avoidable suffering. Psychiatrists and psychologists who are in private practice, despite the general ambiguity of their situation, have a wry advantage here: their therapy is not free. In other words, if one "confesses" to them, it usually *costs* something, sometimes quite a lot, thereby providing a kind of built-in penance which does not, of course, have to be mentioned by name to serve this deeply moral function. If we clearly recognize the realities of this type of situation, can we not choose our own penances and objects of "charity" to better effect?

The policies and practices of Alcoholics Anonymous are particularly instructive on this score. The heart of AA is its twelve-step program of spiritual and moral progress. Here there is much reference to confession and restitution and not one word about "forgiveness." Here it is assumed that each member is going to have to *work out* his own salvation "with fear and trembling" and there will be no "justification by faith only."

Finally, let us consider some related, minor questions.

1. When has one confessed enough?

In a general sense, the answer to this question is whenever there is no felt need for further confession but no fear of having anyone else know the truth about oneself. We continue, all our lives, to make mistakes and to need the discipline of group experience, and when it is useful to other persons as an encouragement to them in their own efforts to become honest, then one should be willing to "share his story" again and again. Practically speaking, however, one rarely feels that anything about himself is much of a "secret" if upwards of half a dozen other persons know it.

2. Isn't there danger of overdoing confession, of getting to the point of boasting about one's sins?

If confession is not directly and explicitly associated with a program of restitution, there is indeed a danger of "overdoing" it, because confession alone and of itself never does enough. But I have yet to see anyone who has *acted* as well as talked about his sins, talk too much or inappropriately. If, in our groups, someone seems to be dwelling unduly upon a past misdemeanor, he is likely to be asked, "What have you *done* about it?" or "What *else* do you need to talk about?"

3. Should you start confession with an individual or before a group?

In general, it is easier to begin with one person who will then "sponsor" you into the open fellowship of a group. But when there are painful problems to be worked through with a marital partner, it is sometimes desirable to have at least one other person present, sometimes a full-fledged group. This provides a kind of "center of gravity" which keeps issues in clearer focus, and helps each of the partners to behave with restraint and fairness.

4. To *whom* shall I talk, confess—everyone I meet, or only a few? And how are they to be selected?

Manifestly there is no need to make a spectacle or bore of yourself with respect to the confession of sins. Do not overestimate your importance—most people aren't that interested in you. So the question is one of pertinence, relevance. How can this be determined? Dr. David Belgum (1963), in his book *Guilt: Where Psychology and Religion Meet* tells the following incident. One of his former seminary students, during a year of field placement, was unfaithful to his wife and became increasingly anxious and concerned. Later, after he graduated from the seminary and had become the assistant minister in another church, he came to Dr. Belgum with the story and a request for help. "Your anxiety," Dr. Belgum told him, "is in effect a fear of blackmail. Whom would you most dread having know your story?" The man replied, "My wife and the senior minister of the church where I am now employed." With Dr. Belgum's encouragement and support, this man was able to go to them with the truth. Painful? Of course, but liberating in a way which nothing else could have been. What a terrible waste of time it is seeing a "counselor" who never counsels us to do anything but continue talking *to him!* And group therapy, while an improvement over most individual counseling, can also fall short of full effectiveness if it becomes ingrown and does not encourage its members to reach out to, and often incorporate into the group, "significant others."

5. And then there is the question, "*What* shall I confess?"

Not long ago a professional psychologist observed (through a one-way mirror, which the patients knew about) one of our hospital groups in action. Later he said, "There were two young women in that group whom I found very 'sexy.' If I had been participating in the group, would I have been expected to confess my thoughts and fantasies about those girls?"

The question was, Had this man *done* anything wrong, and did he have anything about which to feel guilty? Our position, in general, is this. One cannot entirely control the thoughts that pass through one's head, but one *can* keep from dwelling upon them or "acting out" with respect to them. If one simply notes that a given person of either sex is attractive and then passes on to other things, what's there to "confess"? And precious little time is spent in our groups with conversations of this kind. But if one deliberately encourages sexual fantasies and perhaps subsequently uses them as the basis for inappropriate sexual behavior, then that is a very different matter, and the best way to bringing an end to it is to submit oneself to the discipline of absolute candor. (I think our position would also be much the same with respect to "feelings of hostility," although this too is a problem which, in practice, does not often arise. We find that if one deals with one's self-anger, *i.e.* guilt, the occasion to be enraged with others is dramatically reduced.)

Because of the infinite variety and richness of group experience, it is, of course, impossible to anticipate *all* the questions and problems that may arise in this connection. And unless one has actually immersed himself in such experience, *nothing* that others can say will carry complete conviction. There is no substitute for firsthand knowledge of the process. What has been said here is intended, at most, as a rough guide for those who, out of the futility and pain of secrecy and alienation, are ready to try a new way of life, a new type of existence. A "more abundant" life is indeed available for all who desire it and who are willing to make the necessary sacrifice of pride and prejudice.

INTEGRITY THERAPY IN ACTION:
AN ILLUSTRATIVE INTERVIEW

Interviewer: Well, I don't know very much about you. You're relatively new in the hospital, aren't you?

Mrs. Saunders: I came in a week ago today.

I: You've been hospitalized before?

S: No. Not in this type of hospital.

I: I see. What led up to your hospitalization?

S: I have no idea what caused me to do what I did—that's what I'm here to find out.

I: Yes.

S: I've been nervous, and the last two and one-half years I've been having stomach spasms. I've been taking medication for that, and I would say that during the week prior to last Sunday I was under a little extra strain. I *was* tired. I was getting up at four o'clock in the morning and not getting to bed very early. I have my father with me part of the time—he was with me at that time. He's eighty-two and not at all well. But I've been under more strain than that, and I've asked myself, "What led up to this incident?"

It's not unusual for me to have these stomach spasms, although they are rather far apart. They may be six months apart; or I might have two or three rather close together. Then, by watching my diet and watching my rest, I can go for quite some time. But week before last I'd had the doctor on Thursday and Friday for shots to get my stomach settled. And then Saturday was just an ordinary day. Saturday night our youngest daughter, Jessica, had gone to the prom, and I sat up and waited for her to be picked up about midnight by some parents who were going to have a party for these kids. Our church services now start at eight-thirty, and I didn't awaken until twenty minutes of nine and was disappointed because I wasn't going to make church. But I had faced many other disappointments. And I decided that since we couldn't go to church, why didn't we take a long drive out in the country, just to get out and drive. My father could have a coronary at any time —he has had one light stroke. And he had had a heart spell both Friday night and Saturday night. So my husband said, "I don't believe Dad could take the trip today. I think that it would excite him a little too much." And I said, "I'd just as soon rest," and my husband had been working ten hours a day. He said, "And I think you'd better go back and rest; you don't want to have the doctor again." Well, that made me angry at myself. I wasn't angry at him or what he said, but I *was* angry at myself to think that I *had* to have the doctor and that if I didn't be careful even a ride in the country could bring on one of these stomach spasms.

I often get angry at myself, for one reason or another. And then I immediately feel guilty afterwards because I think: "Why can't you control your emotions better than that, or see into a situation better than that?"

So Sunday morning I took two resting pills. I don't know exactly the name of them—but I know they aren't strong. I then lay down but I didn't go to sleep, so I did take a phenobarbital sleeping capsule. Then I went to sleep. I would imagine this was around ten o'clock in the morning—I didn't note the time in particular. I woke up at ten minutes after one, and I didn't smell any food cooking. I have a daughter that's real capable of going ahead and getting a meal—the younger one could help her. I went out in the kitchen and I said, "Why haven't you started dinner? I know Grandpa is hungry." He had been up early. He always gets up real early—he was a farmer and he doesn't know how to sleep in of a morning. I said, "I know Grandpa's hungry, and why haven't you gone ahead then with dinner?" And my oldest girl said, "Daddy said we might wake you up; you'd better have your sleep."

"Well, why do I always have to have my sleep? Why is it always *me* having to sleep?" I said. And I was very clear at that point, because I can remember that just as plainly as anything. We were going to have liver, and I sliced it for my daughter; and I turned to go to another section of the kitchen—I never faint, but I fainted. And I don't remember a lot of things from that point on.

What I'd like to know is whether I don't *want* to remember—this is what I'm trying to find out—and why I am so hazy. It seems that I was in sort of a stupor, because I remember members of the family holding a wet cloth to my forehead out there in the kitchen; and I remember hearing voices. But I don't ever remember being taken from the kitchen back to bed, and I had to have slept again, because it had to be about four o'clock when I got up and went to the bathroom. I was real dizzy, and I know I had trouble getting out of the bedroom. I still felt like I was in sort of a daze. When I stood up I still felt like I was going to faint again. I went into the bathroom—this disgusts me and terrifies me at the same time because I never had any prior thought of it and I don't know what prompted me to have the thought. But as I came back out of the bathroom the door to our linen closet was open, and there was a razor blade laying there on the shelf by my razor. I looked at that razor blade and had this drastic—this impulse to do something drastic. I picked the razor blade up, went back, crawled in bed, and cut this wrist as deeply as I could and started on this one. And I can't remember that hurting; I just don't remember any pain associated with it at all. But my husband had heard me up going to the bathroom, and he came in to see if I got back in bed all right and if I was feeling better. And he caught me just as I was ready to work on my other wrist. And all I remember him saying was, "Oh my God!" and calling for help.

I remember being in the car with him and my sister and going to the hospital. And I remember being next on a cot, I suppose in the emergency room. Also I remember telling the doctor not to sew up the cut. I still had that notion in my mind, that I didn't want it sewed up. I don't remember leaving the emergency room, or going into my hospital room. The next thing I recall was my sister being in the room with me. I knew she wasn't feeling well and hadn't been well for the past week, so I wanted to know why she didn't go home. She needed her rest and hadn't been well. And my pastor came in, and I said, "Why are you here?" And he said, "I came to relieve your sister.' And I said, "What time is it?" He said, "Midnight." And I said, "Why you shouldn't be here, either. You should be home with your family. And I wish you'd take her home. If you go home, I'd sleep better." I don't remember another thing until Dr. Reynolds, my medical doctor, came in the next morning to talk to me.

I: Had things somewhat cleared up by morning?

S: Yes. I could talk to Dr. Reynolds very well. And he said that he had seen me on Sunday afternoon sometime and that my pastor had also been there. Two days afterwards my sister was visiting me and I said, "Was Pastor Hooten at the house Sunday afternoon?" And she said, "Yes." And I said, "I just vaguely remembered seeing him." He's been to see me several times since. He said he talked to me for a half hour, and I don't remember hearing a word he said. He said I was in a real deep, what he called depression, because I had no use for myself. And he said I just kept saying that I wasn't any good, and wasn't any help to my family, and I wasn't any of this and I wasn't any of that. That isn't what I think.

I: Were you drinking Sunday afternoon?

S: No, I haven't been drinking for over a year. I won't. That's part of the thing that has bothered me; I think that might have been one thing that added to my nervous feeling. It certainly hadn't helped. What started me drinking was—well, let's see, it would be about 1960—we built a filling station in 1955, opened it in the spring of '56 and this was the fifth year we had had it. And we were trying to sell it. In the first place we found out we weren't in the most desirable location. We knew this new Interstate was going to come through and was going to cut the station off; and we'd moved into a real old house, expecting to build the station first and then as soon as we got it opened up to tear down this old house and build a new house. But we didn't ever get the job done, because we got the station open and found out we didn't have the right arrangement of the storage tanks, so instead of building a new house, we relocated the tanks and got some new equipment. And for a while we thought, "When we get all this paid out, we'll put up the new house." But by that time we decided we'd better sell and get out of the business.

I know that being in that old house was very much to my disliking; I started to lose weight at that time and Dr. Reynolds suggested that I drink two cans of beer at bedtime or one at suppertime and one at bedtime to try to relieve the tension, and also he said it was a good weight builder. I did that for quite some time, and then pretty soon I thought, "Well, that does relax a person." And perhaps I'd drink one in the middle of the afternoon. I handled all the laundry and what-not; the next thing I knew, if I saw things getting too rushing and I felt real frustrated or anything, I'd think, "Well now a can of beer will calm me down." So sometimes I was drinking five to six cans a day—this would be from six o'clock in the morning till midnight at night. But it bothered me, because it's against our religion in the first place. My husband doesn't drink whatsoever, and I knew that he didn't like it. And so I quit. I'd think, "I don't need it" and I'd pray for help. Maybe I'd go three, four months and then I'd decide, "Oh, I'll get six cans, it'll be all right, I can handle it." Maybe I'd handle those six cans pretty well, stretch them out. But then I'd be back on it again. I think that it was like (pause) not facing reality.

I: Mmmm.

S: It would take me sort of away from my tension, and I could feel good and face the situation, y'know. But it still bothered me. I have a lot of faith in religion, and I began praying about it. I'd go to communion and ask for strength to leave it alone, until finally I said in my prayer, "Well, if you want me to be an alcoholic, I will be one. I'll just give up." And either that was psychological in my own mind or whatever it was, I found I *could* give it up. Now I say "give it up." I stay away from it. Because I still think, unless I can get over some of this, oh, making mountains out of molehills, y'know, being overanxious. . . .

In the last two years I've noticed changes. I used to be very active in Sunday School; I taught Sunday School for about, oh I taught it eight or nine years. And then I was active in the church circle and served in different offices, and I worked in Vacation Bible School. One summer I was chairman of Vacation Bible School, and I got along just fine until the night of our closing program and we had a new minister. Our other minister had been Pastor Seaton and our new minister was Pastor Hooten. And in my remarks, I said it was nice to have Pastor Seaton around all the time. Everyone laughed and laughed. And I went on with my talk and didn't realize until afterward that I had meant to say Pastor Hooten and knew that that was a little bit touchy with him to be caled Seaton all the time when he was Hooten. And that bothered me far more than it should. It did bother me; I'd wake up at night and think about it. And then I noticed that I didn't like to be active as much as I used to. I didn't want to work with Vacation Bible School, although our minister asked me to come back the next year.

Now it was that fall—that would be about two and one-half years ago, two years ago last October—I take my youngest daughter, Jessica, every summer to Avondale for her piano contest; this would be the seventh year that I had taken her. And I came home from the contest very tired and I went into this thing of being sick at my stomach, having the spasms, and couldn't stop. So I went to the hospital for x-rays. I stayed three days, and they didn't find anything. There wasn't anything they could find wrong right away. So I said I couldn't stay at the hospital because my daughter was going to be confirmed and my husband had long planned a trip to Canada with his brother to go fishing, and I wanted to be home for both of these reasons. Well, I went home but I didn't get to stay. I missed the confirmation and my husband missed the fishing, because I had to go back to the hospital and had to be fed through the veins. I was in the hospital fifteen days, and they couldn't find out what was causing my trouble, except "nerves." They tried to find an ulcer but never did. The only thing they could discover was that this little section of the stomach—I believe you call it the duodenum, which connects with the intestine and closes and opens like a fist—will close and stay closed and won't let my stomach empty. And then stomach juices come in and this throws my stomach into a spasm; I just get ill until I get a shot of Demerol® or something to quiet me so I'll sleep and let the little "fist" [sphincter] relax. And since that time I've had these spasms.

I: You've been on quite a lot of medication, have you?

S: Yes, I have. I don't remember the names of the two that I had coming from the hospital. I've been on a liquid I know was Donnatal,® and then from that I went to Librax,® a tranquilizer. And I have a lot of headaches—no, not exactly headaches, but stomachache which will bring on a headache, that's what I would say. And I have a lot of pain with this stomachache, and I've taken codeine capsules for that, and now that my father's been with me I was going heavier on those three. They've changed me from Librax to Librium,® and I was going heavier on both the Librium and the codeine. I don't like to get in the habit of taking sleeping pills, but I found I was also taking—requiring sleeping pills to sleep. And this all built up, this was all going along, and I should have seen the danger signal myself. I should have seen that I was taking too much medication in order to keep going, but a person never wants to admit defeat and give up. But I still am here to find out what would drive me to this, to do this [awful thing].

I: Well, I think we've got a partial explanation. Protracted use of tranquilizers sometimes leads to impaired judgment. Now you'd taken some extra things Sunday, hadn't you?

S: Uh huh.

I: People who have drunk a lot or who have been on tranquilizers a long time, or who are using a combination of the two, often act under the influence of these things quite impulsively. Their judgment is impaired. They don't—they're not concerned, they're not *normally* concerned.

S: I see.

I: And my guess is that this slashing of your wrist is not something that you would have done if you had been . . .

S: Why, no. I couldn't bear to.

I: Yes.

S: But I know Dr. Reynolds felt just very bad when he talked to me Monday morning. He gave me a nice compliment. He said, "You're too fine a person to have let this happen and I'm afraid that perhaps my medication has been wrong for you." He asked me to please come out here because he said, "I don't understand your problem. I don't have the proper training for it. I don't know what your problem may be, and I don't believe I'm getting to the bottom of it."

I: He sounds like an honest man.

S: That's right.

I: Where is your home?

S: In Lewisberg.

I: That's just over west of here, isn't it?

S: Yes, about five miles out.

I: And you say you've previously been hospitalized only for physical reasons. You've never been in a mental hospital.

S: That's right.

I: Well, this has been a very good account of your difficulties, and thank you for talking so freely and so clearly about all this. Your description of the situation permits us to come right to the point of this interview. We think people often get into emotional knots because they have old, unresolved guilts in their lives, things they've been secretly ashamed of and haven't known how to deal with. Have you been deeply guilty about anything? Hiding anything?

S: Definitely.

I: Are you free to talk about it?

S: I don't like to, but I can. I was sexually molested by my brothers as early as the age of eight; I've always felt that somehow my parents let me down, that they didn't see or didn't want to see what was going on. My mother very definitely would never talk to me. We were never close. I can never remember being close with my mother. I had to learn about menstruation from an older cousin. My mother could hardly bear to talk about that to me; when I got older, my older sister realized what was happening and she told me, and an older cousin told me and then I felt terrible. And yet all this time I had felt that this was a very deep injustice. And then I added to it—as I've gotten older I can realize why. In high school I was determined to prove myself, prove I could be something. So I made straight A's, and I was offered a scholarship to college. But I was going with a boy that was—I didn't like high school boys, I always liked more mature people—and he wanted to marry me. I thought it was very important that I get married and have a legal reason for not being a virgin.

So I married him more for, largely for, that purpose. I don't think I loved him—certainly not the way I love my present husband. I didn't feel any of that. And when we became engaged I thought, "Well, at least I'll be honest," and I told him what had happened to me. Well then . . .

I: This was the first husband.

S: This was my first husband. This was when I was sixteen. I graduated from high school when I was sixteen. I was seventeen that summer, but I had gone to school early and skipped a grade. And then, after I told him, he wanted sexual relationships, to know whether he really wanted to marry me. I thought this was terribly important that I get married. So we did that and he decided he would still marry me. But he didn't want anything to do with my family. Well, I could understand that. After all that had happened, I wasn't too sure that I wanted much to do with them.

I: Yes.

S: But we only lived about a half mile from my family, and were all farmers. And living that close you can't ignore your family. And we were married in the summer of the year I was seventeen and that same year, the day before Christmas, my mother and my sister were in a bad car accident; my mother had to stay in the hospital. She was cut from here clear up to here [gestures], her nose was broken, and she was in deep shock. And my sister was in no shape to take care of her, because she too was injured. So the logical thing was for me to stay at the hospital all night with her. My husband was generous with gifts—I think that's probably one reason I liked him because I wasn't used to that sort of thing. And he was waiting up for me this particular Christmas Eve when the car drove in. We'd never had a radio, and he'd bought a radio and had it playing and had gifts all arranged on the table. And he wanted it to be a big surprise for me as I came in. Well, instead of me it was my brother saying that I was going to stay at the hospital all night. My husband took that as a feeling that I thought more of my mother than I did of him, and he was very hurt as well as very angry about it all. I won't say that alone caused what then happened, because a person has to have a weakness of their own to get involved in anything. But along about the next summer he started gambling. He'd stop a little while and then he'd be back at it. Then he started drinking and the drinking and gambling went together.

By now we had been married a year and a half and he'd sometimes be gone as much as ten days at a time, maybe two weeks. I lived only a half mile from my parents and a mile from his parents. They all knew what was going on and they'd sometimes send someone up to find him, check on him. They knew where he was, but he'd refuse to come home until he got ready. But one day he came home—we had a new pickup truck and I can remember he loaded the last of the hogs that we had, to take to market and he said, "Goodbye, I'll see you some day." I knew he was leaving for good, so I went right over to his mother's and said, "I think he's gone for good." And she said, "Oh, no, because he's gone lots of times and come back." But I said, "Yes, but he never said, 'I'll see you sometime'."

He *was* gone! He had mortgaged everything that was to be mortgaged and soon he skipped the country. He was gone for two years, and I had to go out and do housework. I didn't know anything else to do, until eventually I borrowed—then I thought it was a tremendous sum— fifty dollars to go to business school. And I then went to work for a lawyer, and eventually I gave myself a pretty good education, roundaboutwise. But after my husband— I'm getting a little ahead of my story, because—after he was gone two years he came back, but he didn't want to set up a home; he didn't want responsibility. I was still doing housework. I hadn't gone to business school yet, and we would spend some weekends at his parents' home. And then just one day he disappeared again, and no one knew where he went until his folks were notified that he had joined the Army. He joined the Army as a single person and was in Hawaii by this time. Well, by the time I got through the red tape and so forth to let the Army know that he had a wife, they forced him then to send an allotment. And the chaplain made him write one letter and that's all I heard from him for another year.

In the meantime I had gone to business school and started working, and he went from Hawaii to Japan. I worked for the law firm about two and a half years, I think. Then I joined the Navy, and decided I might as well get my freedom because I wasn't hearing anything from my husband, and there hadn't been any marriage to begin with. I filed for divorce and I always did think it was odd that it took both of us to get married but neither of us were present for the divorce.

But I look back now and I wish I had taken the scholarship and gone on to college and not felt as I did. I think I've had this feeling of guilt all my life. First there was this early sexual behavior, and then I was forced to have a partial hysterectomy at twenty-one and the rest of it at twenty-nine. Because of that I was robbed of having children of my own. I always thought that my parents hadn't done a very good job, and when I was twenty-nine I met this man that I'm married to now. But when I had the second operation I didn't want to get married again. I said, "What's the use of getting married; I can't have children and there's no point." Well, Henry said he had been married and his wife died of cancer and they could never have any children, and he would be perfectly willing to adopt children, although he's sixteen years older than I am. So we were married then, later, in 1949.

As a child I was brought up as a Lutheran, and that made a very deep impression on me. After I married the first time I went to my first husband's church because he thought Lutheranism was too much like Catholicism. I drew away from the church until I was in the Navy, but then I came back to the church. When I married I found out my second husband had been baptized a Lutheran and had gone to his wife's church so he was willing to come back as a Lutheran. So that's the first thing we did, and we got married in the Lutheran church. Three years after our marriage we adopted a five-year-old girl, and when she was eight years old we adopted a six-year-old girl.

I now have a wonderful husband. You couldn't ask for a better man; I can't find a fault with him. He's been a good father. He's put up with anything I've done or said or wanted to do. He's given me anything that he could. As soon as we sold the station, we bought the house next door to us. It's completely remodeled; it's a beautiful home. I would never do anything to hurt him. And yet . . .

Last fall my mother had a very unfortunate accident. It was last November, the 23rd, she was cooking supper and like many older women will do, she took her apron to lift the pan off the stove and caught her apron on fire. We think it must have just paralyzed her; she couldn't call out or do anything. My father was just outside the door on the studio couch. And when she walked in to him and said, "Daddy, I'm on fire," everything was on fire. She had some nylon and knit underclothing down to the knees, and they just melted to her skin. She went to the hospital that night and died on the 27th. I was with her the last thirty-six hours straight. I came home after that and slept about five hours, and I got up and started talking to my husband. I think I was feeling guilty because my mother died. I had always felt she hadn't been fair with me. So for some reason I blurted out to my husband about this, what had happened to me as a child. I never had mentioned it to him before, and there was no reason for him to know it at all. He took it real well. He said he'd just as soon not have known it, but he said, "It's happened and there's nothing we can do about it and you should forget about it." He's never mentioned it since and he said, "I won't have any feelings against your father." He said, "I could have," but he said, "He's an old man now and it's too late to have any feelings against him or say anything to him now because he's ill and he's had this shock of losing his wife."

Henry has gone out of his way to do anything he can for my dad. He'll take him in; we keep him, I would say, more than either of my two brothers do. My sister can't because she lost her husband with a heart attack in September, and she's going to school now and she can't keep my dad because he can't be left alone. He is comfortable with us because he has his own sleeping quarters; he leans over backwards to not be any trouble, not to cause you any trouble if he can help it, but I listen for him. I listen for the boards to creak, to hear him if he goes to the bathroom, to be sure he gets back. And that's when I started to take more sleeping pills because I was lying awake trying to listen for him and then in the daytime I was exhausted.

It bothers me now that I did this [make the suicide attempt] to hurt my husband or hurt my children, but they don't take it that way. They take it as an illness, as something that I couldn't help.

When I first came over here I said I didn't know how much of myself to tell. I didn't know how much to unload. And my sister said she and her husband Jason had talked about that very thing and they felt I should tell everything that was in my mind to tell. So I talked as freely with my psychologist as I have with you and I'm glad to have it off my mind. I slept better Saturday and Sunday nights, but only after I'd seen my husband. He came in on Saturday and the minute he had a chance to be with me—he brought our youngest daughter in to see me on Saturday—and when she went out in the other room, the first thing he wanted to know was if I had told about what had happened to me as a child. He wanted to be real sure that I had told that. He felt that this was one thing that was pressuring against my mind and was definitely a feeling of guilt that I'd had.

I've always had a feeling that I didn't quite measure up to the person I ought to be. And I think that's what caused me sometimes to get angry at the world or angry at myself and then feel guilty because I felt, well I've got everything and yet . . . as I said, I feel very strongly about my religion, and I'd think, "I don't have to feel this way." But I'd also like to find out what has caused me to be more and more nervous the last two years.

I: How long have you been on pills?

S: About two and a half years—since I was hospitalized for the stomach trouble. No, I wasn't really on pills that long because . . . I was on codeine that long, off and on. I try not to take a lot of medicine because I'm always afraid I'd be addicted to one or the other, and I would stay away from it as long as I thought I could. But I would take spells when I would get real frustrated or feel real nervous. I had given myself estrogen shots since . . . well, for a long time I took them at the doctor's office and then when they could be spanned out, I gave them to myself. I've also noticed just a little bit more trouble with—my doctor thought it might be a chemical menopause I was going through, because I noticed intense periods of hot flashes, and sleeplessness, and a real odd feeling in my stomach, similar to cramps, stomach cramps. And then

I'd have to give myself one estrogen shot and a couple of days follow it up with another one. And then I'd go for a while until another one of these spells would hit me.

I: Irritability sometimes comes from protracted use of sedatives and tranquilizers. Would you say during this last couple of years your tendency to get angry has increased? Or have you always been a little quick on the trigger?

S: I've always been that way, always! I've got a temper! My husband has helped me tremendously with that. I can honestly say we haven't fought and it isn't my fault.

I: (laughs) Yeah, well it's nice to hear you able to speak so positively of your husband. How old are your girls now?

S: Sixteen and eighteen. They're almost seventeen and nineteen. Again I have learned a lot about psychology in working with them because both of them have emotional problems, as a result of getting them at the age we did. I've been over to this building often enough, that's certain, working with social workers for these children. They've both had casework to find out what their emotional problem was. It helped us understand them better. My oldest daughter still has a problem which she'll always have to cope with, and that's fear. She was so mistreated the first five years of her life that she was—would have been, they told us later—would have been a retarded child out of fear if she hadn't arrived in our home and we hadn't worked so closely with social workers. And I can proudly say she has come a long, long way from the child that we started with. She still doesn't make friends; she may find herself *one;* she doesn't date; she's still withdrawn; she doesn't feel her emotions a great deal. The hardest thing I had to do with her or to her was force her to go to Upton to business school when she was out of high school. That nearly broke her heart. She didn't want to leave home; she didn't want to get away. But we thought she had to; we felt that if we let her go to the local school she'd come home every night, and it was time for her to break away from home. Well, we had a sick girl for about a week. She cried to come back home, and the first weekend she was home she cried all weekend because we were going to make her go back. But she finally whipped it, and she's a different person now.

I: How's the communication between you and your daughters?

S: Very good. Very good with Jessica; Jessica's very outspoken. Jessica has very many of my—what do I want to say, characterizations?—temper, quick-speaking, easy to speak, easy to talk with. Alice finds it very hard to talk; finds it very hard to tell you what her problem is.

I: She's the older girl?

S: She's the older. She'll cry. And I can guess at her problem and I can tell by her expression when I've hit it. But she's coming out of a lot of that now. She got a job about four weeks ago as a private secretary and it's her own capability that is being proven to her. She's gaining self-assurance. But the younger one has given me an awful lot of trouble because she lacks security, and I'm not sure that she's quite convinced that she has it yet. She knows she has it, but she gets very, very angry. She's slapped me, she's kicked me, she's told me I wasn't her mother and that she didn't have to mind me; however, these temper outbursts quieted down after she was confirmed, after she had her confirmation study. And they've gotten farther apart, and she will now come and apologize.

I: Do you feel that your own waywardness in childhood—if you want to call it that—has undermined your security as a mother with these two girls?

S: I wonder about that because often when I have had trouble with the girls I feel I'm not a good mother. I feel, I feel guilty in the sense of, well, God wouldn't let me have my own children, but I was determined to have children so I went and got them anyway. And now, can I measure up to the job of being a mother?

I: The girls don't know, I suppose, about your difficulties as a child.

S: No. But it helped me with Jessica, because she was six when we got her; when she was seven, we found out that she had been exposed to sex in her foster home—not molested, but had seen the foster father, possibly seen the foster father and mother. She drew terrible sex pictures, all out of proportion—drew them at school and put another girl's name on them. I found them first in her book and I was real angry that she should be exposed to this at such a young age. So I went to the teacher and the teacher said, "I can't believe that that girl drew these. She isn't that type of girl." So she took the girl to one side and came back and said, "I don't understand this; I'm convinced this girl didn't draw them."

Well, Jessica was calling for help in her way because the next drawing I found in the wastepaper can. And then I found out that Jessica had drawn the pictures. I didn't know how to talk to her, so young, and so I gave the job to our pastor. I never will know what he said to her; he took her aside and talked to her for an hour, and then I talked to her as much as I could. I talked to her as she got older, and I made very sure that she knew everything. I got a book through the social workers entitled *The Stork Didn't Bring You,* and both girls have gone through that book. What Alice feels or thinks about sex, I don't know, because it's just as difficult for her to talk about sex, in my way of thinking, as it was for my mother to talk about it.

Jessica amused me just no end not very long ago. Oh, it was after Alice had started to school; Jessica came down and said, "That darn book you got over there sure doesn't tell all the answers." And I said, "Well, anything it doesn't answer, I'll answer it if I can." And she said, "Well, what the heck are rubbers?" And I said, "Where did you hear that? In what way did you hear it?" She said that this one girl over at school said that she was going with four different boys and she didn't have to worry because they wore rubbers. And Jessica said, "I thought that it had something to do with sex, but it sure didn't explain it in that book." So I explained it to her and when Alice came home that weekend I thought, "Well now that's a subject I never brought up with them." I had told them how they might be tempted, what might be offered to them, what promises might be made to them, or what argument might be given them, and I'd gone all over that area but I hadn't hit this particular one. So I asked Alice if she knew what they were. Well, she looked like if the floor could open up and swallow her it would be just fine. And before I could open up and explain to her, her face got red and she squirmed in her chair and she said, "Yes, I know!" And I said, "Well, Jessica didn't know." And I said, "You don't talk freely with me and I wanted to make sure you knew." And I said, "I'd failed to explain it to Jessica." I said, "To be sure you know, will you tell me what they are?" She squirmed a little more and finally said, "Oh, it's what those *men* wear!" and got up and went out of the room in tears. Now that's how hard it is for her to talk, and I feel that she has a problem.

I: You say that you wanted to make sure that your daughters knew "everything," but you never wanted them to know everything *about you*, have you?

S: No, I didn't want them to know what happened to me as a child. I did tell them about my first marriage, and I did tell them that I had intercourse before marriage. I didn't tell them why. I did tell them that was wrong because I remember once when my husband was angry he made the remark to me that I'll never forget: "Well, it wasn't too hard for me to talk you into it, I don't think it'd be too hard for any man to." And I said, "Now that's what a man can tell you if you don't wait until marriage." I explained that in that way to them, but it didn't go any farther back than that.

I: Let's go back to this business with your brothers. You say they "molested" you. Now you speak of this as happening to you. But you had some responsibility in this, didn't you?

S: I would imagine so, sure.

I: You could have reported it.

S: I *could* have, but it wasn't the type of thing that I could report to my mother, and my brothers threatened me: "Don't you dare tell Dad about this because he'd really give you a good licking."

I: How old were your brothers? And were you?

S: There's one four years older and the other one, six years older.

I: I mean when the intercourse began, how old were they?

S: Well, I would say, one would be around twelve going on thirteen, and the other would be two years older.

I: So they were sexually mature at this time.

S: That's right.

I: And you were just a little girl, of eight or so?

S: Yes, but I was a *big* girl.

I: Big girl?

S: I was. I weighed twelve pounds when I was born. I was five foot eight when I was in the eighth grade, so I was a big girl.

I: Uh huh. And matured early, sexually?

S: Yes. I did.

I: Yes. So this was full-fledged intercourse.

S: Yes, it was.

I: Yeah. I wonder if you've ever faced up to the full extent of your guilt about that. You talk about it, that they *molested* you and that this *happened* to you. But, in a certain sense, you did it.

S: I suppose I did, and yet when I got old enough to know just exactly what was wrong about it, or why it shouldn't be, I stopped them—I knew enough to stop.

I: Uh huh.

S: Yet, I was probably a coward not to go to my father, wasn't I?

I: Well, it would have taken a lot of courage, and we can't perhaps blame you as a girl for not having done it. But I think that you probably are not very pleased with that situation. I was involved in a perversion when I was in early adolescence. My father died when I had just turned thirteen. He was a retired farmer and we lived out on the edge of town. [The nature of the perversion is described.] I, too, could have done something about it. I *tried* to stop it; I tried praying and I tried making resolutions—

y'know, "This is the last time," and so forth, but I couldn't master it. Having grown up in a Protestant church I had repeatedly heard that we Protestants don't confess our sins and do penance the way those foolish Catholics do. But I couldn't make this work. What I *should* have done was to have gone to my older brother and brother-in-law and said, "Look, I'm in trouble. I need your help. I need your strength." But as I look back upon it, I don't condemn myself particularly for not having been this strong or this wise. But it played havoc with my life, all the same. And about a year and a half after the perversion started, I became quite neurotic, as a freshman in high school. And this in effect *stopped* the perversion. But it took me a long time to get honest and free and liberated from the burden of guilt and secrecy. Now if you and I had both been persons of poor character, I think our perversity wouldn't have bothered us. But we were both people of pretty good conscience and our misconduct did bother us. So I would say that our suffering has been in some ways our strength, our salvation.

S: I see.

I: And we don't think of this kind of disturbance as illness particularly but rather as a discomfort, a discomfort or dis-ease that is trying to get us to grow up and be more mature and open about our lives. So I think if you work this thing through you can perhaps become a whole and wholesome, effective person again, probably more so than you've ever been before. And it's *very* much to your credit that you are willing and determined to talk and not hide these things any longer.

S: Well I definitely—I think this was enough of a shock to bring anybody out of anything.

I: It's a jolt, isn't it?

S: Yes, it is. To think that you could do that to your own person. I'd looked upon people who would attempt to commit suicide either with pity or with scorn because I thought, "Well they were cowards. Only a coward would do that." Or else they were ill. But when I did it myself, I thought, "It's time to find out just how far this was going."

I: Yeah.

S: Just why did it go this far? I mean—How could I, how could I do such a thing? As a Christian, I shouldn't have done this sort of thing. I think my pastor brought that to me just about as clearly as he could because when I came in here Monday, as far as I was concerned, I wanted help, but at the same time it was almost like the end of the world, y'know?

I: Uh huh. It's like death, isn't it?

S: Uh huh. I came in about one o'clock Monday afternoon and Pastor Hooten came out to see me Monday night and I said, "How could I ever face people?" "Well," he said, "I should have been the hardest one to face, and you faced me." And I realized what he meant. As a Christian, it should have been hard to face him for what I tried to do. And I didn't have any trouble facing him and he said, "Why did you feel free in coming out and talking to me?" I sat and thought that over, and I said, "Because I feel very deeply that you're my friend." So, then as he left, he said, "You aren't guilty about this in particular." He said, "I don't know what your problem is. But I know you've been feeling guilty about something for a long time." So he said, "As a friend to a friend, will you be as cooperative as you can, while you're out here?"

I: But you had never been able to confess this early sinful period in your life in the church?

S: No. I couldn't. When I heard about group therapy and thought I'd be discussing it with a group of individuals, I thought, I can't possibly. I can talk with a psychologist; I could talk with a doctor. I *don't* know if I could talk to my minister about it. I've never *felt* like I could. And I sure don't feel like I could talk to a group about it.

I: You've felt like something of a hypocrite, is this it?

S: Hu huh.

I: Well, you can imagine what a hypocrite *I* felt like. I was a Sunday School boy, and made good marks in school, and lived in the big white house out on West Main Street. And when I walked down the street everyone was sort of proud of me as one of the promising young men of the town. But I knew, underneath, what I was involved in. I think hypocrisy is a great illness. You remember Christ had some of his sharpest words for the hypocrites.

S: That's right.

I: And it's too bad that our society isn't more helpful to us on this score. If we see somebody suffering in this way, we say, "Oh, you're sick," y'know. Well, it would probably be more helpful if we could ask each other, "What sin are you hiding?"

S: That's true, isn't it, when we look at it that way.

I: Come right out with it. But we say, "Oh, y'know, she's a nice person; there couldn't be anything wrong with *her;* she's just sick." This way, we make a *mystery* out of something that really makes quite a lot of sense when you understand it.

S: Well, why would this build up so? For a long time I lived very well with it. I was able to be active among people, and my husband and I have a wonderful marriage together. There's nothing wrong with it whatsoever. And I think we've made a success with these two children. So why would I start having these stomach spasms two and a half years ago? At that time I quit going to groups because I'd get real tense, and when I get real tense and nervous, next thing I know I am having a stomach spasm. Now why, all of a sudden?

I: Well, I don't know, I'm sure, but you know there's a saying from the Old Testament, "The Lord is slow to wrath." The Lord has given you a lot of time. . . .

S: Uh huh.

I: Or conscience has given you a lot of time. And it may be simply the fact that you are now the mother of teen-age girls, and you want them to be honest with you, I'm sure.

S: That's right.

I: But you have not been fully honest with them. Mind you, I don't think you've done a real bad job with your girls. Considering the fact they were adopted and so forth, you've probably been very, very good for them. But it's conceivable that your hypocrisy has been piqued a bit by having to pose as a . . .

S: A good mother!

I: As a little better mother than you in fact are.

S: Uh huh.

I: This may be the thing that kind of threw you.

S: Then perhaps some of my guilt at not being a good mother isn't altogether that I didn't do a good job with the girls, but I'm not a good person.

(Pause)

I: And there's something here, because of what you said when you were so heavily under the influence of those pills Sunday, "I'm no good," y'know, and so forth.

S: Uh-huh. (long pause) And I *never* would have said that to the pastor. I mean I don't know what I said to him. No one told me too much of the things I said. But I would like to find out. I'll ask the pastor exactly what I did say to him. He said, "I never thought, I'd hear some of the things from you that I heard." I don't know exactly what all I might have told him.

I: So that your taking the pills and talking out of your head may be a little like your daughter drawing the pictures, mightn't it?

S: That's what he told me he thought this was. He said I'd reached the limit and I wanted help and that's how I went after it.

I: Yes.

S: But it just appalls me to think that I wanted to die. Because I sure don't.

I: In light of our discussion, don't you think that we may be able to understand a little better now why you were angered when your husband said, "Be careful, or you'll be sick again"? You are— you want to be strong. You are afraid of getting nervous, getting anxious, afraid of your conscience maybe.

S: Probably so.

I: And I think this was maybe a little threatening to you. (pause) Had you ever feared insanity?

S: Yes, and I think that stems from way back because my mother said that she had two sisters, one of whom died in a sanitarium. But that was a long time ago. There were a lot of girls in the family and this was one of the older girls and mother was one of the younger girls so I never knew her. And then my mother—maybe in 1950—had a very bad case of eczema. She was allergic to something, and she started breaking out and her face swelling and what not; a doctor we had where we lived at that time started giving her cortisone and she just began to get worse and worse, so we took her out to the University of Iowa Hospital. They said that she had an extreme overdose of cortisone and they gave her shock treatments and said that she had a certain amount of brain damage. And my mother was not a well person from that day. She had lapses of memory.

I: Uh huh.

S: I wouldn't say that she was like . . . that there was anything wrong with her mind. When she was clear, she was very clear, but she would have these periodic lapses of memory like, for a moment when she'd see me, she didn't recognize me. She'd try to say who I was but she didn't know me.

I: Blocks!

S: Uh huh. And people that she hadn't seen for a while, they were distorted completely when she was having one of her bad days. And then somtimes she would repeat herself. Well, this was not a mental illness. I know it had to do with. . . . But in the back of my mind, I remember her saying there were two sisters who had had mental illness, and she had a form of mental illness. So I think I feared it.

I: Well, I would say probably that (chuckles), not that mental *illness* runs in your family but I would say *secrecy* runs in your family. And that this has probably encouraged insecurity, guilt, and so forth. (Pause) You apparently didn't feel that you could go to your father or your mother with this thing you were involved in. Your brothers were forcing dishonesty and secrecy upon you, and I would say the thing that wasn't valued highly maybe in your family was openness.

S: That could very well be.

I: And so I wouldn't worry at all about having "inherited" mental illness. But it may be that there were some character traits and some virtues that you didn't acquire very easily.

S: That would be like when I first found out what my stomach trouble was diagnosed as, I said, "Don't tell me I inherited the type of stomach my father has, because they 've had to take his stomach out, turn it around and put new openings on it, and cut off a piece of the esophagus and so forth." And the doctor said, "No, you didn't inherit that, but you probably inherited the nervous system that makes that kind of a stomach."

I: Well, I'd push it back one step further. My guess is your nervous system is all right. But your life hasn't been quite right, in some ways.

Well, now, I would regard this as really a very satisfactory interview. You've been able to talk quite freely. I've told you a little bit about my life; there is more to it than I have told you, but in order to save time I won't go into this. But I often share with people quite extensively about my life, particularly where it seems necessary or helpful to getting them to come out. You were ready to talk, y'see, and not everybody is. *You* apparently want to get out of this place.

S: I sure do.

I: And some people come in here and they've been so miserable for so long outside that they don't care whether they get out or not; they don't care whether "school keeps" or not.

S: Uh huh. I certainly don't feel that way, and I feel sorry for those that do.

I: Of course. I talked to a woman this morning who'd just as soon draw the curtain down on everything.

S: Well, we have a girl on our ward that I wonder about—Ann, Ann, I can't remember her last name.

I: I don't know either. You see, I'm just here on Mondays and I don't get down on the wards very much.

S: But I tried to talk to her, and all I can get out of her is "Oh, I wish I could drop dead."

I: Um.

S: And it's the third time she's been in the institution, and she built up my morale real good, I would say, when she said, "Is this your first time?" and I said, "Yes," and she said, "Oh, well they don't keep you very long the first time." And I thought, "Oh boy, if I get out of here the first time (laughs), I don't intend to come back for a second, if I can get to the basis of what caused the first time."

I: Yes. Well, this is why we'd like you to come into group therapy, and do a very thorough job on this. Because they often get people patched up and out of here, with medication and so forth, but they often don't get to the root of the difficulty and things get worse and they do come back. And we're very concerned that when people go out that they *stay* out. And moreover, when people leave the hospital who've been in our group, if it's at all possible for them to do so, we like for them to come back on Mondays and participate in the group, helping with others and so on as a means of helping themselves. You live so near-by this would be quite possible for you, I should think. Now my guess is that if you do have the strength and determination to come into group therapy that you'll be out of the hospital pretty fast.

S: Well, I'll come into it. I'm not very brave about it, but I'll do it.

I: Well, why don't we go in there and just. . . . I'll sit down in there with you, and we'll just watch what's going on for a while.

S: Okay.

I: Very good!

EXPLANATIONS, INTERPRETATIONS, AND COMMENTS

Since this section will consist of a series of somewhat unrelated observations rather than a sustained argument, it will be useful to list each of the following brief comments by number.

1. It should be noted, perhaps first of all, that the interview with Mrs. Saunders was not, in certain respects, "typical." Usually a person who has gotten into serious emotional difficulties is much more resistant, much more entrenched in secrecy. The interview with Mrs. S. moves with such rapidity (despite the inclusion by her of some unnecessary circumstantial detail) because she was very highly motivated and because she already had a "running start" on the process which we sometimes have to initiate, in the face of considerable distrust and opposition. Because Mrs. S. was "in motion" (in the right direction) before I saw her, it is much easier to *see* the process of recovery through self-authentication in the course of a comparatively short interview. A deeply disturbed person is often very guarded, in the beginning, about what he or she will spontaneously reveal, and modeling by the interviewer is necessary in order to loosen resistance and provide much-needed encouragement and reassurance. But in any case I like for the other person to go as far as possible in the direction of self-disclosure before I model. There are several advantages in this practice, among them the fact that it permits one to see where the other person is, in terms of the capacity for and the practice of openness, and also it permits one to see the often very dramatic *effects* of modeling—in the sense of releasing material which might otherwise be quite inaccessible. In the present situation, atypically, the modeling was not necessary as a precondition for the disclosure by Mrs. S. of very deep and painful material.

2. Some surprise may be occasioned by the fact that in the interview with Mrs. Saunders I still "modeled" despite the fact that it was not necessary as a means of getting her to talk freely. This was not an inadvertance. My speaking as openly about at least a relevant segment of my life as she had about hers was a deep "behavioral" indication that I accepted and approved her openness. At no point in the interview did I attempt to reassure or "forgive" her, as far as her past misdemeanors were concerned. In fact, I

even suggested, as regards the incest, that she had probably not recognized the full extent of her own accountability and guilt. But I made it very clear from beginning to end that she had my full support in what she was trying to do *now*. And I reinforced this stance, as powerfully as I knew how, by indicating that I myself try to practice radical honesty, when the occasion is appropriate, with respect to my own life—and have found it a good discipline, strengthening, and redemptive. When Mrs. Saunders and I joined the larger group, immediately after our interview, she encountered a similar atmosphere of acceptance and approval—not, to be sure, with respect to her past errors but with respect to her present resolution to be open and authentic. Here she found further support, of a most unequivocal kind, in the fact that these people were also willing to share their experience as candidly with her as she shared her experience with them. But over and beyond these advantages in an interviewer's telling another person who *he* is —even though that person has already spoken at length, there is always the possibility that some last pain-packed cranny of experience has not yet been explored. "Modeling" by the interviewer, even though it comes relatively late in the interview, may have the effect of releasing such residual material which will otherwise remain untouched and a potential source of further trouble. Thus, even though modeling is not needed to release most of the material another person needs to talk about, it may nevertheless be highly useful (1) as a means of support and reassurance—"Confess your sins *one to another* . . . that ye may be healed" (James 5:16), and (2) as a means of encouraging a really thorough job of self-disclosure.

3. Although Mrs. Saunders had gotten into a very serious predicament from the use of alcohol and drugs and had made what could easily have been a successful attempt at suicide, she was still relatively intact psychologically. This, I think, can be largely attributed to the fact that her past dishonesty had not been total. It will be recalled that prior to her first marriage she had had the integrity and courage to tell her prospective husband about the history of incest, and after the death of her mother she had "blurted out" (her words) the truth to her present husband. Moreover, since entering the hospital she had told her story with

considerable candor to both the staff psychiatrist and the psychologist who had interviewed her. She was therefore, even prior to the suicide attempt, not a totally secretive or alienated person. If her secrecy had up to this point been total, I would have expected to see, in all probability, much more serious signs of personality disorganization. Her partial honesty with significant others had, in other words, protected her from a more total form of disintegration.

4. But why the crisis now? Why, as Mrs. Saunders herself asked, had it not come years earlier? As the interview brings out, the crisis actually had begun some two and a half years prior to the suicide attempt and hospitalization. For a while Mrs. S. had more or less successfully fought it off with the aid of beer and various kinds of drugs. But the stress (identity crisis) had obviously started at the time when her two daughters were approaching or were in early adolescence. Knowing the difficulties into which she herself had gotten as a girl, she was eager to avoid a similar fate for her daughters, but she was not able to be entirely genuine with them—and they, in turn, were not able to be fully honest with and close to her. She undoubtedly wished them to be free and open with her, and although she went to great lengths to give them sexual information of an impersonal nature (note that, even so, she had turned a part of the task over to the minister), it was obvious that in a more fundamental sense she was being something of a hypocrite with them. It is probably correct to say that on the average, parents do not get their children to be any more honest with them about their personal lives than the parents have been with their children about theirs (*cf* Smith, 1966). Mrs. Saunders saw that her daughters were withdrawn and secretive in the area of sex, and this she undoubtedly took as a rebuke on the score of her own secretiveness—and it also activated fears as to what *they* might be hiding.

5. At this juncture a general word about "sex education" may be in order. I often suspect that when young people get into sexual difficulties it is not because of things their elders know about sex, in the sense of formal facts or "scientific knowledge," and have not told them, but rather because of things which youngsters themselves know about sex, experientially and behaviorally,

and have not told their elders. Probably the best way to bring about the happy state of trust which permits a reversal of this situation is for parents to share with their children, at an appropriate age, their own sexual misadventures and failures. After all, the race managed to reproduce itself fairly adequately for several millennia before there were books and illustrated lectures on the subject, and the difficulties that our youth today get into are not, it seems, nearly so much from a lack of abstract knowledge about sex as from a lack of awareness of how dangerous it is to fall into secrecy and evasion. A youth may have all the knowledge in the world about sex in its anatomical and physiological aspects, but if he lacks the character and ego strength that come from the discipline of personal openness, his "knowledge" may merely make him feel "prepared" for behavior which wisdom and strength born of openness would hold in check. It is not, in other words, lack of formal information that gets our youth into sexual difficulties, but a lack of truthfulness: a failure of communication *with us.* And openness, truthfulness, and authenticity on their part is best fostered by a reciprocal honesty on the part of parents with them. One of the great appeals which the "sex education" approach has had for many parents probably lies in the fact that it promises to get them off "the hook" by permitting them to substitute mere information-dispensing for personal candor and real wisdom in this area.

6. There is, of course, sometimes hesitation on the part of parents to share with children their own moral failures, particularly in the sexual area. Often they feel that an admission of error on their part will be taken by children as sanctioning, or at least condoning, similar behavior on their part. The fear often is that children will say, "Okay, you did it, why shouldn't we?" But when Mrs. Saunders ultimately told her two daughters about the history of incest, she was able to do so with the added injunction: "And you see what it *cost* me!" When patients tell professional therapists about shameful guilt-engendering acts in their lives which they have kept carefully hidden, a common tendency on the part of therapists is to point out that this or that deviant action "isn't so unusual"—with the implication that it is, therefore, not really wrong or worth worrying about. (Just at the moment—

midsummer, 1966—mass murders are in vogue. Does *that* make them desirable, right?) When, in the context of integrity therapy, a parent shares deeply with a son or daughter, or when a more experienced group member "models" for a newcomer, it is not at all with a view to implying, "I've done that (or some equivalent act), too, so you needn't worry about it." It is rather with the implication: "Yes, I've done some pretty stupid things myself, and they didn't work out well for me, either. But now I've found a way of resolving this kind of problem and I'd like to tell you about it." This kind of openness with children about our own mistakes (when they are commensurate with a child's experience) is, we believe, the best possible way to keep them in communication with us about their mistakes—actual and potential.

7. It seems likely that one of the reasons why Mrs. Saunders was so sensitive to her own inadequacies as a mentor for her daughters in the area of sex was that she had herself indulged in a good deal of criticism of and resentment toward her own parents in this connection. Had she not been handicapped by a history of deviant action *or* if she had been less inclined to attribute blame to her parents, the task of guiding her two girls through adolescence would probably have been considerably easier. (She was, in other words, uncharitable as well as unchaste.) When we have resentment toward others for failings which we ourselves display, criticism and anger can sometimes recoil upon us with terrible impact. It is one thing to be guilty of deviant behavior, admit it, and take responsibility for it, but it is quite another thing to be guilty, deny one's own role in the situation, and harshly blame others. It seems that in scientific and professional circles we have often fallen into the trap of encouraging people to see the "causes" of their deviant actions as lying *outside* themselves (either in "society" or in the "unconscious"). We are now discovering that sometimes the only hope of recovery for a disturbed person is in coming to see himself as an agent rather than a mere passive reactor or recipient. The term "change agent" is gaining currency today as a substitute for the term "therapist," and as a part of the same trend is the growing realization that the *principal* agent of change in an identity crisis must be the individual himself. If his

resources for self-redirection are not mobilized, no amount of "treatment" by others is likely to accomplish much.

8. One area in which the tenets of integrity therapy are often misunderstood is that having to do with the role of *the past* vs. *the present* in the causation or powering of a "neurosis." The case of Mrs. Saunders is very much in point. The initial alienating action in her life was the incestuous relationship with her brothers. But this behavior was eventually abandoned. For years she had not indulged in it, it was truly a "thing of the past," and from one point of view it was no longer of any importance. But what was *not* past, and thus still important, was this woman's practice of concealment, her lack of openness and full authenticity. This was an ongoing reality, a fact of the present. And when Mrs. S. discovered that in the realm of sex her adolescent daughters were not "talking to" her, it must have been a painful, near intolerable reminder that *she* had not "talked to" them—except in a very impersonal, objective way. In other words, Mrs. Saunders' problem, here and now, was not incest but insincerity. And being a person of basically good character, *i.e.* having a strong sense of consistency and integrity, she was understandably bothered by this ambiguity. Thus, our position is that an ongoing guilt always, in some sense, represents an ongoing form of inappropriate action (or inaction). If past action is indeed past *and* if it has been appropriately acknowledged and amended, there may be continuing regret and sadness with respect to it, but the painful urgency which unresolved guilt always has about it is gone. Mrs. Saunders, I may say, has now fully authenticated herself not only with her daughters but also with a number of other persons; she is taking no form of medication, the stomach "spasms" are gone, and life for her and her family is better than it has ever been.

9. A further word may be in order concerning the course of Mrs. Saunders' "therapy" after the recorded interview. Basically, it was uneventful. She went from the interview with me into the room where a group of some ten or twelve persons were meeting; at an appropriate point she was introduced in a more or less conventional way; and she then had an opportunity to "tell her story," which she proceeded to do, courageously and without self-

defensiveness. Her subsequent improvement in the hospital was rapid, and she was shortly discharged. However, she has continued to come back to the group meetings as a "graduate" with considerable regularity, occasionally with her husband; she and he attend and actively participate in a similar group which has spontaneously formed outside the hospital. In no sense overzealous with respect to this approach to psychotherapy, she has, nevertheless, become a loyal and effective devotee and helper of others. One of the weaknesses, we feel, in much conventional individual psychotherapy is that when it is terminated, the person has "no place to go," nothing in particular "to do." We believe that a person who has successfully negotiated a return to community, in the full sense of this term, has both the competence and a deep obligation to help others. This sense of mission often serves as a source of amendment, restitution, and rehabilitation. We believe that one of the best ways to prevent *self*-punishment, after radical honesty with respect to oneself, is for the individual to have something constructive to do, something significant to become involved in, a service to render. Ongoing work with others in a group provides such an opportunity and, as suggested earlier, may be one of the best possible ways of implementing the community mental-health movement, generally.

10. Because we encourage people who have benefited from experience in an integrity therapy group to continue indefinitely in such a group (or to form new groups), it is sometimes said that this type of procedure does not really "cure" anyone, basic difficulties supposedly remain "untouched," and the group is "just a crutch." (The same criticism, incidentally, is also made of Alcoholics Anonymous. Here it is often said that one addiction, alcoholism, is just replaced by another, AA meetings.) The assumption behind this type of objection apparently is that a "well" person ought to be able to find the Good Life without benefit of continuing human intimacy, deep sharing, and the discipline as well as support that derive therefrom. Thus anyone who elects to maintain his affiliation with and participation in a group must still be sick— or at least not very strong. Everyone is certainly entitled to his own views in this regard, but long ago Aristotle reminded us

that man is a *social* animal;* and some of us still feel that man's natural state is *in* community, not out of it, and that the real thrust of "therapy" ought always to be in the direction of helping alienated persons to become able once again to participate in deep and meaningful social interaction, not to be able to get along without it. This is not to say that an I.T. group, Alcoholics Anonymous, or any other similar enterprise ought to take the place of the "natural" groups and associations in a person's life, and it has not been our observation that they do. What happens, instead, is that these special groups serve as "schools" or "laboratories" in which people learn new attitudes and skills which materially improve their sense of responsibility and their capacity to relate meaningfully to other persons in "real-life" situations. And since there is such great need for this sort of thing today, I can see no reason why a formerly disturbed, "lost" person should not make this sort of thing a continuing avocation if he wishes—or even a full-time vocation!

11. Integrity therapy, on at least one occasion, has been called "nudity therapy"; it has been criticized, not infrequently, as an "invasion of privacy." A commonly neglected distinction needs to be made between *privacy* and *secrecy*. Those of us who are associated with integrity therapy have great respect for privacy. Privacy, in the sense of being able to keep certain parts of one's body or certain actions out of the public view, is a part of good taste, common decency, and civilized, refined living. And in no sense do we disparage or disapprove this sort of thing. Our campaign is rather against secrecy, that is, the *abuse of privacy.* Human beings, we believe, get into emotional trouble, *i.e.* lose their integrity, their innocence, their honor, when they begin using the cloak of privacy to do things which are in violation of the trust that others have placed in them. Pratt and Tooley (1964), in the paper previously cited, define an identity crisis

---

* A passage often quoted from Aristotle in this connection is the following: "Man is by nature a social animal, and an individual who is unsocial naturally and not accidentally is either beneath our notice or more than human. Society is something in nature that precedes the individual. Anyone who either cannot lead the common life or is so self-sufficient as not to need to, and therefore does not partake of society, is either a beast or he is a god."

(neurosis, psychosis) as the state a person gets into as a result of the secret, unilateral violation of an interpersonal contract, *i.e.* *cheating*. Obviously privacy and secrecy are *not* the same thing. One may enjoy the privilege of privacy and yet make no attempt to "hide," in the sense of deny, anything that the privacy protects from the discriminate eyes of others. It is only when we begin to do things, in private, which we also keep secret that trouble arises—not infrequently in the form of paranoia—which involves the delusion that one has *lost* one's privacy, is being constantly "watched," and other illusions (*cf* Mowrer, 1966d).

A therapist who would make even the smallest sexual advance toward a patient is, in our judgment, doing much more in the nature of "invading privacy" than we, by our modeling, ever do in encouraging people to give up their painful, pathogenic secrets. The abandonment of secrecy is not at all the same thing as loss of privacy. In fact, it sometimes happens that this is the only way to *recover* the security and enjoyment of privacy, to become fully trustworthy and "open" with respect to *the facts* regarding one's "private life." Therapy, we believe, calls for an abandonment of cheating, deception, phoniness, and secrecy and a steadfast quest for consistency, candor, and integrity.

12. I am sure some readers, at this point, will be asking, "But are there *always* guilty secrets in a neurosis?" The term *identity crisis*—and this is why we prefer it—tends, of course, to presuppose such a condition, namely a discrepancy between what one genuinely is and what one is pretending or claiming to be. And the task of therapy, thus conceived, is obviously to *close* such a discrepancy by self-authentication and the surrender of "false pride" in the sense of a pride that betrays us, leads us to a "fall." But are there not *some cases* of emotional disturbance which do not involve this state of affairs? A recent review of empirical research findings (Mowrer, 1967b) shows that, if not all, at least the great majority of so-called neurotics are, in fact, suffering from irresponsibility rather than from the over-socialization and from inappropriate instinctual gratification rather than inhibition, as Freud posited. This is not to say that there may not be a *few* Freudian neurotics. Thus, in the context of integrity therapy, when we have the first interview with a person we do not, by any

means, *insist* upon our view of his situation. If the other person in the beginning categorically denies "secret sin" (or "duplicitous deviance"), we tentatively accept his report and say something like this: "Perhaps so, but I have had some experience with emotional disturbance, and things were different with me." Then we "model." In a surprisingly high percentage of cases this procedure releases the other person enough to become much more honest and to begin the painful and liberating process of real self-disclosure. The striking regularity with which modeling "uncorks" a history of deception and hypocrisy generates considerable confidence in the general validity of this point of view. But we do not absolutely exclude the possibility of "innocent" neurotics—although I must personally say that if such exist I do not really understand them and do not think I know anything to do for them or that they can do for themselves. Manifestly they require some other kind of "treatment."

13. But we are not by any means saying that emotional crisis can arise only from secret "sins of commission." "Sin," in the sense of irresponsibility, may obviously involve *omissions* as well as commissions. In order to get into serious trouble with conscience one does not have to violate a contract, or interpersonal commitment, in the sense of doing something *else*, something that is *wrong;* one may simply fail to do "what is right," what has been agreed upon. For example, I was dilatory in getting about the task of writing this chapter and, as a result, have not met the accepted deadline for completion. Fortunately, the chapter—now virtually finished except for final typing—will not be more than a few weeks late in reaching the editor. But I have nevertheless been quite uncomfortable at times about the situation. And if I had continued to renege on my commitment in this regard, I have no doubt that I would soon have been sufficiently "sick" (sick of myself) to have had some very inconvenient "neurotic" reactions such as depression, loss of appetite, or insomnia. Thus, we do not at all suppose that making a clean breast of what one has done .that is actively wrong is enough to insure emotional serenity now and forevermore. We are, indeed, expected to be honest, to keep faith with the significant others (or reference group), and not to do deviant things; however, just being "good" in the moral sense

is not enough. We have, in addition, to be "good" in the sense of positively productive. That is, we have to *work*. And one of the many things wrong with the whole notion of disease, treatment, and hospitalization in the mental-health area is that both of these forms of responsibility tend to be minimized: one is permitted to be indolent as well as falsely innocent. Small wonder our conventional mental hospitals have not been great places of personal rehabilitation and "recovery"! But in one sense the sins of omission are not as perilous as the sins of commission. If we are lazy and don't work, *others* are likely to know about it, or soon find out. But the "actively" wrong action can be kept indefinitely concealed, and thus serve as the source of progressive personal disintegration. In fact, there is reason for thinking that dishonesty with respect to deviant actions often comes first, and the laziness, demoralization, and inaction come as secondary results. If we stubbornly keep our silence with respect to guilty actions, no form of work, in the ordinary sense of that term, will permanently satisfy us, and we may ultimately stop working and become socially dependent (regressed) because we have previously been so morally "*in*dependent."

14. As the reader may have noted, I failed, at the time of the interview with Mrs. Saunders, to make anything of her apparent overconcern with the incident of having called Pastor Hooten by the name of the former minister, Pastor Seaton. She cited this as an instance of her tendency to "make mountains out of molehills." At the moment the probable meaning of the incident simply escaped me. Some psychotherapists would take such a tendency at its face value, as a characteristic of neurotic persons, as a part of their "sickness": they are supposedly too senstivie, oversocialized, excessively conscientious. And if this premise is accepted, therapy should be aimed at reducing the severity of the superego and liberating the patient from such obsessive moral concerns. There is, however, a more valid and operationally far more useful way of viewing this sort of "symptom." It is not, I think, without significance that Mrs. Saunders made the "slip" concerning the minister's name in the context of presiding at a church meeting of sufficient importance for the minister to be present. Here she was giving all the outward appearances of being a woman of full piety

and virtue, but secretly she knew she was not such a person. She was tacitly denying the facts of her earlier life, and also not acknowledging the dilemma these facts currently placed her in with respect to the real education and guidance of her two teen-age daughters. She was, in short, being a hypocrite. Thus in the form of the slip, conscience was able to get a message "out" to the public that there was something "wrong" with this woman, appearances notwithstanding. An intuitive understanding of what had thus happened was, I conjecture, what made Mrs. Saunders subsequently so uncomfortable over the incident. If conscience could trick her in this way and make her say something she did not "intend to," it might force the whole truth out of her—as indeed it eventually did! Thus, in this case, as in many others I have seen, the problem is not that the neurotic makes mountains out of molehills; his difficulty arises instead from an *attempt* to make molehills out of mountains.

15. Throughout this chapter, and as an integral feature of integrity therapy in general, there is an emphasis upon the responsibility of the individual himself in an identity crisis: *he* has done some deviant thing (things) and *he* has systematically concealed it (them). The chances are that no one forced this person to commit the questionable act in the first place, and almost certainly no one could have prevented him from later reporting it, if he had so desired. But having once fully recognized the reality of individual responsibility in this area, it is also true that our mid-twentieth-century American culture is not very helpful either in keeping people out of an identity crisis or in telling them what to do once they have gotten into such a predicament. In the case of Mrs. Saunders, it is noteworthy, first of all, that her "neurosis" flourished right in the midst of an institution which once knew how to redeem lost souls—and hopefully will again become able to do so —but which is today very largely impotent in this regard. Pastor Hooten sensed that Mrs. Saunders' problem was one of unresolved guilt, but he lacked the confidence and skills to get on with its resolution. As a result he permitted, perhaps encouraged her to consult Dr. Reynolds, who, being a physician, made a physical, *i.e.* chemical, assault on the problem with near tragic consequences. And even Mr. Saunders gave his wife no real sup-

port or encouragement when she desperately confided her painful secret to him. His rejoinder was "I'd just as soon you hadn't told me, but now that you have, forget it." Thus from no quarter did this woman, in her daily-life setting, find support for the one course of action which her own intuition urged her to follow. Can it be that common sensibilities and untutored inclinations in this domain are sometimes sounder than the theory and practice of the helping professions?

REFERENCES

ALBEE, G. W.: No magic here. Review of R. Glasscote; D. Sanders; H. M. Forstenzer, and A. R. Foley (Eds.): *The Community Mental Health Center: An Analysis of Existing Models.* In *Contemporary Psychology, 10:* 497-498, 1965.

ANDERSON, P. A.: *Church Meetings That Matter.* Philadelphia, United Church, 1965.

BELGUM, D.: *Guilt: Where Psychology and Religion Meet.* Englewood Cliffs, N. J., Prentice-Hall, 1963.

DABROWSKI, K.: *Positive Distintegration.* Boston, Little, 1964.

DRAKEFORD, J. W.: *Integrity Theory: A Christian Evaluation of a New Approach to Mental Health.* Nashville, Broadman, 1967.

ERIKSON, E. H.: *Young Man Luther.* New York, Norton, 1958.

FRANK, J. D.: Review of O. H. Mowrer: *The New Group Therapy.* In *Amer J Psychiat, 121:* 829, 1965.

GLASSER, W.: *Reality Therapy—A New Approach to Psychiatry.* New York, Harper, 1965.

JARVIS, P. E.; and NELSON, S. E.: The therapeutic community and new roles for clinical psychologists. *Amer Psychol, 21:* 524-529, 1966.

JOURARD, S. M.: *The Transparent Self.* Princeton, N. J., Van Nostrand, 1964.

KANTOR, R. E.: Review of O. H. Mowrer: *The New Group Therapy.* In *Family Process, 4:* 325-326, 1965.

KLINE, D. R.: The retreat of the church from pastoral responsibility. *Religion in Life, 32:* 116-131, 1962.

LAKIN, M.: Guilt and groups. Review of O. H. Mowrer: *The New Group Therapy.* In *Contemporary Psychology, 10:* 50-51, 1965.

LONDON, P.: *The Modes and Morals of Psychotherapy.* New York, Holt, Reinhart & Winston, 1964.

MOWRER, O. H.: *The Crisis in Psychiatry and Religion.* Princeton, N. J., Van Nostrand, 1961.

MOWRER, O. H.: *The New Group Therapy.* Princeton, N. J., Van Nostrand, 1964.

MOWRER, O. H.: Learning theory and behavior therapy. In B. Wolman

(Ed.): *Handbook of Clinical Psychology*. New York, McGraw, 1965, pp. 242-276.

Mowrer, O. H.: Abnormal reactions or actions?—An autobiographical answer. In J. Vernon (Ed.): *Introduction to General Psychology*. Dubuque, Iowa, Brown, 1966a, pp. 1-42.

Mowrer, O. H.: The basis of psychopathology: Malconditioning or misbehavior? In C. D. Spielberger (Ed.): *Anxiety and Behavior*. New York, Academic Press, 1966b, pp. 143-156.

Mowrer, O. H.: Mental health study requires historical dimension. Article in Champaign (Ill.) *News-Gazette*, June 19, 1966c, p. 2.

Mowrer, O. H.: The behavior therapies, with special reference to "modeling" and imitation. *J Assn Advancement Psychothery*, 20: 439-461, 1966d.

Mowrer, O. H.: Integrity therapy: A self-help approach. *Psychotherapy—Theory, Research, and Practice*, 3: 114-119, 1966e.

Mowrer, O. H.: Conscience and the unconscious. *J Commun Dis*, 1967a (in press).

Mowrer, O. H.: New evidence concerning the nature of psychopathology, 1967b (in press).

Parlour, R.; Cole, P. Z., and Van Vorst, R. B.: Rediscovered dimensions of the psychotherapist's responsibility. In O. H. Mowrer, (Ed.): *Morality and Mental Health*. Chicago, Rand McNally, 1967

Pratt, S., and Tooley, J.: Contract psychology and the actualizing transactional field. *Int J Soc Psychiat;* (Congress Issue): 51-60, 1964.

Reiff, R.: Mental health manpower and institutional change. *Amer Psychol*, 21: 540-548, 1966.

Shelly, J. A., and Bassin, A.: Daytop Lodge—A new treatment approach for drug addicts. *Corrective Psychiatry*, 11: 186-195, 1965.

Smith, M. B., and Hobbs, N.: The community and the community mental health center. *Amer Psychol*, 21: 499-509, 1966.

Smith, R. E.: Integrity therapy and parental opportunity. Urbana, Ill., 1966 (Mimeo).

Sullivan, H. S.: *Conceptions of Modern Psychiatry*. Washington, D. C., William Alanson White Psychiatric Foundation, 1947.

Tkacik, A.: Conscience: Conscious and unconscious. *J. Religion and Health*, 4: 75-85, 1964.

VI

EXPERIENTIAL GROUPS

Instructions for Groups

EUGENE T. GENDLIN AND JOHN BEEBE

THE emphasis in this chapter is set forth in a series of eleven propositions or Ground Rules for Group Sessions, written so that each participant in a group can take a copy of it home, study it, bring it back, discuss it, and tentatively operate by it. (There is insufficient experience with these rules, and group members should be so informed.)

The ground rules cut across the usual orientations in psychotherapy and group methods: they fit both therapeutic and task groups, and they fit various settings such as clinic, church, industry, school, and so forth. How can one set of rules cut across all these differences and still characterize anything? The answer lies in the theory of experiencing (Gendlin, 1962; 1964), that is to say, in being concerned with the concrete experiential process rather than the different words people use, or the different social roles which different settings involve. The crux of the current group movement is not words and roles, but the experiential process.

The scope of spontaneity has greatly widened in modern society. Almost every situation today requires large portions of spontaneous, direct, unplanned, individually devised behaviors. Some generations ago, prescribed routines were required. Some now view the lack of prescribed routines as a breakdown in social forms and, indeed, the strain on the individual is very great. If there is going to be continuing multiplication of forms and conflicting values, *i.e.* a breakdown in prescriptions and ever widening scope for spontaneity, then either humans will become very much more

190

proficient at the process of spontaneously revising and devising forms, or the percentage of people and portions of each life "not making it" will greatly increase. At present, both trends are discernible. The group trend is the former.

A powerful group process is being discovered and used under different names in different settings. Some of its names are sensitivity group, T group, brain-storming, creativity group, encounter group, development group, group psychotherapy, marathon group. Some of its settings are schools, churches, industry, campus politics, hospitals, consulting offices, private homes.

The different approaches and settings involve the same experiential process. Of course, people speak differently in a religious group dedicated to more open communication about personal and religious conflicts than they do in a middle management development group devoted to more perceptiveness of others and one's own feelings toward them. But both groups involve expressing and pursuing creative ideas even when at first these may not seem correct, and in both cases individuals are breaking out from routine role behavior. In both instances, direct and spontaneous expression is valued, taught, and made safe. In both cases, individuals discover their own good sense, capacities for originality, sensitivity, interesting reactions, deserving of the respect of others, and so on. In both cases, individuals break through to—and then gain steady control of—a more spontaneous, live, real, experiential manner of process. They still speak the same English words and live in the same American patterns; the content of what is said and done is not always startlingly different, but the manner of process is an interplay between concrete experiencing on the one hand, and roles or words on the other—rather than mere empty roles with minimal deadened, or silent, private, removed experiencing.

Neither group is the same as a psychotherapy group. But these differences in words and roles must not obscure the fact that in each instance, the individuals are seeking one and the same process, variously called "seeking to overcome alienation," "seeking to be more alive in roles and words," and (to make the roles and words stretch to permit this) "seeking to be more open, more in touch with what they live and feel," "more expressive," "more spontaneous," "more real and genuine," "more honest with themselves and others," and "more in the world rather than silent, dumb, isolated, and frozen in mere empty role-playing." Note that each of these phrases refers to the same concrete process occurring in an individual, even though these phrases stem from different fields and verbal contexts and are at home in quite different social settings. The manner or verbal and institutional behavior is changing from alienation to experientially interactive.

Thus, in presenting the following analysis of experiential groups, I am cutting across social settings (industry, churches, schools, hospitals) and theoretical vocabularies (group dynamics, psychoanalysis, client-centered therapy, existentialism, sociology).

EXPERIENTIAL GROUPS

Phases

One way to characterize the concrete process common to all these settings is by the following phasic description.

Breakthrough phase. This phase lasts from six weeks to six months and consists of an explosive freeing and growth process in the individual. (The individual describes it as one of the most important occurrences in his life, or in many, many years.)

Sustaining phase. If new members come to the group, the old members in the sustaining phase consider it valuable to help the new members. For themselves, the older members no longer need the breakthrough experience, but they can help others have it. Although they are convinced of the great value of the group process, (if new members keep arriving and breaking through) these old members get increasingly tired, since the group is now doing little that is directly meaningful for them. On the one hand, the sustaining phase is both rewarding and needed for new members. On the other hand, a *continuing* life-sustaining group fails to occur in many cases. We think that this failure happens when *different* times and places are not provided for the excitement of inducting new members, and for sustaining feelings of depth when old members meet alone. When this separation is not successful, the sustaining phase (which should continue indefinitely) gives way to the tired phase.

Tired phase. If new members constantly come into a group, and there is not also a quiet continuing group of old members, the old members cannot indefinitely sustain the group. Eventually, the old members get tired of trying to make the breaking through have meaning long after they are done with that phase.

Experiential Expressiveness

These three phases (breakthrough, sustaining, tired) can be observed in all groups cited above; for example, in the student political groups. The first phase for a new student in the political group is explosive. He discovers he can speak well, have new ideas, influence others, relate meaningfully, reason for himself, help and appreciate others—all this not in his usual role-playing way as in most of his classes—but in a new spontaneous way that is natural, experientially expressive and, it turns out, quite safe—really safer than the routine social controls embodied in his more habitual behavior. Naturally, all this is very exciting. And if the political group is seeking to bring to the society as a whole the same sort of change (participative democracy), then concrete experiences and political programs support each other. And, indeed, politics has developed considerably from the days when the political program was everything and the mode of organizing did not matter at all so that idealistic freedom-oriented programs were agitated for by rigid people in authoritarian groups. In today's left politics the Ghandi insight has caught on, that is, the movement is itself a miniature of the sort of society it can help create.

Why the political example in the middle of a psychological article? The shift from words and roles to an experiential manner is itself a shift in current political thinking. But a shift in religious thinking is also brought about by the same experiential trend and the same group process now considered in that setting: it asserts "renewal," the breaking out of the words and routines that have become empty. So also in education where, for example, "the new

math" teaches by making sense and not by rote, or in the psychotherapy area where discussion no longer rages so much as to the
supposedly basic contents (the patient must talk about sex, self
concepts, power drive, life style, separation anxiety), nor so much
anymore about the supposedly right therapist role (transference
engendering, neutral reflecting). Client's words and therapist's
roles have given way to the more basic question of the experiential
expressiveness, working through, and real open interaction of two
persons.

These are not separate and unrelated developments in separate
and unrelated fields. The same manner of experiential process is
being developed in all of them, and it is making one basic change
in the manner of living—a change which, if it becomes dominant,
will change thought and action in all these areas from mere roles
into an interplay, a zigzag from role to spontaneous person and
back to revised role.

But how can there be a back-and-forth, an interplay between
words and roles, and some concretely felt process called experiencing? One seems external and precise; the other, neither. To
understand this group process one must know that the individual
is not an entity, not only a thing inside a box or inside his skin,
but the individual is an experiential interplay with the environment. "An experience" is not something located in the eye, the
mind, or the gut, but an experiencing of something outside the
situation one is in. It is not really true that we feel our feelings—
that repeats the word "feel" as both a verb and then a noun that
is the object of the verb. Really we feel our situations. When I am
scared, I do not fear my fear, but rather I have a fear *of* the thing
coming at me. The very nature of a human personality *is* to be
this interplay process and not a thing inside. Once we know that,
we can grasp how what a person is will be different in different
situations, in different relations to others, and hence in a group.
To be alive differently is already to have been changed. One does
not first have insights, and then apply them to oneself. Rather,
one could not have that insight the way one was alive before—
that way of being made that insight impossible to have, to feel, to
see, to be—for we cannot "grasp" or say "Oh!" or "A-ha!" except
physically, bodily, with a breath and a directly felt sense of "mak-

ing sense." The way one is alive must, therefore, change first before
he can have the insight he lacked before (Gendlin, 1964).

SOME SAFEGUARDS CONCERNING THE GROUND RULES

Closeness

Note in the ground rules that contact or closeness is not at all
the same thing as revealing intimate facts. The latter is content;
we are concerned with process, *i.e.* a certain manner of process.

Closeness comes before unmasking. Contact or closeness is the
sort of experiential sense you have when another person is looking right into your eyes and you into theirs; it is an unavoidable
concrete sense of knowing yourself seen by another person, and
has nothing to do with whether or not you know anything *about*
him.

The example of looking into another person's eyes and being
seen by him is *only* an example. The point is that closeness is independent of what one knows about someone.

Sometimes we take off our masks and thereby become close.
But, more often, we feel like taking off our masks with those with
whom we already feel close.

It is never necessary or possible to take off another person's
mask against his will, and it can never make for closeness to try to
do so.

The rule, "closeness comes before unmasking," phrases for us
the learning that it is useless and harmful to claw at another person, insultingly insisting that he is "not being real," "not opening
up," as groups unfortunately sometimes try to do. Much of these
desires to hear from the other person are highly artificial, throwing the difficulty of the process onto the other person. Sharing
oneself becomes a forced parlor game in which facts are shared
and inward loneliness is not at all relieved. But, while "opening
up" is made into something artificial, the attacks on some members are perfectly real attacks. People claw at some person's supposed "mask," but that is really his face, at least for the moment.

Leader Support

The leader supports against too much attack. Whatever the

members and leader may think of one member's being attacked, someone in the group must support the member who is being attacked. This is best done by quickly inserting time in which the attacked member is asked and helped to state his view, feelings, good sense, intention, honesty, and so forth. Every person makes some sense and, whether one agrees with him or not, one can see his point if one wishes. A member can tolerate being attacked by nearly everyone in the group if his own good sense also emerges and is recognized by at least someone in the group. It is the leader's obligation to do this.

Anyone can be the leader. He might be elected, his role might be rotated, he might be picked out on some other basis. What counts is that there be someone recognized as the responsible person to make room for a member not then being heard rightfully, that is to say, in the name of the group as a whole.

The ground rules are written to apply to any situation and therefore we also included (under number 8) the situation where the leader really does command more attention (because he is really the teacher, or the doctor). But the leader could be simply any member who, for the given period of time, has been given the role, and who thus, for that period of time, makes it his first order of business to watch carefully each person in the room, and to notice when someone is not being heard, or might want to speak, or is being misunderstood or out-argued, and the like. Thus, as leader he may say and do much less than he would as a member; nevertheless, he may be very busy just paying that sort of responsible attention.

People Before Purpose

People first—and that expedites purposes. A group may have this or that purpose, but when other things are in the way, then these other things must be dealt with or the purpose cannot be served. Thus, putting the individual first permits the same rules for all sorts of groups.

If the group is a therapy group, but a participant is all involved in some event that happened to him, he must first be allowed to talk—thus is he welcomed by the group. Then he can turn with the others to the therapeutic task.

Conversely, if it is a task group, but two participants fight and undercut each other, the task will not get done effectively until their problem is resolved. Or, if a member cannot do well because of some private painful problem, the task will be done better if the group sustains its members when they need it.

If the purpose is ideological, much more communication and effective arguing will occur if contact and caring for each other come first. The usual discussions never convince; whereas, personal closeness makes for being able to see and sometimes adopt the other's political outlook, and the like.

Quite often it may seem that all this personal self-expression is inappropriate or distracting in a group devoted to completing some task. If the group wants to complete a task and nothing stands in the way, then they will constitute a simple task group. Yet, when or if something is obstructing, the assumption that it will be considered, that anyone's expression of it will be welcomed, is a powerful aid to getting the task itself completed. Just consider any task group you know and some of its difficulties, and think how it would be greatly expedited if the group knew and quite naturally fell back onto the sort of openness and working through described in the ground rules which are presented later in this chapter.

Why force a group of rules to be only one thing or the other, when so evidently any group has times for both? Take, for example, when a psychotherapy group is devoted only to that purpose, the very insistence that everything must be therapeutic, deep, and meaningful makes it all somewhat artificial and also rules out the quiet times, and the times of sharing seemingly irrelevant things—the things that matter *only* because they matter to someone there.

Consider, as another example, a group of therapist trainees that tries to decide once and for all whether or not it will be a "process group" or a "case-conference group." These seem like two different things. In one they talk about themselves; in the other they talk about their therapy cases. But why would they want to talk about therapy cases? They do so only to learn—to work through difficulties they feel as therapists.

It is necessary, therefore, to have a climate of free expression, openness, and willingness both to express and to listen. If we have trouble with each other, we do not have such a climate; therefore, what is the use of playing tapes and using discussions of cases as mere gambits in bad moves between us? On the other hand, once these things are worked through, and as long as no new ones exist, *must* we manufacture issues between us just so we can say we have a "process" group?

Of course, there are often "official" purposes; for example, the above group may actually *be* a case-conference group, or a therapy group. Other things being equal, we return to our official business, but with the understanding that we must do all these different things as needed.

GROUND RULES FOR GROUP SESSIONS

The following rules have been found to be helpful for groups. They are an informal kind of "constitution."

(One might phrase some of these things differently, and one might find different helpful rules.)

1. *Everyone who is here belongs here just because he is here, and for no other reason.* (This is our top rule. It depends on nothing else. Nothing changes it.)

If everyone in the group is angry at one person, that does not change his belonging in it. If he gives up on himself, the group does not give up on him. If he is unfair to everyone, the group says so and tries to help him with whatever troubles him. If he has something hopeless, the group keeps company with him and it.

(Since this is so basic, it is fitting for anyone to remind us of it if we seem to act or feel as though it were not so.) The group leader should do the reminding, but sometimes the group may have to remind him. Any person whose belonging is somehow being questioned can and should remind us, but this may be hard for him just when he is made to feel shaky. (It is easiest for someone who at the moment is not part of the argument, but it is equally fitting for anyone to do this reminding.)

2. *For each person, what is true is determined by what is in*

him, what he directly feels and finds making sense in himself, and the way he lives inside himself.

Everyone does a lot of living inside himself. No one knows more about how a person really is than the person himself. For instance, when someone says, "I feel pain," no one can say, "You're wrong!" When someone says, "I like this," no one can say, "No you don't!" On the other hand, anyone can say (and we will say), "Can you tell us more? Is that *all* you feel? Don't you feel some other things, too?"

We try to help each person get to know even more clearly what he feels and thinks. We do this by listening more closely to how he feels and lives inside himself—and only he can tell us more of this. We tell each other whatever we think might be useful. Whether or not it actually turns out to be useful, only the person himself can determine; he does this through determining if it makes any direct sense to him in the feelings and meanings of his living inside. When what we say seems useless to him, we ask him to say more of what he does feel. Of course, not always will everyone state the truth of what he feels. Sometimes he will not be able to (though we try to help him say it). Sometimes he will not want to, and we respect that. Our living inside cannot all be put into words, anyway. We can only say a little about it, or from it.

3. *Our first purpose is to make contact with each other. Everything else we might want or need comes second.*

We will often have other needs or purposes or jobs to get done. They will get done better, faster, and more fully if we make contact first. There may be someone in the group who values some aim or purpose he has above everything else and above all of us. We will try to make contact with him first. We will respect his purpose just because it is *his*. Later, when we have contact, it will become possible for him to tell (and for us to feel) what this purpose means to him. Then we can see (and say) what we feel about it. That will mean a lot to us *then*. It would only be empty arguing *now*. Contact comes first. Contact is something felt. It is like looking someone in his eyes and knowing that he sees you. It is a direct feeling for the other person's living inside himself.

Contact occurs despite differences in upbringing, viewpoint, and even when two people cannot speak each other's language. Contact is a feeling for the other human being. Contact, feeling close, and caring occur not because of what someone is like, but for him, for who he is.

If one of us seems to be only pretending, lying, or very cautiously hiding behind a false front, we assume that this person still feels distant. We would like to know him. But we may first have to get across more of ourselves. We hope to make more contact with him and get to the point where we feel some caring for him, and he for us. By that time, he will be more direct with us. When we feel contact, it is because we sense the other person's living inside himself. This may occur without words, with few words, or with many words.

4. *We try to be as honest as possible and to express ourselves as we really are and really feel—just as much as we can.*

My own honest, real self-expression is the fastest way to make contact with others. Any self-expression is always welcome in this group. (In other places, what we feel does not "fit" being said. Here it always fits because making contact as the people we really are is our first aim.) Any expression of anyone's feelings or thoughts is equally welcome whether good or bad, smart or foolish, ugly or pretty, friendly or angry, strong or weak. It is welcome and fitting because *he* feels it and for no other reason. We try to express what is difficult, hard to say, what hurts or is puzzling or troubling, what we usually cannot say because it is not fitting to say.

If we feel something toward what is happening in the group, or if we see that another person has feelings about it (perhaps from looking at his face), we try to say it. The more difficult it is to say, the more we will all appreciate someone's saying it aloud. We try —and we try to help others—to speak and live here as the people we really are and feel inside.

5. *We listen for the person inside living and feeling.*

We always assume that any person speaking to us is really speaking from a living and feeling place inside. What he says is probably just the first thing, the opener for a lot more which he could say if we invite him to. We tell him what we sense about the way he is living inside at a given moment. When he tells us more, we will have a clearer idea. What he says may not make sense to us at first, but we ask to hear more about it. We know it makes sense to him, and we hope to see the sense it makes. If he says it not at all clearly, we guess at it; perhaps that helps him find better words for it.

We force no one to be more honest than he wants to be at a given moment. If he tells us that he wants to say no more for the time being, we respect it. If we see someone being pressured to talk more, we may say to the group, "Maybe Joe doesn't *want* to say more about it." We let Joe then say if that is so. We try to sense this living and feeling part of each person, and to see what is there at a given instant in time. We know that what is there is always felt, and it is always much more than anything he says.

6. We listen to everyone.

Sometimes just from seeing someone's face change, we know he could say something—and might want to. If it seems he might want to, we invite him to do so.

The person who interrupts someone needs to be heard. What does he feel so strongly that made him interrupt? Did what was being said make him angry? Did it scare him? Did he think what Mr. A. was saying was all wet? Did he feel Mr. A. was hurting Mr. B.? But, if we stop to listen to the person now interrupting, and we find out what made him feel so strongly, who will remind us to go back to Mr. A., who was talking and did not get a chance to finish what he wanted to say? Anyone in the group can remind us and invite Mr. A. to finish if he so desires.

And meanwhile, perhaps I notice Miss C. frowning. I wonder what she is frowning about. *I can say,* "I notice Miss C. frowning. I wonder what she is frowning about. Will you tell us, Miss C.?"

Perhaps one of us makes a comment. Right afterwards someone else makes another comment. We all discuss the second comment. No one paid any attention to the first one. Anyone in the group who remembers can bring us back to the first comment. "Miss D. said earlier that so and so . . . and nobody said anything about it. I didn't really understand why she said that." (Or, we may state what we think about what she said.)

We do not bring the group back to every unfinished start, or every uninterpreted facial expression, but we do when we feel it might be important, or when we wonder about it. When we notice people who are usually quiet starting to say something, we make very sure they get heard. We want to be sure that we listen to everyone.

7. *The group leader is responsible for two things only: he protects the belonging of every member, and he protects their being heard if this is getting lost.*

The group leader makes it his special task to pay attention and notice when someone is not being heard, ignored, or attacked to the point where his belonging to the group needs reaffirming. It is the group leader's responsibility not to get his own feelings *so* involved that he can no longer notice these things. (Even so, sometimes he will get so involved that he will miss what is happening to certain members.

All of us do these two things, but we do not have to do them.

The group leader does not speak between *every* two members. He is not a switchboard or funnel through whom everything must go. The group leader does not tell us what to do. He may suggest it, but everyone else has the same right. We do not do anything just because the group leader suggests it. His only special rights are to affirm belonging and to let everyone be heard.

8. *Realism: If we know things are a certain way, we do not pretend they are not that way.*

By being in this group we do not stop being whatever we are on the outside. Therefore, we do not pretend we are not what we are. If, in our group, there is a husband and a wife, a father and a daughter, two good friends, or an employee and his boss, we do not expect them to act as if they did not have the relationship they do have.

We do not pretend that the leader is not the leader, and *if* we try to do whatever he wishes, then we do not pretend that we are not trying to do what he wishes. (Of course, we do not have to do it, but if we feel we should, then we say so.) We probably pay more attention to what he seems to want than to what others want.

We do not pretend that we want to do something if we would

rather not. For example, we do not pretend that we want to share feelings with each other if we would rather talk ideas or plans.

If there is research going on, or if there are observers present, we do not pretend there is no research or that the observers are not present. It is fair for anyone to know all he wants about any observers or research.

If some people in the group know each other very well, they do not act as if they did not. In fact, we hope they will talk with each other much as they would if we were not present. We hope they will talk intimately and with a feeling of closeness. Of course, this means they may not fill us in on some of the things they introduce. In this group, we do not think this is impolite. We are glad they are permitting us to be present while they are close with each other. (It lets us all feel closer to them than if they saved it until they were alone and talked here as if they were strangers.)

With these ground rules one's capacity for deep feelings toward others grows markedly. Since we expect and want this, we will not be surprised when it happens toward others in the group. Realism means that we will not violate the long-term relationships in which we live the major part of our lives, even though growth is slower there. A group member's marriage may currently be hostile, distant, or empty, but he must not damage it further by anything that he does in the group or in relationships engendered by the group. As his new capacities develop further, his marriage will also change and may become closer, although currently it may seem impossible, and another relationship may seem safe and intense. One must know in advance not to act in ways that will introduce long-term damages or obstacles into his marriage, unless he has really decided to leave it.

Similarly, we make realism include any other type of case in which outside consequences might temporarily be lost sight of without really being dealt with. For example, if two competitors for a promotion are in the group, they will be moving to a real closeness only by talking honestly about whatever realistic cautions they must excercise.

The above are examples which illustrate that we try not to pretend anything we know is not so.

9. *What we say here is confidential: no one will repeat any-thing said here outside the group, unless it concerns only himself. This applies not just to obviously private things, but to everything. After all, if the individual concerned wants others to know something, he can always tell them himself.*

But will all of us really keep everything confidential? We will have to get to know each other before we can be sure. We will not say anything which would *greatly* hurt us, meanwhile, or hurt others, if it were repeated by those here. (We need not tell private facts when we do not want to. We can just say, "There is *something* in my life which makes me feel so and so . . . ," or "Once *something* happened to me which scared me so much that I felt I didn't have any guts, and . . . ," or "Once *something* happened which hurt me so badly that even now I still. . . .")

Honest expression is not so much a telling of private facts, as it is a telling of what we feel and what we are as persons.

But, anything whatever—feelings, events, ideas, plans, troubles, hurts, joys, views, anything that means something to one of us here—is welcome and worth telling just because it means something to one of us here. Whatever means the most to you is what you should tell.

10. *Decisions made by the group need everyone taking part in some way.*

If a person is quiet throughout the time we make a decision, it means that what is happening is all right with him and he has nothing important to add. If what is decided is unpleasant for anyone, it is his right *and duty* to say so, even if it means back-tracking for the rest of the group to hear arguments or opinions we thought we had already finished.

We try to find a way that everyone likes. At least in the begin-ning it is important to us all to hear what anyone does not like. He might bring in something we forgot that is important to us also. And, he is part of the group; we cannot make a true group decision without him. We might then have to settle for something not all of us like, but at least something all of us can accept.

If we absolutely have to do something, we might have to agree to a way which some said they could not accept. . . . But we will not be content until we know what they do not like, then we may be able to find a better way. To find such a way, they will have to tell us more and exactly what thing or part of it they cannot accept. Then we will avoid that specific thing and probably find a new way.

Sometimes the group is making a decision which concerns one person more than any other, because it is for him, or because it is his idea, or because he will have more to do with it than anyone else. In such a case, what he wants counts more than what any other group member wants (including the leader), and we remind ourselves of this if we forget.

We are here to be really ourselves, and so in all cases we let the group know when some decision or turn of events makes it hard or impossible for us to be really ourselves in the group. We never let ourselves be twisted into what we are not. We do not let the group become something which will not permit us to be ourselves. We do not put up with it and stew about it later, or never come back. We tell the group (and quickly).

But how do we decide the purpose of the group? The answer is that it is *for us*. This means that when we make decisions about what to discuss or to do, we are guided by what those of us here really feel, need, and care about. We try to help each member with what *he* cares about at the moment. He may want to discuss with us some situation, decision, task, personal feeling, or view of his. He may want to show or tell us something of his life just because it is his.

As a group, we may find that we all come to feel a given purpose. Then we arrange to act together to fulfill it. Therefore, we may sometimes look like a discussion group, an action group, a social group, a therapy group, a political group, a religious group, a task force, a class, or a group of friends—yet throughout we remain really the same kind of group because our purposes come from us and what we come to care about.

11. *New members become members because they walk in and remain. Whoever is here belongs.*

We look at a new person with a feeling of "I want to sense who you are"; perhaps we say something of the sort. We cannot tell new people what we do here, but we can give them the ground rules and we can show them what we do, and engage them in it.

But if we constantly have new people, then some of us need to set a time when we can be together without new members, so that we can move in depth . . . not only experiencing the excitement of novelty and new humans. We let that be *another* time of the week, so that we can have *both* new people *and* depth with each other.

If a very large number of new people come, and keep returning so that they are then no longer "new," we may suggest that they too set a different time so that they also can move in depth as another group.

SUMMARY

This chapter includes a brief presentation of the "theory of experiencing" with special application to the small group. The phases (breakthrough, sustaining, and tired), which characterize the concrete process common to all experiential groups, are described briefly followed by a further explanation of the phases through the use of the paradigm of student political groups.

The essence of the chapter is the inclusion of a set of ground rules for experiential group sessions. Preceding the rules, certain safeguards in using them are set forth.

REFERENCES

GENDLIN, E. T.: *Experiencing and the Creation of Meaning.* New York, Free Press, 1962.

GENDLIN, E. T.: A theory of personality change. In P. Worchel and D. Byrne (Eds.): *Personality Change,* New York, Wiley, 1964, pp. 100-148.

VII

FOCUSED FEEDBACK WITH VIDEO TAPE: EXTENDING THE GROUP'S FUNCTIONS

Frederick H. Stoller

WHENEVER a field opens itself to technological innovation, both opportunities and pitfalls are simultaneously faced. While the previously impossible or difficult now becomes feasible, unforseen chains of consequences may be set in motion. Above all, a conceptual framework is required to insure that the new inventions will be appropriately incorporated and their full potentials exploited. At the same time, there must be some awareness of process alterations which may ensue. The group field, with its interest in facilitating personal change through interaction, is now faced with these issues.

The introduction of the audio tape recorder has permitted therapists to obtain records of the verbal content of therapeutic sessions in a relatively simple manner. Previously difficult studies of interaction can now be conducted. To aid their continuing development, therapists are now able to confront their own functioning (Ruesch and Prestwood, 1949). Most important from a therapeutic standpoint, the client is able to listen to himself, an extension of group therapy's attempt to give a person information about himself as he interacts with others. In practice, many groups have utilized the tape recorder to listen to themselves (Armstrong, 1964; Cameron, 1958). However, there is little by way of organized study of the effects of doing this, nor any extensive attempt to systematize or conceptualize such mirroring activity. Because the audio tape recorder has been used fitfully, its incorporation as a meaningful part of the group's resources has not developed in a meaningful way.

Video tape recording represents an augmentation of electronic tapes in which visual as well as audio records can be obtained by means of a television camera. Except for the necessity of adding a viewing monitor, video tape operates in much the same fashion as the more familiar audio tape: it is available immediately upon recording; it can be moved forward or backward with the same ease; and it can be erased while a new recording is made over it. (Because of their greater cost, video tapes are less likely to be saved for future reference.) Although the video tape recorder (VTR) has been available for some time, the high cost and size of early equipment made it impractical for application to group therapy. However, small and relatively inexpensive equipment is now available. The near future promises a proliferation of VTR systems for home use which make them practical for most group settings.[*]

Because it captures the whole expressive range used in social intercourse, the VTR has more power than the audio tape recorder. Introducing it into the group situation is also more complex than conventional tape recorders. Television cameras are more imposing than microphones and require more accommodation on the part of group members. Involvement in group interaction, however, becomes so absorbing that participants adjust to the equipment with surprising ease. There is much evidence that the introduction of television equipment does not grossly modify group interaction (Farson, 1966; Stoler, 1965).[†]

[†] Focused feedback is a technique which has been developed for utilizing the VTR within the group therapy situation, particularly in enhancing the presentation of information about self. The group provides the arena for behavior as well as the opportunity for reflection upon the impact on others of this behavior. Video tape is capable of extending such a process. So much information is made available that selection becomes necessary. In order to appreciate the rationale for this particular approach, some atten-

---

[*] Approximate prices range from about $1500 to $2,000 for very modest equipment to about $20,000 for a more than adequate VTR and television camera. A VTR designed for educational TV costs about $4,000.

[†] The relative quiet of television equipment is also a factor in rapid accommodation. Lighting requirements for modern equipment are relatively modest though consideration must be given to preventing shadows.

tion should be given to the concept of feedback and to theories of personality development emphasizing social interaction.

THE ROLE OF FEEDBACK IN THE GROUP

Feedback,* as an important ingredient of a group's work, has been dealt with most extensively by the exponents of training laboratories. From their point of view, it is one of the unique elements which the T group has to offer as an educational technique. To the degree that psychotherapy encompasses the function of feedback, it has tended to place it in terms of confrontation: facing a patient with inconsistencies in his motivations or evasions. In the present context, confrontation represents one of a number of ways of presenting feedback.

As a working definition, the one provided by Benne, Bradford, and Lippitt (1964) is useful: "Feedback, as used here, signifies verbal and nonverbal responses from others to a unit of behavior provided as close in time to the behavior as possible, and capable of being perceived and utilized by the individual initiating the behavior" (p. 24). There are three important elements of this definition which should be examined in more detail.

1. Feedback may include verbal and nonverbal responses to a unit of behavior. The emphasis upon behavior is a more explicit procedure than interpretation, which is generally more speculative and broader, often bridging a series of behavioral units viewed as representing a pattern. While much feedback is given verbally, it is possible to present it in another fashion. A participant may attempt to imitate the unit of behavior of another, the "mirror technique" of psychodrama (Moreno, 1959). Video tape viewing, in which the individual watches his own behavior, represents another nonverbal means of providing feedback.

2. The feedback is provided as close to the unit of behavior as possible. Early T groups incorporated feedback by participant

---

* It is tempting to draw upon the extensive use of feedback in technology for pointed analogies. The possible confusion such parallels can foster is stated by Berlo (1960) in treating communication processes: "There is one difference between the engineer's meaning and the communication man's meaning for feedback. In engineering, feedback often is a "bad" word—engineers try to avoid feedback. In human communication, feedback is a very "good" word. When we communicate we constantly seek feedback" (p. 104).

observers who presented their comments in special sessions set up for this purpose. Experience suggested that the feedback was best given within the group session itself and should come from as many of the participants as possible (Benne, 1964). Benne, Bradford, and Lippitt (1964) lend additional support to the need for immediate feedback when they state, "A closely related notion from learning theory is the powerful effect of instantaneous feedback concerning the effects of the learner's exploratory response. In learning about the effect of his behavior on other people, the learner needs to have some more or less immediate report of the effects of his response on the others" (p. 25). There is a basic assumption that contiguity is important when facilitating learning about oneself. Video tape, because of its immediate availability, has the capability of presenting the feedback as close to the behavior as desired.

3. The information provided the individual is comprehensible and usable if the promotion of change is desired. Whitman (1964) makes the following point: "Feedback implies only understanding what has been said. The crucial test of understanding is whether the person can utilize what has been said to create a new thought or insight" (p. 319). Learning about oneself is probably the most difficult educational task there is. Promoting conditions in which the individual is motivated to free his own self-perceptual capacities represents one of the more time consuming tasks of therapy. The clearer the feedback format, the more likelihood there is of piercing the perceptual defenses of the individual. A response to a group member may be valid but it is pointless unless given in usable fashion. Insofar as it is his own behavior, recently displayed, an individual seeing himself on video tape is receiving the clearest, least distorted, and most comprehensible feedback possible. The ease with which the behavior can be shown repeatedly also makes possible greater clarity of information which can be made available to the group members.

Interpretation is a form of providing information about a participant which differs from feedback. Its major characteristic is its speculative nature placed within a theory of motivation. In form it can be stated as follows: "You behave this way because . . . ." To a considerable extent, its usefulness depends upon the acceptance of the theoretical framework by the individual for whom the interpretation is intended. When the behavior under discussion encompasses a great many units developed over a period of considerable time, the individual's perception of what is being told is subject to distortion. As a consequence, interpretation unlike focused feedback, as a means of providing information to the individual about himself, is subject to more problems in terms of its usefulness.

A group setting provides a valuable opportunity for participants to give reactions to their fellow members. Hill (1965) writes of the value for group members in partaking of the growth aspects of the therapist role: it encourages them to reach into their own potential for honesty and courage as well as helpfulness. Insofar as interpretation requires considerable training in a particular theoretical structure, as well as extensive experience in its appropriate application, this mode of providing information about others is not the most appropriate way of being mutually helpful. Unless group members are especially sophisticated, their interpretations tend to be inappropriate and difficult for the recipient to utilize. Since the group provides an occasion for people to learn new styles of interaction, adapting interpretation to use outside the group situation can be highly inappropriate. On the other hand, feedback, particularly where it involves specific behavior and concrete responses, is a natural though covert part of conventional social interaction. Verbalizing the feedback or making group members aware of what it is to which they are reacting is one of the functions of a therapeutic group.

It is not the primary purpose of the present discussion to defend the value of feedback over interpretation as part of the therapeutic armamentarium. What is important is that feedback is indigenous to the group and has a much more important role there than in individual therapy. The behavior elicited in the dyadic situation is highly colored in that it is in reaction to one specialized individual: the therapist. A great deal of the content of individual psychotherapy concerns behavior which is talked about with the therapist helping to organize it into a meaningful structure. Since the group member reacts to a variety of people, the most important information he may bring is his way of behaving within this setting. Thus, the group can deal with direct behavior rather than with behavior as described in secondhand fashion. Although interpretation may still have a very important role to play, a great deal of the group's efforts can involve personal feedback and this can be a function of all the group members. By providing this kind of help to the other participants, members learn to adopt a more appropriate social manner than that of "junior therapist."

In employing focused feedback, much of the emphasis is placed upon the feedback that the group members and the group leader can provide for each participant. Employing video tape is meant to enhance this important aspect of the group process, not to supplant it. It is important to stress this since VTR is an intriguing piece of equipment which has a fascination all its own. Should the group learn to lean too heavily on video tape, it will rob itself of a very important facet of the growth process: personal participation. However, when the feedback provided by the group could be improved by more explicit information than can be provided verbally, the utilization of the VTR can become an extremely valuable asset.

When a group member receives personal feedback from other members, the situation is unique because such information is rarely expressed overtly in interpersonal interaction. Looking at himself on the television monitor is an even more special circumstance: it is probably the only chance one has for seeing himself in interaction with others. Photographs do not provide this information and motion pictures are rarely used for natural social interaction. A person may see himself in the mirror every day, but the minute he starts looking at his reflection he stops his natural interaction. Thus, he confronts himself on the video tape. To appreciate the importance of this special situation, it is necessary to examine certain aspects of personality theory.

THE THEORETICAL FRAMEWORK FOR SELF-VIEWING

More than anyone else, George Herbert Mead has appreciated the importance of interpersonal perception in the development of human personality. Although his views have exercised considerable influence on such theorists as Sullivan (1953), there has been little direct clinical application of his work. Mead's emphasis on normal development and his sociological bent has not been as meaningful for therapists as other approaches. Consideration of personal feedback and self viewing, however, calls for a fresh look at Mead's possible contribution to therapeutic innovation. It is presented, not so much as an alternative to current clinical theory, but rather as a new emphasis upon relatively neglected features of the change-inducing process. Above all, it provides a conceptual structure for considering such technical innovations as video tape.*

One of the central characteristics of humans in shaping behavioral patterns is the picture of one's self that is developed. The self-image emerges out of the attitudes and reactions of others directed toward the individual, particularly of significant others who represent important sources of interaction early in life. Through the incorporation of these reactions and attitudes, a person develops the ability to react to himself as an object and to take the role of others as they might respond to him. It is this self-consciousness which is the unique characteristic of the human as differentiated from animals. In Mead's words:

> Self-consciousness, rather than affective experience with its motor accompaniments, provides the core and primary structure of the self, which is thus essentially a cognitive rather than an emotional phenomenon. The thinking or intellectual process—the internalization and inner dramatization by the individual, of the external conversation of significant gestures which constitutes his chief mode of interaction with other individuals belonging to the same society— is the earliest experiential phase in the genesis and development of the self (Strauss, 1956, p. 228).

Physical characteristics represent an important basis for the development of self-concept since they contribute to the kinds of responses one will receive. Not only are a person's external and

---

* The relative infrequency of discussions of Mead reflect a long-term neglect of his views. Most of the ideas relevant to his analysis of personality are found in *Mind, Self, and Society* (1934). A useful collection of his writings has been compiled by Strauss (1956). A very adequate presentation of his theory, presented in considerable detail from a contemporary point of view has been made by Shibutani (1961). Much of this presentation is based upon Shibutani's discussion though the organization and emphasis have been altered.

internal physical movements important in the personification of self but also the consistent manner in which he is treated by others. Since it is essential for him to retain the support of those who are important in his life, an individual will inevitably learn to anticipate the reactions of others and guide his conduct in such a way as to insure their positive behavior. Thus, he learns to take the role of others toward himself and to control himself in such a way as to make more likely a response which will not violate his self-image. Much of human endeavor is directed toward maintaining the conception of self once it has formed, particularly when physical gratification is fairly predictable and no longer an overriding concern.

Because a threat to the self-image arouses anxiety, the individual will strive to maintain a consistent self-concept. A self-concept must be confirmed by others since this represents the reality testing to which it is always being subjected. However, it is not necessary for the confirmation to come from everyone with whom one comes in contact. One way in which self-personifications are maintained is the selection of significant others who will maintain reactions which will not violate this picture of self. In addition, people tend to react selectively, to attend most closely to that which will be consistent with what they want to receive from others.

Important in this version of human behavior is the ubiquitous reaction toward self which continuously occurs, both with and without awareness. Once having stabilized, self-conceptions are attuned to the *imagined* audience rather than to the actual one. Though there is often considerable overlap, a picture of self does not necessarily correspond with the way in which a person is actually seen by others. Consistent behavior develops because a man behaves as if he were a particular kind of person with specific characteristics, even though he may exhibit a variety of conduct with different audiences. Assumptions about self and expectations from others shape his inclinations to act. Conversely, changes in inclinations to act represent changes in one's personification of self. In self-conceptions, the person is both the subject and the object—a subtle relationship is constantly maintained between his experience of himself and his initiation of action.

Presuming how others will react towards oneself represents a very important facet of interpersonal behavior. As Shibutani (1961) states:

> Thus, a man becomes conscious of himself as a distinct unit through role-taking; he responds to his own activity as if he were someone else. He responds covertly to his own behavior in the same way in which he expects others to respond overtly. The capacity to form self-images, then, makes self-criticism and self-control possible (p. 91).

Prediction of the behavior of others permits people to engage in a cooperative endeavor with confidence as well as helping to maintain a stable self concept. The potential reactions of others are decided through imputed attitudes which are constantly being evaluated.

When engaging in role-taking, people project their own inclinations to action upon others and pay close attention to the gestures produced by others. Since there is no way of obtaining an accurate reading of the internal feelings of others, inferences must be made on the basis of the sounds and movements they make. Registering the gestures of others and interpreting them is a constant activity, though not always a conscious one. People frequently can describe their feelings about the intent of another person without being able to specify why.

Verbalizations play a vital role in evaluating one's own behavior. They are particularly important because the individual can hear his own remarks in much the way others hear him. In Mead's words:

> I know of no other form of behavior than the linguistic in which the individual is an object to himself, and, so far as I can see, the individual is not a self in the reflective sense unless he is an object to himself. It is this fact that gives a critical importance to communication, since this is a type of behavior in which the individual does so respond to himself (Strauss, 1956, p. 206).

Important as verbal gesturing is, it is still a limited form of role-taking. People monitor their own verbalizations so that only part of what they say is heard and attended to by themselves. When they hear themselves speak on a tape recorder, people are generally surprised at how they sound and at all that they have communicated without quite realizing it.

But verbalizations represent only a portion of the fund of gestures. Facial and body movements are another important dimension for calculating the intentions of others. Such physical gestures are generally outside the perceptual field of the one who is generating them and cannot be adequately utilized in role-taking. Such gaps in communication are responsible, to a considerable degree, for the discrepancy between self-perceptions and the perceptions of others.

Scanning the gestures of protagonists is an almost constant part of social interaction so that people develop considerable skill in "reading" others. In reaction to this, men develop a variety of protective devices to divert attention from their internal events. Consequently, considerable allowance is made in the interpretation of gestures. Since it is important to anticipate another's reactions, the involuntary gestures involved in expressive movements receive a great deal of close scrutiny.

Under the circumstances where evasion, rather than directness, is to be expected, a person's style frequently reveals more about his intentions than the content of his reactions. Expressive movements, because they tend to be involuntary, represent an important component of personal style. People generally attempt to control their communication of feeling and to divert attention from their inner reactions, particularly when they sense this might give others an advantage in dealing with them. Nevertheless these expressions of feeling are generally difficult to hide completely, and the average person becomes highly skilled in making inferences about the feelings of others from small expressive gestures. This becomes particularly important in the development of role-taking because important information about oneself which is being utilized by others is unavailable to the individual. Ekman (1965), for example, has conducted a series of experiments which suggest that head cues are used to identify affects while body cues reveal information about their intensity.

Action which is not communicated to the initiator of the act can be considered unconscious and a considerable proportion of any individual's behavior falls under this category. That which is outside self-awareness is also beyond control. Self-control is important because it involves forming images of oneself in relation to an anticipated audience and redirecting behavior in the light of this. The more communication there is with oneself about the behavior that is being undertaken, the more control can be exercised. To quote Mead once again:

> Here we should call out in ourselves the type of response we are calling out in others; we must know what we are saying, and the attitude of the other which we arouse in ourselves should control what we say. Rationality means that the type of response which we call out in others should be so called out in ourselves and that this response should in turn take its place in determining what further thing we are going to say and do (Strauss, 1956, p. 213).

Without self-control and responsibility for one's action there can be little of a cooperative nature in man's activities. From a personal point of view, a man's self concept is closely related to his perception of the field over which he can maintain some degree of control. Increasing his self-awareness of the gestures he generates towards others widens his capacity for role-taking and enhances the development of a self-image that is more attuned to the image perceived by others.

Consensus occurs when a number of people can agree as to the definition of a situation. Unless an individual enters into such a consensus, continual misinterpretation between himself and others is inevitable. When people are involved in a common situation, consensus is the result of a sharing of gestures throughout the mutual relationship. The agreement implied in consensus is not the same thing as conformity but rather the buildup of motives and intentions which can be clearly interpreted by all the parties concerned. Self-control becomes an important characteristic because it enables people to anticipate reactions to their behavior and to stop behavior which might interfere with cooperation. The ability of a person to appreciate the feelings of another and to take them into account, to empathize, bears an important relationship to his effectiveness in the social sphere.

Anticipating the reactions of others toward oneself is a central feature of behavior. Such areas of behavior can create difficulties in a number of ways. An individual may grossly misinterpret the way in which others will react to his behavior. More often than not, the gestures he actually exhibits differ somewhat from that which he intends; he means to give out one message but actually generates a different one. This may be a constant feature of his behavior with others or may only occur when specific types of interaction are involved. More common is the tendency to narrow expectations of what others would approve in one's behavior. The continued practice of evasion concerning the expression of certain feelings or tendencies prevents testing their actual reception. A self-image of how one would appear to others develops and one rarely attempts to test it. All too often, this becomes so much a part of people that they are rarely aware of the discrepancy between their actual potential and that which they show to others; they become unaware of an aspect of themselves.

Ultimately, it is the tremendous investment of energy in evasion that is the concern of this method of psychotherapy. To the degree that defensiveness does not really keep one's motives from others, that one reveals himself more than he cares to admit, it represents an expenditure that is largely wasteful. Clarity and honesty in interpersonal dealings is the immediate goal, but the much more important purpose is increasing these qualities in the internal dialogues which all have within themselves. Thus, the video tape will be used mainly for self-confrontation within the field of group behavior.

THE ROLE OF THE VIDEO TAPE IN THE GROUP

It is helpful to think of a therapeutic group in terms of a system. The elements of the system consist of the group leader and the group members filling, at different points of time, the roles of patient, therapist, and spectator. At any given moment in a group's life, someone has become the focus of the group and is receiving help, others are attempting to give help, and still others are quietly sitting by. Utilizing video tape introduces a number of extra elements into the system: the television camera, the VTR, and the television monitor. An interesting parallel to the expanded arrangement is made by Wiener (1954) as he discusses a machine system: "This control of a machine on the basis of its *actual* performance rather than its *expected* performance is known as *feedback*, and involves sensory members which are actuated by motor members and perform the function of *telltales* or *monitors*—that is, of elements which indicate a performance" (p. 24).

Within the group system, the monitor indicates a performance of any of the group members (including the group leader), in any of the three major roles,* *i.e.* patient, therapist, and spectator. Thus, the choice of where and how to use the playback facilities of the VTR can become relatively complex. The initial tendency is to pay most attention to the group member as he becomes the focus of the group and as he begins to talk about himself in characteristic fashion, either exploring or defending himself. Experience has shown that there is considerable merit in attending to the other roles which the participant enters. One's manner of questioning another, of providing feedback or of confrontation, that is, one's way of being involved and helpful to another can be of considerable importance. In addition one's manner of listening, of showing interest or disinterest, while not actively participating, provides important clues to his true intentions. The opportunity to provide feedback for the group leader in the various roles should not be overlooked; however, less attention should be given to the leader roles.

The occasions for providing feedback are frequent. If used indiscriminately, video tape feedback could conceivably overwhelm the group members and swamp the natural group interaction. The natural group interaction, of course, should always remain the primary requirement of a therapeutic group. Where an overwhelming amount of data are provided, group members may have difficulty in assessing relative importance. Unless there is some way of highlighting certain information, the value of that information decreases. It is out of this requirement that the concept of focused feedback grew: the centering of participants' attention on that aspect of video tape feedback which would seem to be most relevant for beneficial behavioral change.

In order to use efficiently the material in a video-taped group, a strategic rationale is required. Otherwise, the group leader is in danger of using the mass of information in a clumsy manner that

---

* Although the three major roles to be filled in therapy groups are stressed, it is not meant to imply that these are the only roles which occur. Bach (1954) has listed a number of roles which are frequently found in therapeutic groups and these, as well as others, should be the object of feedback with video tape. Generally, these roles are special instances of the three major ones.

is ultimately dissatisfying and unenlightening. Without a strategic structure to depend upon, a preoccupation with the mechanics of the VTR may occur. In this sense, focused feedback represents a strategy for using video tape in a meaningful fashion.

The essential interval comes between the intended reception that the individual imagines and the response he actually elicits from his audience. Generally unavailable to him is the family of gestures he generates which the others use to process their own responses. To the degree that there is a discrepancy between what he intends to receive from others and what he actually gets, a message is being sent of which he is unaware. In a video-taped group this message is being recorded simultaneously with its reception by the other group members, and it is then available to the initiator. One of the most opportune points at which to introduce the video-tape feedback occurs when it becomes apparent that a group member is getting discrepant responses in terms of his own goals.

Despite the fact that the image he is shown on the monitor represents clear and unassailable data, the individual may respond as if this were not the case. As in any attempt to clarify an individual's behavior to himself, resistance to change always has to be considered. The immediate playback of video tape represents a solution to one of the problems involved in providing feedback: that of presenting the material in as clearly defined a manner as is possible. By itself, it does not solve the problems of timing and appropriate preparation. The recipient of the feedback must be reasonably ready to assimilate the material fed back to him in a manner that bears some resemblance to the way others see the same material. He must be ready to react to himself in analogous fashion to the way others react to him. Judgments as to when a person is approaching this readiness require as much art with the VTR as it does with any verbal interpretation.

When an individual becomes receptive to the video-tape material, he often becomes more self-conscious; he will lose some of his smoothness and display hesitation and faltering. Such stumbling is an indication that someone has become aware of incongruent elements in his own conduct. A frequent immediate consequence, then, of increased self-awareness is less adequate behavior, an essential step in halting action which ordinarily flows without hesitation. Finding alternatives for the behavior which is in the process of being dropped becomes a necessity at this phase. Unless he is helped in this, the individual is in danger of responding to the unrewarding consequences of his new self-awareness and either returning to his former behavior or reaching for other forms of conduct in a less than adequate manner. It is at this point that the providing of alternatives by the therapist and other group members becomes an important part of the process. It is not always necessary to provide substitutes which will be adopted; it is the attempt to help in a moment of stress which is important and which encourages the individual's further search for more rewarding conduct.

When a participant begins to evidence new forms of behavior, another occasion for focusing feedback is presented. An individual should have the same chance to confront himself at a time when his acts are congruent with the response he would like to elicit as he does when he is shown his incongruent behavior.

One of the major decisions to be made under focused feedback is the nature of the material to be emphasized. It is natural, particularly early in the course of therapy, to emphasize behavior which engenders undesired responses from others. It is tempting to speak of this as negative feedback. However, such a term would be too easily confused with servomechanism terminology in which negative feedback causes some function of the system to reverse itself while positive feedback causes the function to continue on its course (Sluckin, 1954). Stability is the goal. The results will be the same in therapy except that stability of behavioral patterns is not the goal; negative feedback is not expected to lead to reversal as much as it should lead to the abandonment of one pattern and a shift to another. Therefore, positive feedback might be expected to lead to stable behavior while negative feedback leads to change. It is preferable to refer to the latter as *discrepant feedback, i.e.* feedback concerning behavior leading to responses to this behavior different from that which the actor intends to receive. Feedback concerning behavior seen in a positive light will be referred to as *nondiscrepant feedback:* acknowledgement of behavior leading to responses from others which is in line with what the actor intends to receive.

Opportunities for providing nondiscrepant feedback should not be disregarded. There is considerable merit in helping an individual enhance those aspects of this functioning which tend to foster interpersonal reactions in line with his overall goals. One of the prime functions of a therapeutic group is to help a participant move his self-image and expectations closer to reality. A self-image represents many facets so that there are a variety of expectations in different interpersonal situations. The same individual may require discrepant feedback under certain circumstances and nondiscrepant feedback under others. It should be emphasized that the therapeutic goal is not necessarily to develop a more acceptable self-image but to decrease the differences between expectancies and actuality. Focused feedback, through video tape, is capable of enhancing such changes over and above what the group, itself, can provide.

Providing feedback data for more than one person is also utilized. Individual group members develop patterns of interaction toward one another which become recognizable and which suggest important elements of their life styles in relating to particular individuals. The presence of family members in a group represents direct evidence of the development of important relationships, though other participants can represent such central protagonists. Behavioral interaction of this type is referred to as *relationship feedback:* information about recurrent interaction between two group members which generally differs from either participant's overall behavior toward other group members.

Still another type of feedback can occur when the group as a whole functions in certain nonproductive ways. The aim here is to help the group readjust its overall manner of conduct by considering how they are colluding in order to subvert significant movement. It is appropriate to refer to this as *process feedback:* information about group functioning which is intended to be considered by all the group members simultaneously. Both of these types of feedback, *i.e.* relationship and process, can be described in discrepant or nondiscrepant terms.

THE PHYSICAL ARRANGEMENTS FOR VIDEO TAPE

Introducing a VTR with camera and monitor presents certain complications over and above the usual arrangements for a therapeutic group. Besides the equipment, there is often the necessity for additional personnel to handle it. A number of arrangements are possible, depending upon the nature of the resources.

The original work with focused feedback took place in a closed-circuit-television studio of a mental hospital (Stoller, 1965; Stoller, 1967). The studio setting represents an elaborate arrangement including two television cameras on dollies which circled the group. The cameras were mounted so as to shoot over the shoulders of the participants. In this case, the cameras were manned by hospital patients who were also members of the crew of the television station. In addition, a sound boom in which the microphone was directed toward the one who was speaking, was manned by another crewman. When televising an encounter group over commercial television, Farson (1966) used the same arrangement. Under studio conditions, the cameramen were given instructions by a director who was placed in the control room, viewing the group interaction through monitors. The group leader used a signal light to the crewman operating the VTR in the control room whenever he wished to take note of a portion of interaction. With such an arrangement, a self-viewing session was arranged following the regular group in which participants sat in front of the VTR and monitor and viewed segments of the session just completed. Those portions of the tape noted by the group leader could be recovered with minimum delay.

A somewhat more advantageous arrangement is feasible where adequate funds are available. It is possible to obtain remote-control equipment for the television cameras, two or three of which could be ranged about the group. Control over the cameras and decisions as to what would be taped would be exercised by a director who would not have to be in the same room. If a monitor and a remote control device for the VTR were made available to the group leader, he would be in a position to make use of the video tape at any point during the session or afterward. Maintaining control over the playback features of the VTR enables the group leader to make maximum use of it with minimal interruption of the group's flow of interaction. A group room with remote controlled television cameras has many advantages for research of group processes—it provides capability for capturing much of the group's behavior with minimal interference.

The most practical arrangement, the one that will probably prevail in most settings, is made possible through recent developments in VTR designed for home use. Not only are these new sets much less expensive, but their relatively small size enables the camera, VTR, monitor, and microphone all to be placed with the group. Experience has suggested that the most advantageous method is to employ a cotherapist on the camera who becomes an integral part of the group. Both group leaders can alternate manning the camera and leading the group. Together, they can contribute to the focused feedback phase of the group. The one manning the camera uses the monitor to guide his camera work and can merely turn it around to face the group when the video tape is to be viewed.

Incorporating a cotherapist gives adequate latitude for the most subtle use of the potentials of video tape in a group situation. Such an individual is in the best position to make judgments concerning what aspects of the group to focus on at any particular time. As indicated earlier, in addition to relationship and process feedback, there are three major roles any participant assumes, all of which can be seen in terms of discrepant or nondiscrepant feedback. Appropriate selection as to which of these features of the group system to capture on video tape can only be made by someone who has a firsthand familiarity with group development. It is obvious that only someone qualifying as a cotherapist could fill such requirements adequately.

A further advantage of using a coleader with this modest equipment is the flexibility it permits. Whenever the group leaders (or group members) decide an opportune moment has arrived to view the tape, they can do this with a minimum of complication. The cotherapist is also frequently in a position to take note of events in the group which the group leader may not notice.

One of the more surprising aspects of working with television equipment is the degree to which group members become accustomed to its presence. A certain degree of self-consciousness is inevitable when a group first encounters this equipment. However, group interaction and involvement generally reduces this in a matter of minutes. Group leaders play vital roles in reducing self-consciousness since their attitude toward the presence of the television equipment is generally communicated to the group members and will markedly affect their reactions. Even when a certain degree of self-consciousness persists, most of the individual's style tends to be captured and it is upon this that the emphasis is placed.

THE PROCEDURE FOR FOCUSED FEEDBACK

The primary point to be stressed is that focused feedback is ancillary to the group process, attempting to enhance what the group does rather than replacing it. At all times the emphasis should be upon the ebb and flow of the group interaction. Fostering of group development should never be subverted because of the presence of cameras and VTR.

Emerging from the material provided by the group's interaction, focused feedback goes through three phases. These phases include choice of materials, presentation of feedback, and the development of alternatives.

Choice of Material

Not only must decisions constantly be made as to what aspects of the group interaction will be video taped, but also there are choices concerning which part of the tape should be viewed. There is an enormous amount of material to be viewed and reviewed within an hour's tape. Attempting to deal with all this material at one time would flood the participants with more than they could adequately handle. Even when the more relevant interpersonal data are stressed, selectivity is necessary to maximize impact.

A structured view of feedback is helpful but does not replace judgment. It is obvious that it would not be possible to provide rigid rules for selection since the variables with which a group leader must deal are far too complex. Nevertheless, some idea of the kinds of choices to be made can be developed through an examination of samples of the different group roles that are possible in terms of the two kinds of feedback.

Discrepant feedback is likely to be stressed early in the group life. When the group places a participant in the role of patient, there is ample opportunity for observation of his self-presentation. A group member may elicit anger or rejection when he wishes to receive sympathy. His self-justification or defensiveness may repel or dissuade others from trying to help him. Feelings such as anger, injury, or even empathy may be disguised and encourage others to make inferences about his internal state. When confronted, he may typically attempt to alter the direction of the interaction while insisting he is eager for help. Such discrepant behavior may not occur consistently but may emerge under specific circumstances; he may be defensive, for example, only when dealing with certain subjects or only when interacting with particular group members.

Taking on the therapeutic role also provides ample opportunity for discrepant feedback. An important element of the group process calls for the participant's being helpful and interested in the welfare of other members. Under the guise of fulfilling the therapist role, a person may point out others' shortcomings with such hostile glee that the response can only be rejection regardless of the appropriateness of the observations. Rushing in to support in an overzealous manner, which has the effect of placing the recipient of this help in a weak and childlike position, can also be inappropriate. Under the disguise of being interested in helping others, participants often engage in strategies which actually serve their own ends to the disadvantage of the others. Focusing feedback on such action not only clarifies for a member his participation in the group but also suggests how he extends help in other situations. Permitting him to become aware of this enables him to free the more mature side of himself, that part of himself which is strong enough to forego strictly advantage-seeking maneuvering.

Because of its passivity, the spectator role is often overlooked in the heat of more volatile interaction. Only when a spectator grossly ignores the group or in some way interferes with the ongoing process is he likely to receive attention. However, a person's manner of paying attention to others gives considerable information about his actual motives and so enters into judgments made about him. Focusing on discrepant feedback in the spectator role can take place when a group member appears consistently disinterested in what is going on, yet professes to be involved with others. Another type of important information occurs when a group member distracts through whispering, joking, and otherwise giving evidence of striving for attention in an indirect manner. Some may show undifferentiated gestures so that it is impossible to distinguish between their various levels of involvement. It is important to realize that people provide important information about their intentions, motives, or internal feelings when they are not in the center of the stage. Video tape offers a unique opportunity to appreciate important ingredients of what contributes to others' judgments about oneself.

Addressing the feedback to more than one member can involve relationship feedback of a discrepant nature. Here, two or more participants show a pattern of being together which inevitably results in unrewarding outcomes in terms of long-term growth. Thus, two participants may begin an argument whenever anyone shows a possibility of movement, their noise drowning out any possibility of continuing the movement. Others may engage in extensive seductive play, freezing their ability to proceed to further depths of communication. The way in which a married couple deal with one another, particularly where they enter routinized game-like enounters, can often be shown to them in a manner so striking that they inevitably must reflect on their own conduct. The possibilities for relationship feedback are almost endless and extremely potent when captured on video tape.

Group behavior which seems dedicated to the maintenance of a stalemate should also be the subject of feedback. A group may engage in intellectual sophistry, lead each other into topical discussions or, more insidiously, engage in sophisticated analyses of "problems" without addressing themselves to specifics. Since such developments generally involve the entire group in collusion (including those who do not like such activity but do nothing to change it), the group as a whole should be given this feedback.

While nondiscrepant feedback often becomes predominant in the later phases of therapy, it has a relevant place throughout the group life; its reinforcing quality tends to stabilize and strengthen the object of focus. A participant may show behavior which is so effective and appropriate that there is a natural tendency to support it—in this case, provide nondiscrepant feedback. Strategically, such data may balance an overabundance of discrepant feedback for a participant, but the greatest value of nondiscrepant feedback will occur when a group member has changed his behavior so as to elicit reactions which are more congruent with his goals. The use of nondiscrepant feedback is an excellent way to support growth and change and to give an individual an opportunity to see himself in a new light.

Nondiscrepant feedback, in the patient role, is most appropriate when a group member requires a minimum of effort to explain himself away: his actions and his intent are not too far apart. Not only will he talk about himself in comprehensible ways, but he will listen in such a fashion as to indicate that he is giving consideration to what is being told to him, rather than automatically raising his defenses. Even when rejecting someone else's contribution about himself, he will use it as an opportunity to introspect further. Above all, he is likely to be taken seriously and treated with empathy when discussing his difficulties, and his presentation of his problems will be considered in the light of his dealings with the group. Comparison of improved behavior with earlier behavior of a different order can be very rewarding by way of showing the extent of growth.

In the therapeutic role, nondiscrepant feedback will be illustrative of the manner with which a person presents his help or how he interrogates other members. Concern, helpfulness, and an absence of serving his own needs at the expense of another are important attributes of the person attempting to influence another. As a helper, honesty and directness, as reflected in the gestures he shows, also markedly affect his impact on others. It is not infrequent that the first evidence of change for a person may come as he fulfills the role of therapist, and nondiscrepant feedback could reinforce and encourage a wider range of growth.

Spectator roles probably provide the least obvious material for nondiscrepant feedback. When the participant's spectator gestures facilitate rather than inhibit or interfere with the style of relationship he wishes to maintain, he can be said to be generating messages which are congruent with his goals. Such behavior has particular merit in a therapeutic situation, either when it represents a change on the part of the individual or when it offsets much behavior the impact of which is different. Where the usual passive behavior on the part of the group member represents a discrepant image to an audience, an opportunity for nondiscrepant feedback provides a change for the person to react to another aspect of himself, to see the differences within his own behavior, and to get some sense of his own potential for being different. As with other group roles, any change on the part of the participant which can be considered to be moving in the direction of nondiscrepancy should receive the positive support of feedback.

Interchanges between members that are honest and direct and yield satisfying outcomes can be shown in terms of nondiscrepant feedback. As with other feedback of this nature, it has a particularly reinforcing nature when it represents a visible change in a significant relationship. In some instances, group members literally do not know what is meant by game-free conduct, and feedback to the group of an example of this could contribute to the modeling of appropriate action. The opportunities for nondiscrepant feedback on a process level are often very frequent. Group behavior which generates movement and gain for the participants is rewarding in its own right and rarely requires the reinforcement of feedback.

It should be clear that any session provides an enormous amount of material for possible selection, particularly if one considers each of the group member's contributions to the pool. Exactly what will be stressed within a single session is a function of the group's or individual's therapeutic phase. Selection of material for feedback can never be done in an automatic or routine fashion. Instead, proper selection is based on the sensitivity of the group leaders and their capacity for relating group behavior to life styles.

Presentation of Feedback

Once the choice of material for focusing has been made, the next problem is to select a method of showing this material to make it most meaningful. As with the situation of therapeutic interpretation in general, the mere presentation of the video-tape image is often insufficient. At times an individual is capable of looking at himself on the monitor and of grasping exactly what will be relevant to him from an interpersonal point of view. However, this is infrequent, and help generally is required to aid observation. Verbal specification and repetition are often necessary to give structure and meaning to self-observations.

There are two basic opportunities to present video-tape feedback (it is assumed that verbal feedback is a continuous activity of the group). One occurs within the group session itself, where the normal proceedings are halted as the group observes something on the monitor. The other occasion comes at a viewing period immediately following the group session.

Viewing the video tape within the group session itself will affect the course of group interaction following it. Continuity is disrupted and a qualitative change is likely to occur when the group resumes. Experience has suggested that the effect of video-tape viewing on the group process is not necessarily an undesirable one. It may push the group toward concentrating on immediate confrontation relating to group behavior in place of discussions of behavior external to the group. It should be recognized, however, that it is a disruption, and too frequent interruption of the group interaction changes the nature of the group. In view of the probable effect upon the group, the utilization of video tape within the group itself has to be considered with caution and full awareness of what may occur.

Since video-tape viewing does change the direction of the group interaction, at least temporarily, it can be used purposely to affect its course. Given a group that seems to be bogging down in empty verbalisms and automatic "contributions" to discussions of problems, the introduction of video tape could effect a change.

Process feedback during the group session can be expected to change the group's focus and manner for a period of time. If used for such a purpose, the video tape should be utilized very rarely, and then only when the group leader feels he has used all other means of helping the group attain a new level on its own.

A more pertinent interference with ongoing group interaction occurs when an individual is being confronted by the rest of the group about some aspect of his behavior and he refuses to consider what they are trying to tell him. There are points at which this struggle becomes stalemated and the group member loses, whether he gives in to group pressure or whether he refuses to reflect on what might be very important information about himself. At times, the clarity of what the group is trying to tell the participant, and his immediate defensiveness, stands out in such stark contrast that almost any intervention would be welcome. Discrepant feedback via video tape seems to be a natural intervention at this point. It is as if it were saying, "Why don't you look at what the group is talking about? See, that is what they mean!" Stopping the group to look at that portion of the video tape which illustrates the behavior the group is commenting upon can have the effect of capping the group struggle with significant movement, thereby significantly strengthening the therapeutic impact of the group process.

Opportunities to enter meaningfully the group process itself with the video tape are relatively rare. Much appropriate focused-feedback material does not warrant interfering with the group process. As previously indicated, there are numerous points at which focusing the feedback would be relevant so that a continuous interference with the ongoing nature of the group could well occur. For these reasons, most focused feedback occurs in a viewing period which follows the group proper. This can be considered to be a new phase of the group session itself in that interaction and discussion are encouraged. However, what goes on within the viewing period will revolve about what is being shown on the television monitor and relevant to the kind of feedback that is being attempted.

During the group session, the cotherapist, who is handling the camera and VTR, will keep a running record of parts of the interaction which might be appropriate for review. A form has been devised with columns for every group member. Within the appropriate columns the meter number on the VTR will be noted to indicate the place on the video tape at which the significant behavior occurred. A coding system has been devised indicating whether it is discrepant feedback (d) or nondiscrepant feedback (n) as well as the kind of role participated in at the time: patient (p); therapist (t); spectator (s). In addition, process feedback (pr) and relationship feedback (f) can be noted. Thus, an entry may be placed under a group member as follows: 186 dt, indicating that the place on the tape can be found at 186 on the VTR meter and that it involves the participant in discrepant behavior in the therapist role. Feedback which is considered to be particularly important by either of the group leaders will be starred so it will not be neglected. Other brief symbols can be used to give an

With such information available, the group leaders are in a position to focus their feedback on what is considered to be indication of what is being captured on the tape.
significant within that session. The monitor is placed before the group and sections of the video tape are played back. When a section of video tape is reviewed, the group leaders will often point out what they feel is important about the behavior being viewed. The recipient is given an opportunity to react to this feedback. On the basis of his reaction, the group leader may continue with a restatement of what he has pointed out. Depending on how close the participant is to comprehending the feedback, the group leader may move on or may replay what has just been shown. Replay may occur a number of times as a way of emphasizing significant behavior. At times the replay is made without the sound, an effective way of emphasizing the nonverbal aspects of the message he is conveying. Reduction of the channels of information through the VTR places greater emphasis upon what is actually being transmitted.

It is a principle that the attempt to provide a unit feedback will be pursued as long as the recipient would seem to be in a position to make use of it. If he is still too resistant to utilize the videotape material effectively, the group leader should move to other material. The VTR has a number of capabilities, *i.e.* its replay capacity, its ability to pinpoint a very specific bit of behavior, and the complexity of channels of information (there are times when it is advantageous to remove the picture and play back the sound alone, in effect, to make use of the audio-tape-recorder capabilities of the VTR).

Following the participant's opportunity to react to himself, the rest of the group should be given the chance to discuss what they saw take place. There usually will be further conversation concerning the group member as he affected the others in the group. As a result, the level of confrontation often will be enhanced; to the degree that the group member can accept what he sees, the other participants can talk with him with less struggle and with more mutual empathy and understanding. When the recipient still cannot accept the feedback, other group members often find more strength and assurance in their own observations. When a specific bit of feedback seems to have exhausted its maximal impact, it is best to move on to another participant. It is important to realize that too much input at one time about the self can dilute rather than enhance change.

A further word about resistance is in order. Defending against discrepant feedback is obvious and expected. Reactions to nondiscrepant feedback would seem to require no defense on the part of a participant because of its generally positive flavor. In the main, it does not meet with the same kind of struggle and is usually reinforcing as previously indicated. There are individuals, however, whose reactions to nondiscrepant feedback do give evidence of considerable resistance. These are people who seem to revel in the negative aspects of themselves, who become uncomfortable when seen by others in a positive light. An odd struggle can ensue in which a person is helped to accept himself in a more pleasing frame.

The Development of Alternatives

The immediate effect of discrepant feedback which enters significantly into a person's self-conceptualization is an increase in self-consciousness. Instead of an immediate improvement in behavior there is likely to follow a period of less adequate performance. It is often necessary for an individual to stop his accustomed course before he can develop something new. As beneficial as it may be ultimately, it is, nevertheless, an uncomfortable situation for the person and those around him.

An extremely important feature of focused feedback is the attempt to provide alternatives. This may consist of direct suggestions on the part of the group leaders or the other group members. Conceptualizing alternatives is a very difficult and subtle task. Doing this adequately tries a therapist's skill to the utmost, since he is often reduced to supplying inadequate suggestions at the point when the individual's need is greatest. As indicated earlier, the attempt to help the person is often more important than coming up with a concrete answer. In the process of offering alternatives, as inadequate as they might be, an individual is often encouraged to search further, arriving at his own solutions.

More meaningful than providing suggestions is the attempt, on the part of the group and the group leader, to help the individual engage in new behavior. This often will take the form of the group leader or some of the group members entering into a new type of interaction with the recipient of the feedback. They will try to engage him differently or attempt to elicit an aspect of himself which has not yet become manifest in his behavior with others. Such interventions are similar to other therapeutic activity. They are stressed here because focused feedback should be considered incomplete unless attempts of this nature are made. A considerable danger exists that the presence of television cameras and other equipment could make the providing of feedback more important than the development of alternatives. Unless the third step of focused feedback is seen as an integral part of the technique, the means rather than the ends will have gained dominance.

THE PRODUCTION OF CHANGE THROUGH FOCUSED FEEDBACK

Above all, focused feedback represents an enhancement of one of the important ingredients of the group therapeutic process. The main agents of change are considered to be the major forces inherent in group psychotherapy: the opportunity to see oneself in operation with others, the support of a group, the verbalized reactions of those with whom one interacts, and the chance to sample the range of behavior which a group of people represents. It is not so much a new technique as it is an attempt to heighten the mirroring effect which the group ordinarily provides.

Basic to this modification of group therapy is the opportunity it provides to permit role-taking toward oneself. In his being able to evaluate the style he presents to others, which determines their reactions and subsequently their behavior toward him, an individual heightens his capacity to adjust his own course to be more in line with his goals. When he can visualize and conceptualize the differences between what he intends to present to others and what he actually presents, a participant is in a position to make concrete and specific adjustments. Similarly, when he can see himself behaving in line with his intentions, such behavior receives support and a person obtains an enhanced view of himself.

Much of what focused feedback is directed toward is already part of an individual's repertoire. Normally, the rehearsal for an intended audience takes place without conscious awareness and is presumed to occur whenever one interacts with others. Confronting part of his behavior which is ordinarily unavailable to him, the group member is in a position to make this part of his behavior more purposeful. With more self-awareness, he is in a position to modify his readiness to behave in a particular manner and to develop alternatives.

The process by which a person becomes more aware of his own contribution to the world's treatment of him is presumed to require guidance. Such guidance is represented by the focusing which is an integral part of this technique. People generally develop a learned insensitivity to much of their own behavior. Learning about oneself would seem to require somewhat different conditions and circumstances than learning about anything else. This is partly the result of the long history of biased self-attitude with which a person has to contend. But it is also a function of looking at oneself in a particular way, of seeing only those aspects of himself which tend to maintain a level of comfort. In order to counteract such long-term perceptual styles, a particular kind of presentation is required. Such a presentation is attempted through the highlighting that is an integral part of focused feedback. Finally, the attempt to help the individual seek out alternatives, once he has developed self-awareness, represents a facilitation of the growth process.

THE GOALS OF FOCUSED FEEDBACK

Focused feedback concentrates on developing a greater awareness of self. Its aim is to improve a person's ability to direct his own behavior, to increase his ability to "read" himself so that he is in a better position to close the distance between goals and actuality. Ultimately, there should be a reduced distance between his own perception of himself and the way others see him (Leary, 1957), a moving together of his idealization of himself and his actual self as perceived by others (Rogers, 1964).

Directed self-viewing of important facets of an individual's behavior, as manifested within the context of group interaction, makes such goals much more feasible than conventional therapeutic practice. Conceivably, measures of self-perception, idealized self, and the self as perceived by others could be made before and after exposure to focused feedback. Such research should be attempted only within the boundaries in which the technique should be utilized.

The material upon which the feedback is focused emerges out of the group interaction. It is presumed that an individual's behavior within the group represents a valid sample of his behavior within the larger world. By focusing, narrow aspects of a person's conduct are highlighted. Generally, the significance of the information about self to be highlighted is selected in terms of its effectiveness in eliciting desired responses from others. Consequently, the individual has an opportunity to look at himself within a relatively narrow and pointed range, rather than through a wide spectrum. Should changes in self-perception occur, it may not be in a total shift but rather in a "filing down" of elements that most negatively affect how one currently moves through the world.

Focused feedback is too recent a technical innovation to have been the subject of any extensive research. The earliest attempts to investigate the process quickly ran into a problem: most instruments for measuring self-perception are too global. Margaret

Robinson, in close cooperation with the author, is currently developing research into this technique while working on her doctoral dissertation at the University of Southern California.* An instrument is being developed for measuring changes in an individual's placing of the locus of responsibility for his fate. Subjects will be asked to make statements about themselves and their problems, and these statements will be rated along a variety of continua—reflecting the degree of closeness to self an individual places the responsibility for his fate. The results of this research, however, are not yet ready for publication.

Robinson is also attempting to measure the effect of video-tape viewing upon the group process through the application of the Hill Interaction Matrix (Hill, 1965). Preliminary results suggest that self-confrontation on video tape tends to push the group into a period of heightened interpersonal confrontation which concentrates on behavior within the group, rather than upon behavior which is removed from the group.

Finally, attention will be given to the proportional involvement of participants in the various group roles following different types of feedback; qualitative as well as quantitative features of these roles will be studied. The capacity of the video tape to capture much of the ongoing group behavior for more leisurely (later) investigation will be exploited.

Currently, there is no other formal investigation of focused feedback beyond the planning stage. But there has been interest in the effects of feedback upon a group. Gibb has conducted a series of studies of T-group laboratories involving different kinds of feedback. Feedback that was feeling-oriented rather than task-oriented tended to decrease defensiveness and promoted the widest group participation (Gibb, 1960). Another study (Gibb and Platts, 1950) suggested that role-playing combined with feedback is more effective than verbal feedback alone, an interesting finding in view of what video tape offers. Miles (1958), studying in the same area, concluded that, in my terminology, change was greater when feedback focused on discrepancy rather than non-discrepancy; interpersonal behavior was more responsive to feed-

---

* She is currently on the staff at Camarillo State Hospital, Camarillo, California, where her research is being carried out.

back than was task-oriented behavior, and that, in contrast to task-oriented feedback, interpersonal feedback needed alignment with the participant's motivational structure.

Visual feedback has been used experimentally. Cornelison and Arsenian (1960) had psychotic patients look at themselves in movies and photographs. Changes in the psychopathological states were found among a wide range of reactions. Moore, Chernell and West (1965) attempted a similar procedure with video tape and found a greater degree of improvement for those who viewed themselves than for those who did not. Counselors' self-perceptions grew closer to those of their supervisors and they also gained confidence in their interviewing as a result of viewing their work on video tape (Walz and Johnston, 1963). Not only has counselor training been facilitated through video tape, but therapy has been also through the use of a stimulated recall method by Woody, Krathwohl, Kagan, and Farquhar (1965). A unique feature of the work of Woody *et al.* was the effectiveness of using hypnotic suggestion during the recall phase, possibly related to the presentation of alternatives described in this chapter. A similar team has viewed the use of video tape in individual psychotherapy as a methodological breakthrough (Kagan, Krathwohl, and Miller, 1963).

A finding paralleling the "focusing" of the present technique was made by Geertsma and Reivich (1965) in repeated presentations of video-taped therapy interviews to a patient. While changes in self-perception were noted, it was frequently necessary for the therapist to direct the patient's attention to the cues which he felt were important.

UNIQUE CONTRIBUTIONS TO TREATMENT

Information about the self is an essential part of every form of psychotherapy. Very often, the principle differences are to be found in what is considered to be important data and the method of presentation. In most cases the applicable material is selected through the filter of theoretical structure. The organizational framework within which the therapist operates orders what he will see, and shapes the manner in which he will transmit this information. A major struggle of the therapeutic arena concerns itself with the acceptance of the therapist's framework, an essential feature of many methods of persuasion, according to Frank (1961).

Group psychotherapy diminishes, to some degree, the need to indoctrinate the client. Since feedback comes from a number of people, it is not so exclusive a product of the special perceptions and terminology of the therapist. But therapist influence prevails, and group members tend to emulate the leader, so that they often couch their reactions in the professional's terms. Unfortunately, this is often done in a naive and clumsy fashion, blunting the participant's natural effectiveness. In addition, adoption of the therapist's style is not necessarily the most appropriate one for most social situations.

Perhaps most unique about the introduction of video tape is the feasibility of introducing information about the self which is almost unbiased. What is seen on the VTR can be denied, of course, but it takes considerably more effort on the part of the individual than turning away from a verbal picture of self. A picture represents communication of a different order than the spoken word and must be responded to in a dissimilar fashion. An individual is confronting information about himself that varies from what he is accustomed to receiving, and he must react to himself somewhat analogously to the way he reacts to others. The fact that this is immediately available to him, within the same context as the behavior itself, adds to the power of this kind of presentation. Frames of reference, theories of personality, and knowledge of psychopathology are less essential for processing this information.

It should not be inferred that the video-tape material presented to the individual is completely free of bias. It is merely less biased than the usual kind of verbal interpretation. Focusing represents a selection of material and therefore is inherently subject to shaping on the part of the group leader. The information is shown on a television screen, which, as McLuhan (1964) has suggested, presents a picture with less definition than a photograph or motion picture, and therefore forces the perceiver into more active projection and interpretation. Thus, the medium changes the situation in ways that are difficult to appreciate. In addition, the television screen is a restrictive area which tends to bring one closer to a subject than one might ordinarily get in actual life: the close-up is equivalent to being nose-to-nose with a person. Group members view it in a lighted room in the presence of others so that their overt reactions upon seeing themselves are public rather than private. All of these conditions define a situation which is uniquely different from the purely transactional one. Adding the medium of television extends the tools of learning which are so important a part of the therapeutic process. In doing so, it inevitably alters the process in subtle ways. Such changes must be ultimately understood and maximally used to the advantage of those seeking therapeutic help.

MODIFICATIONS OF VIDEO-TAPE FEEDBACK

At the time of writing, focused feedback represents the only organized attempt to utilize video tape within a group-therapy situation. It has been used considerably within the field of family therapy (Spitzer, Jackson, and Satir, 1964). Such a pheonomenon as the "double bind," in which the mother may say one thing and indicate the opposite with her gestures, can be shown to her in a way that is otherwise difficult. Alger (1966) reports using video tape with families. He video tapes the first ten or fifteen minutes of a family session, plays it back, and bases the rest of the session on the reactions to the playback and what emerges from it.

The author has been using the technique of focused feedback as a training device for group leaders. Video tape is being utilized in psychotherapy training in a number of settings as reported by Schiff and Reivich (1964). The author and his colleagues are developing a program to use focused feedback as an extension of consultation. Instead of using the VTR continuously, it is used for a few sessions when the group feels the need for it. Both the group members and the group leaders are provided with these specialized data, and thus consultation becomes a therapeutic tool when both the group leader and group members go through their feedback together. In this way, the group leader can help model fearlessness of self-criticism.

Plans have been formulated for the utilization of focused feedback within executive training programs. A parallel development within the industrial field is represented by the technique of structured feedback (Griver, Robinson, and Cochran, 1966) in which new learning is inserted at the moment when the feedback is received and acknowledged by the individual. For the most part, structured feedback deals with performance and bears the same relation to it as focused feedback bears in interpersonal behavior. In meeting the interpersonal needs of industry, the two techniques approach one another.

A recent innovation involved the introduction of video tape into a two–day group (see chapter on marathon therapy). Cameras and VTR operated continuously as the group stayed together. Viewing of the video tape was employed whenever it was felt necessary, particularly when the group and the individual were in disagreement over behavior. In this instance, a semi-professional television studio was used, and the hot lights and complex television paraphernalia almost overwhelmed the group. In addition, the presence of eight crew members through the two days represented a meta-group; they could observe but could not interact, and they needed group attention themselves. Despite these many difficulties, the group was considered to be a very successful one, suggesting the power of group involvement over distracting environments.

It is obvious that video tape can be used in a multitude of ways. Because experience with it is so narrow it can only be considered to be at the beginning of a proliferation of innovation, limited only by a dearth of imagination and ideas.

GROUP LEADER AND MEMBER ROLES

For the most part, the roles required of the various participants in a group featuring focused feedback are identical to those found in most therapeutic groups. In this setting, however, immediate feedback on the part of the group members is highly valued and stressed. The group situation is seen as an opportunity to exhibit a significant portion of one's characteristic behavior with others and to have it mirrored back to one. As a consequence, a focused-feedback group stresses the behavior within the group over and above interpretation about behavior external to the group, that is, behavior that is talked about. Emphasis upon group behavior and upon the immediacy with which it is dealt represents a guiding principle for certain therapeutic groups (see chapter on marathon therapy, for example) and is not merely to serve the purposes of video-tape feedback. Focused feedback was developed to serve this principle rather than vice versa.

Because of this view of group psychotherapy, group members will learn to give immediate reactions, as explicitly and as devoid of psychological elaboration as possible. The same approach will be carried over into the viewing period. During the group session, the group leader has to attend to the group itself as much as possible, paying as little attention to the VTR as he can, though he may occasionally signal the cotherapist to make note of a particular bit of interaction. A practiced cotherapist will often relieve the group leader of this necessity and will be able to see things that the group leader cannot because of his involvement with particular members.

Although the coleader tends to stay in the background during the group session, playing a more dominant role in the viewing period, he is free to enter the group interaction. In the first place, he is an integral part of the group and cannot remain completely out of it. Also he may make extremely valuable contributions at a number of points in the group development because of his special vantage point. And finally, there are times when he will suggest that the video tape be incorporated in the group session because of a special situation. The coleader must, at all times, be a comfortable and valued member of the group.

QUALIFICATIONS OF THE GROUP LEADERS

Focused feedback places a greater burden upon the group leaders than conducting a group without it. It should be obvious that it is necessary for someone using this technique to be accomplished in and accustomed to the group situation. One must have considerable awareness of how a group operates and particularly how to relate behavior within the group to significant observations about life style and its relationship to one's course through the world. One must also have a clear understanding of the theoretical structure within which he is operating and possess flexibility and imagination for the presentation of the material selected and the alternatives being sought.

The presence of television and the use of gadgetry always presents a danger of overwhelming the human aspects of the group. There must be a constant awareness of such a tendency and the group leader must possess the resources to counteract this pull. His first involvement must be in people and not in machines. Oddly enoughly, he must also have a thorough acquaintance with his instrumentation, not only so he can operate and incorporate it into the group more smoothly, but also in order to have satiated his fascination.

Working in an open setting in which his actions are under surveillance is a situation many therapists abhor. It is necessary that the group leader be comfortable with the eye of the television camera and the self-observation he must, himself, undergo. Not only must he be open to the self-correction that is available to him but also his attitude toward using cameras is crucial; to a considerable degree he will set the tone for the rest of the group.

GROUP COMPOSITION

There are no special requirements for the makeup of a group involving focused feedback. The use of one television camera does tend to limit the group somewhat in that a group of eight to ten is easier to handle than a larger group. Two cameras enable larger groups to be accommodated more easily but this adds to the complexity of equipment. Zoom lenses make one camera more flexible and enable a larger number to be included.

Most populations, including chronic mental-hospital patients, seem to be able to benefit in varying degrees from focused feedback. Despite the fact that hospitalized patients often have the least motivation for self-observation, they can benefit. Two other groups deserve special mention.

Experience of a limited sort has suggested that sociopaths, with their frequent sharp ability to "spot a phony" will be able to utilize focused feedback much more readily than conventional group therapy. Of course, one still has to contend with their basic motivation; what might be discrepant feedback for others becomes nondiscrepant feedback for certain types of social deviants.

Another possible population which may show a surprising affinity for focused feedback would be those from lower socioeconomic levels who generally find little attraction in conventional verbal psychotherapy. They are accustomed to watching television and may find it a more meaningful and comprehensible modality than that of "talking it out." There is a fascination to watching oneself which everyone possesses, and which may provide an opportunity for involving those who are more visual than verbal. Plans are currently being drawn to experiment with this modality in programs dealing with such populations. Considering the possible gains that could result, more extensive exploration with this group is definitely in order.

LIMITATIONS

Video tape is potentially a powerful instrument and, as such, should be used with discretion. When the viewer looks at himself too frequently, a possible consequence is that he ceases to observe in the same manner. If used steadily for too long a time, there is a decided danger of dissipating its power. It is similar to the phenomenon that occurs when one looks in the bathroom mirror every morning; people generally cease to really look unless there is some unusual situation which pulls their attention. In groups that continue for indefinite periods of time, it is recommended that focused feedback, involving video tape, be used at intervals when it appears to be advantageous. Under these circumstances it should be used for a specific number of sessions, stopped, and then be reintroduced at a later time for another series of sessions.

Motivation remains as much a problem with this technique as it does with any other. Some people have a definite disinclination to look at themselves. Under the circumstances, no one should be forced to view video tape who expresses a clearly stated resistance to it. Such an attitude sheds light on the individual's motive for entering group therapy and should be examined within the context of the group. However, until there is a shift in the group member's attitude, attempting to force video-tape viewing on him could negate the possible gains that could be made.

Some find it difficult to deal with specific bits of behavior toward which focused feedback directs itself. They would prefer to remain on fairly rarified levels of abstraction or else find themselves so rooted in the past that they resist shifting to concrete behavior in the present. As in the case with resistive behavior, this is a matter which should be dealt with in the group session though video-tape viewing can aid in helping them shift.

OTHER READINGS

The most complete presentation of focused feedback to date has been made herein. Because of its recent formulation its development is continuing and it will undoubtedly undergo further evolution. However, some of the underlying considerations upon which the procedure is based may require deeper study.

Mead presents the bulk of his viewpoint with which we are concerned in *Mind, Self, and Society* (1934). It is however, not a completely satisfactory treatment in contemporary terms. A representative selection of Mead's writing has been made by Strauss (1956). Shibutani gives a very well organized presentation of Mead's view in *Society and Personality* (1961), a work which concerns itself with a much broader spectrum than was relevant for the procedure under consideration.

A very informative treatment of the general topic of feedback is found in Sluckin's *Minds and Machines* (1954). Feedback in engineering, electronics, and communications is discussed, as well as implications for psychology. Probably the most extensive treatment in group terms (though not necessarily for therapeutic purposes) can be found in many of the chapters of *T-Group Theory and Laboratory Method,* edited by Bradford, Gibb, and Benne (1964). Dorothy Stock's chapter, A Survey of Research on T-Groups (1964), gives an outline of the kind of research conducted on feedback within the laboratory movement.

Extremely provocative speculation can be found in Marshall McLuhan's *Understanding Media* (1964). McLuhan deals with the impact of various media of communication on society and, in doing so, deals with the character of the media. His discussion of television raises many intriguing questions concerning the style of perception this medium forces on viewers, which should be the subject of investigation within the context of focused feedback.

SAMPLE PROTOCOLS

The following interchange occurred in a two-day marathon group utilizing video tape. The following represents one of the first opportunities for self-viewing. It involves discrepant feedback in the patient role and indicates the kind of interaction that often follows video tape feedback. The group is one-hour old.

Leader: I was wondering—you feel people don't talk to you the way you would like them to talk to you.

Bill: Yeah, I do but——

Leader: I was wondering—I would like you to look at yourself. I have a feeling about you—that there're two messages coming out to people. There's one saying, "There's a lot going on inside me." And the other is saying, "Don't step into it too deeply—you'll get yourself in too deep." That's the message I get. I don't know if other people get it. How about looking at the tape. (The group looks at a short portion of the video tape covering the last few minutes of interaction in which Bill has been in the patient role.) Bill just had a chance to look at himself and the last thing we said was—I said at least, I got a feeling of two messages coming out of you—and I would like to know what was your initial reaction?

Bill: I saw myself as—not being someone real easy to get at. And this was different than my self-perception before.

Charles: You think you're real easy to get at?

Bill: Yes.

Leader: In a sense you think you invite people to come to you and when you look at yourself—there is a kind of invitation but it's sort of half you.

Charles: How did you see yourself extending so that you invited?

Bill: I thought of myself as a pretty open person—you know—and—I like to relate to people and—you know—I don't particularly care if they say nice things—you know just open—and I don't see that Bill up there as being very open.

Mary: But I can't understand—I've had other experiences with you.

Leader: What you are saying is that he is capable of being otherwise.

Mary: No, I'm saying more than that. I'm saying that on two occasions when I was under great stress and I had an alternative of a number of people in the classroom or a number of people in the group that I could turn to and express great feeling that I chose Bill to express it to. And that's what I am saying and that's a little different, you see, and that's exactly what I was trying to get at. That's why I made the remark before when someone asked him, "Do you have this with your wife?" and he said: "Yes." I said to myself, in fact, I said to the group, "I'm sure he does."

Leader: But Bill also said that people in general did not talk to him the way he would like them to.

Mary: I don't know—Did I talk to you the way you would like me to?

Bill: Yes.

Mary: OK.

Bill: But this may be something in you. What I was concentrating on was what is it in me that is inviting some people and cutting off a lot of other people?

Charles: Well, I feel I can talk to you. We drove together a few times and we talked to each other.

Leader: I think it's still interesting for Bill to have a chance to explain how he saw himself up there because this is certainly a unique opportunity.

Mary: I wanted to say the picture as presented is not a total one.

Leader: Oh, by no means! We know that this isn't all of you, but this is one aspect of you and this is one aspect you have a tendency to show to the world at large, perhaps. But it certainly is by no means all of you.

Charles: Can I ask a question? Is it just because of this kind of a setup in this group that you're this way? I wonder if the others feel this way about Bill outside the group—has nothing to communicate, or he is not that open?

Alice: I have never been able to talk to him. One night I had a dream about you and I was going to tell you the next time I saw you and I sat right next to you in class and I couldn't even tell you. I didn't feel open enough to be able to tell you. This was kind of interesting to me because I had planned when I woke up —and I didn't even know your name—and I was sitting right next to you—and I didn't feel—you know—that you maybe wanted to talk—I don't know what it was—but the kind of thing we're talking about here is the kind of picture I have of you because I haven't had much contact with you.

Charles: Well, why didn't you have much contact with him? Why is it hard for you to talk to him? Is it something you do or something he does?

Alice: I don't feel any responsiveness from him.

The following represents a portion of the tenth hour of the same group. Following discrepant feedback in the patient role, the participant is aided in exhibiting alternative forms of behavior.

Sam: Just like in saving money—either I'm real thrifty or just blow it.

Coleader: You really put your finger on something that makes it concrete for me—that somehow the guy who has fun can't be the guy who has feeling inside himself about something else. Switch into one and the other is all gone.

Leader: Yeah. That would be why you talk about being one person one time, another person another, when what you are really talking about is that there are different parts of you that come to the surface and it's as if all of you can't be serious, work hard toward a goal, have simultaneously or in one chunk of time, one segment of time. One or the other. Now, in a way what you're doing is kind of putting a big part of yourself out of the picture. You kind of—let me ask you—Is there a side of you that doesn't like people?

Sam: I think I'm high or low—I have a lot of hostility.

Leader: Do you?

Sam: I think.

Leader: Who are you angry at? Did you get irritated at anyone here?

Sam: No. I had a dream last night—I can't remember it too closely but it was almost in a nightmare form because—I think I was venting hostility toward everyone in the group here and I woke up and for some reason I was saying Yes or No—that's about all I can remember. And my wife perceives me as having a lot of hostility in me at times towards her or toward my son. I just blow my stack a lot.

Leader: So you sense that there is some kind of hostility toward us that you have not expressed.

Sam: Well, I think I expressed it last night—in the dream.

Leader: That doesn't do us any good.

Sam: I don't feel any hostility toward anyone right now. If I do, I'll try to let you know.

Leader: Would you like to look at yourself?

Sam: Well, I saw myself yesterday.

Leader: But we didn't concentrate on you, did we?

(The group looks at the last few minutes of video tape in which Sam is the focus.)

Leader: Just looking at yourself now—if you were someone else—

if you were on the receiving end of you—how do you think you'd feel—how do you think you'd be affected?

Sam: I don't think I would be affected at all. Just a person talking and that's it.

Charles: What would you tell this person? What would you suggest to this person.

Sam: What I would suggest is—what has already been mentioned —I don't know if I would have suggested that before it had already been mentioned but I—I—I—have a tendency to say to myself, "Speak up!" No matter what the subject matter is—its coming out in the same tone. Just the same.

Charles: Even now.

Bill: You're right. Maybe I'm particularly sensitive to this. I feel this a lot in myself. I find myself a lot of times modifying and sometimes almost apologizing for what I said and when I see myself doing that—it really burns me up. You know, I say, "You said it! Why the hell are you taking it back for and trying to be apologetic about it!" And I think you do it. You talk about dreaming and "I can't remember it so clearly." And lots of times you say, "or something like this" or "This isn't the way I feel." You said it and that's what counts and it bothers you like it bothers me to see myself modifying it and apologizing.

Sam: It would be better to—what I thought you were going to say —when you saw yourself you were surprised that you didn't come up with too much and this is—can also apply to me. Not necessarily there but very often I'm really feeling something and I'm trying to convey it to somebody—on paper, or in person. And— from the reaction I get from other people or from reading over what I had written it's not there.

Bill: You use words like "hostility" and "anger" which aren't nice words but you say them nice.

Leader: They are nice words. "Hostility" is a nice word for "anger" or "pissed off." It's way up here. "I have hostility for you." So it is a nice word.

Bill: It has the connotation—I can be angry or hate one thing or one person but I have hostility I have a free floating—––

Leader: A textbook word! If you weren't in this field you wouldn't say it. Right? These are the qualities that certainly Sam has, I think more than you. You seem to be bugged more by it. Sam doesn't seem to mind this quality of his which doesn't affect people that much. Leaves it mild, sort of unaffected, in a narrow range. You want to leave it that way?

Sam: Uh—what—you say—I don't mind that I'm not communicating with people.

Leader: Let's leave that word communicate out. You're not affecting people very strongly, one way or the other. You said yourself if you were listening to you, you would not be that much moved by it—one way or the other—bland.

Sam: I don't like that—If I'm trying to comm—talk to a person—to the way that I want them to be—to receive what I—––

Leader: You seem to be struggling right now. Is there something going on?

Sam: When you take me away from the textbook words, I don't know how to express myself.

Leader: You don't know how to express yourself? I don't believe you. That's learned very recently. There's something before that.

Sam: Well, for instance, if I tell my wife I love her—(chokes) I hope to God that she understands that—that she feels what I feel toward her. If—I—I—if I feel strongly about something that's happening and I'm trying to communicate to someone or some people the importance of it—the importance of it to me, I want them to know it.

Leader: Do you love your wife?

Sam: Yes.

Leader: Can you tell us how you feel about her?

Sam: I—I—I'd cry if I told you. I can't seem to talk emotionally without crying.

Leader: Take a risk.

Coleader: You know it's really—I kind of get the feeling that you're really full of feeling—and all different kinds of feeling, not just hostility that you have to mask. That's what—what happens; there is suddenly a big discrepancy between the way you talk and what's welling up inside you.

Leader: I would like to hear about your wife.

Sam: Well—she's my—my life—she's sacrificing—working real hard and raising our child and—going to school while I am—and sacrificing so much so I can go to school and—(tears)—when I get a lot of bitches—things like that—she seems to be able to—to—adjust and still—love me and—uh—she's a—I call her a—a—puppydog—because I somehow—what I feel about a puppydog is the quality she has—cuddly and—someone who needs me and can give out a lot of love—peppy and she's petite and—(sigh)—and sometimes I feel I don't deserve her—she's a—I guess—a—well—one of the most special people I ever met and—uh—how I ever ended up with her I don't know—and—uh—it kind of scares me when I think—that—I need her so much. Maybe I feel so—pained that I— have—haven't given her what she deserves——

SUMMARY

Focused feedback is a procedure to be used within therapeutic groups which exploits the self-confrontation possible with video tape. Its underlying assumption is that people monitor their behavior with an internal rehearsal which provides an image of how an intended audience will react. Their actual behavior contains gestures which are generally unavailable to the actor but which shape the actual reactions of others to a very significant degree. For the most part, it is upon the discrepancy and agreement between what is intended and what is received by others that the technique concentrates. The feedback available on the video tape is considered to be an extension of the kinds of feedback that are often made explicit in a therapeutic group in that it relates to retrievable behavioral data rather than interpretation of recalled behavior.

Focusing consists of selecting and highlighting the particular aspects of the group interaction to be viewed on the monitor. This is accomplished through consideration of the kinds of feedback which are applicable in terms of the various roles that are ordinarily carried out within the group.

As much as is feasible, group members are aided in developing new behavior to aid them through periods of increased self-consciousness, which frequently accompany awareness of behavioral trends hindering the individual's goals. The group process is considered to be of primary importance so that the requirements of the video tape are always secondary to the human needs of the group members.

REFERENCES

ALGER, I.: Involvement and insight in family therapy. Paper read at Los Angeles Group Psychotherapy Society Annual Meeting, Los Angeles, 1966.

ARMSTRONG, R. G.: Playback technique in group psychotherapy. *Psychiat Quart Supplement*, 38: 247-252, 1964.

BACH, G.: *Intensive Group Psychotherapy*. New York, Ronald, 1954.

BENNE, K. D.: History of the T-group in the laboratory setting. In L. P. Bradford; J. R. Gibb, and K. D. Benne (Eds.): *T-Group Theory and Laboratory Method*. New York, Wiley, 1964, pp. 80-135.

BENNE, K. D.; BRADFORD, L. P., and LIPPITT, R.: The laboratory method. In L. P. Bradford; J. R. Gibb, and K. D. Benne (Eds.): *T-Group Theory and Laboratory Method*. New York, Wiley, 1964, pp. 15-44.

BERLO, K. D.: *The Process of Communication*. New York, Holt, 1960.

BRADFORD, L. P.; GIBB, J. R., and BENNE, K. D., (Eds.): *T-Group Theory and Laboratory Method*. New York, Wiley, 1964.

CAMERON, D. E.: Ultraconceptual communication. In P. H. Hoch, and J. Zubin, (Eds.):*Psychopathology of Communication*. New York, Grune, 1958.

CORNELISON, F. S., JR., and ARSENIAN, JEAN M.: A study of the responses of psychotic patients to photographic self-image experience. *Psychiat Quart, 34*: 1-8, 1960.

EKMAN, P.: Differential communication of affect by head and body cues. *J Personality and Social Psychology, 2*: 726-735, 1965.

FARSON, R. E.: The use of audiovisual input in small groups. Presented at VRA conference on The Use of Small Groups in Rehabilitation, San Diego, 1966.

FRANK, J. D.: *Persuasion and Healing*. Baltimore, Johns Hopkins, 1961.

GEERTSMA, R. H., and REIVICH, R. S.: Repetitive self-observation by video-tape playback. *J Nerv Ment Dis, 141:* 29-41, 1965.

GIBB, J. R.: Defense level and influence potential in small groups. *Research Reprint Series,* No. 3. National Training Laboratories, Washington, D. C., 1960.

GIBB, J. R., and PLATTS, GRACE N.: Role flexibility in group interaction. *Amer Psychol, 5:* 491, 1950.

GRIVER, JEANETTE A.; ROBINSON, MARGARET, and COCHRAN, B. B.: Structured feedback: a motivational theory and technique for improving job performance and job attitudes. Symposium at American Psychological Association Convention, New York , 1966.

HILL, W. F.: *Hill Interaction Matrix.* Los Angeles, Youth Studies Center, U. of Sou. Calif., 1965.

KAGAN, N.; KRATHWOHL, D., and MILLER, R.: Stimulated recall in therapy using video tape: a case study. *J Counsel Psychol, 10:* 237-243, 1963.

LEARY, T. F.: *Interpersonal Diagnosis of Personality.* New York, Ronald, 1957.

McLUHAN, M.: *Understanding Media: The Extensions of Man.* New York, McGraw, 1964.

MEAD, G. H.: *Mind, Self, and Society.* Chicago, U. of Chicago, 1934.

MILES, M. B.: *Factors Influencing Response to Feedback in Human Relations Training.* New York, Horace Mann—Lincoln Institute of School Experimentation, Teachers College, Columbia, 1958.

MOORE, F. J.; CHERNELL, E., and WEST, M. J.: Television as a therapeutic tool. *Arch Gen Psychiat, 12:* 217-220, 1965.

MORENO, ZERKA.: A survey of psychodramatic technique. *Group Psychotherapy, 5:* 14-19, 1959.

ROGERS, C. R.: Toward a science of the person. In T. W. Wann (Ed.): *Behaviorism and Phenomenology.* Chicago, U. of Chicago, 1964. pp. 109-133.

RUESCH, J., and PRESTWOOD, A. R.: Anxiety: its initiation, communication, and interpersonal management. *Arch Neurol Psychiat, 62:* 527-550, 1949.

SCHIFF, S. B., and REIVICH, R. S.: Use of television as an aid to psychotherapy supervision. *Arch Gen Psychiat, 10:* 84-88, 1964.

SHIBUTANI, T.: *Society and Personality.* Englewood Cliffs, N. J., Prentice-Hall, 1961.

SLUCKIN, W.: *Minds and Machines.* Baltimore, Penguin, 1954.

SPITZER, R. S.; JACKSON, D. D., and SATIR, VIRGINIA M.: Resource paper: A technique for training in conjoint family psychotherapy. American Psychiatric Association Meeting, Los Angeles, 1964.

STOCK, DOROTHY: A survey of research on T-groups. In L. P. Bradford; J. R. Gibb, and K. D. Benne (Eds.): *T-Group Theory and Laboratory Method.* New York, Wiley, 1964, pp. 395-441.

STOLLER, F. H.: In TV and the patient's self-image. *Frontiers of Hospital Psychiatry,* 2 (7): 1-2, 9, 1965.
STOLLER, F. H.: Group psychotherapy on television: an innovation with hospitalized patients. *Amer Psychol.* 22: 158-162, 1967.
STRAUSS, A. (Ed.): *George Herbert Mead on Social Psychology.* Chicago, U. of Chicago, 1956.
SULLIVAN, H. S.: *The Interpersonal Theory of Psychiatry.* New York, Norton, 1953.
WALZ, R. G., and JOHNSTON, J. A.: Counselors look at themselves on video tape. *J Counsel Psychol,* 10: 232-236, 1963.
WHITMAN, R. M.: Psychodynamic principles underlying T-group processes. In L. P. Bradford; J. R. Gibb, and K. D. Benne (Eds.): *T-Group Theory and Laboratory Method.* New York, Wiley, 1964, pp. 310-335.
WIENER, N.: *The Human Use of Human Beings.* Garden City, N. Y., Doubleday, 1954.
WOODY, R. J.; KRATHWOHL, D. R.; KAGAN, N., and FARQUHAR, W.: Stimulated recall in psychotherapy using hypnosis and video tape. *Amer J Clin Hypnos,* 7: 234-241, 1965.

VIII

CONJOINT FAMILY THERAPY: FRAGMENTATION TO SYNTHESIS

Virginia M. Satir[*]

TRANSITION IN PSYCHOTHERAPY AND THE DEVELOPMENT OF FAMILY THERAPY

A LL things grow out of something. Nothing grows out of a vacuum! It only looks that way because the connections between then and now are not evident. The present reflects the connections to the past, specifically that which was useful and seems still to be workable and believable. Unfortunately, much of the present represents the "shoulds" of the past. Because of inevitable changes in time, place, situation and person, acquisition of new knowledge, and the passing of yesterday's experience into today's memory and tomorrow's fantasy, no formula in relation to human situations can be applied twice with exactly the same results.

There must have been a first time when one human being looked at another, did not recognize that other as like himself, and then felt frightened. Perhaps he ran away, killed the different one, captured and caged him, ate him, developed a protective myth, or labeled him a god whom he then worshiped. *Whatever happened,* he needed to protect himself in the presence of difference and explain the existence of the differentness.

Probably since the beginning of man's existence, he has observed and pondered upon the similarity of, and more important the differentness from, one person to another. Throughout history, the questions of what should be done about the latter, how it

* The author wishes to express her thanks to Richard L. Miller, Joan E. Zweben, and Susan M. Powers for their editorial assistance.

should be explained, what it should be called, and how it should be treated, must have arisen. On the other hand, the observation of similarities may have brought recognition, feelings of connection with the other, and a sense of personal security that over time may have become unnoticed or even boring.

If differentness were pleasing, interesting, or useful, it would have been desirable and something to acquire. If it were fearful, destructive, or strange, it would be undesirable and something to destroy. Perhaps the roots of modern psychotherapy were formed from the efforts to make the strange familiar, and to eliminate the destructive.

Originally, persons experienced as strange or destructive were regarded as deviants and consequently as trouble makers and outcasts. In the past the deviants of society acquired names that were identical with diagnoses—witch, idiot, pauper, criminal, and the sick. They were the *different ones*. These categories have been modernized: psychotic and neurotic, mentally retarded, public welfare recipient, indigent, the physically ill, and the physically handicapped. Perhaps the first recorded treatment of differentness was killing. In some ways we have not progressed from that. It is difficult in this year of 1967 to imagine a time when man acted only from instinct, with no awareness of how he functioned. For example, there was a time when man did not connect intercourse with conception. Children were thought to be born because of the way the sun or moon behaved. It is conceivable that some of the connections we are making today may look equally incongruous to future generations.

With the acquisition of new knowledge about how man's body works, how it gets sick, how it stays well, how man is related to other men, what makes this relatedness come out pleasant and productive, what makes it come out unpleasant, unproductive, and destructive, how man develops and educates his senses, deviancy became more and more understandable, and being more understandable, one knew how to label it, but not necessarily how to change it. The need for change became increasingly apparent, yet humane and successful ways were, and have been very much too long in their coming, probably because they are very difficult to achieve.

During the past century, *psychiatry* developed from taking care of the bizarre and unfamiliar; *psychology*, from the idiots who obviously had mind problems; *penology*, from the criminals; *social work*, from the indigent; *medicine*, from the physically ill; *sociology*, from the way man's context influenced his behavior; and *anthropology*, from man's curiosity about his own genus. The last two have only recently become pertinent to the practice of psychotherapy.

Each civilization has had deviants. At one time, labels were designated, causes ascribed, and treatment prescribed. This made sense at the time, given man's available knowledge about himself. A highly simplified overview of label, causation, and treatment in time emerges something like the following: Beginning with the labeling of deviancy such as witch, idiot, criminal, pauper, and the physically ill, the first theory of causation was probably unexplained, and the treatment resulted in death by direct or indirect means. As man progressed, he theorized that something from the supernatural entered the body that explained the deviancy. The treatment consisted of exorcizing the evil spirits by whatever method existed.

Later, theory pointed to genetic causation for which the treatment was again death by direction or neglect. A further step was to see deviance as a result of man's bad intentions, the treatment for which was corporal punishment and banishment. This approach appeared later in the philosophy of imprisonment, which unfortunately still exists today. The concept that deviancy was the result of living in an undesirable place or with undesirable persons, particularly in the case of children, led to a new form of treatment which was removal to an institution. Thus, custodial care came into being. Present day foster-care programs have derived from this background. Recently, deviancy was explained on the basis of man's unconscious, that is, a recognition that behavior was not altogether under conscious control. The treatment for this was to make the unconscious conscious.

Now, we are beginning to believe that the interactions between people are powerful shapers of the happenings between them. The obvious treatment is to change the interaction. It is just a next short step to noticing that over time people develop predictable actions and interactions toward each other—the human system concept. Again, the obvious treatment would be to change the system.

We are just now beginning to see that all the deviant labels have something very basic in common—a defective self concept, which is learned and maintained in interaction with others. This observation points to the fact that previously labeled categories of deviancy are but different forms of the manifestation of a defect in the self concept. For instance, mental retardation, delinquency, physical illness, and indigence can all occur in the same person at different times in his life, or be present simultaneously. Almost all forms of treatment known are still being used: death, punishment, removal, institutionalization, working with the unconscious, and dealing with interactions and human systems.

The etiology of deviancy has some relation to all previously known causes; part is unknown; part, genetic; part, intentions; part, environs; part, the people one lives with; part, the unconscious; part, the interaction between people; part, the system of their family, and part, the legal, social, and moral system which surrounds them. The diagnostic question is how are these parts interrelated? I think the major shaping factors are the family system and human interactions.

Initially, the individual who manifested the deviancy was the one who was treated. The person and his symptom were one. Furthermore, that person was all there was to explain the symptom. When the time came that a differentiation was made between a child and an adult, and it was known that adults, particularly mothers, had something to do with how children perceived themselves, the mother and child pair came to be used as the unit of treatment. This was the beginning of the recognition that interaction between people had something to do with how each behaved. The child guidance clinic came into existence. Fathers were introduced into child treatment much later, because it took a longer time to see that fathers also had something to do with how the child perceived himself. Through perhaps the awareness that one person could influence the behavior of another, symptomatic persons were brought together in groups of unrelated peers. Thus group therapy was born. Somewhere completely unrelated to this main stream, the marital unit was discovered. Gradually, the use of the marital unit was worked into the official mainstream of psychotherapeutic practice.

Starting with experience with the individual, then adding the parental—filial and the marital unit, it was but a next step to the use of the family as a treatment unit from which we have been evolving for the last ten years. Ways are now appearing as to how to use a whole community as a treatment unit.

The first officially recognized "therapists" probably came from religion. Religion concerned itself from the beginning with man's relationship to life, death, himself, and other men. As such, the official model for how man should be, came from religion. Different religions have developed different explanations and different models. These models have shifted and changed over the years. We are in a changing period now.

The development of knowledge in medicine, derived from physiology, suggested another model based on the health and ill health of the body. At a point in time, the religious model and the physical or medical model were opposed to one another. Sometimes a person would find himself in the conflicting situation of what would fit for his religion would not fit for his health. We seem to be in a stage now where there is the recognition that the needs of both must be met, and some bridges are being made. To meet one without the other is destructive in either case. Man has both a soul and a body. Each therapist had to put this together in some way. The way he does it cannot help but influence his therapeutic efforts.

Everyone has to start someplace. The innovations happen when one looks anew at things taken for granted, challenges past beliefs, experiments with hunches, trusts the senses, and is willing to act on new findings. Having done this, I find some past learnings remain valid, others assume different meanings and consequently have new uses. Some need to be totally discarded. I am continually sorting and shifting, not because of *who says it*, but because of what seems to work and fit. I hope the reader does likewise. This requires the willingness and courage to be wrong and alone at times. There are no right or single answers for all time, only those enabling us to act confidently now. If we keep our eyes and ears open and are willing to use what we perceive *now*, these answers become stepping stones to future questions, and create innovations.

This current period is an exciting time in which to be living. It is a period of obvious and rapid social change. The challenges and the potentials for meeting these challenges are infinite. At no time in the past have we had more knowledge about how man lives, grows, and works with others. Despite this, we have exploited all too little of this knowledge for better human living on a world-wide scale.

We human beings are a stubborn lot when it comes to changing. We represent centuries of seeking the *one* right way, assuming a face that shows we found it, and then denying reality to the contrary. The effect of this righteousness and masking obscures and retards learning about how human beings really are. New knowledge that does not fit in with the *one right way* could easily be suspect and therefore left unused. It is too easy to rationalize not using what one does not want to use.

Current innovations in psychotherapy exploit new as well as past knowledge and resources for the purposes of treating man's problems and enhancing his growth. How can man be helped to unlearn and learn anew when it has been amply demonstrated how tightly he hangs on to old learnings? How can he connect with his growth potential when much of this is obscured by his past learning, even though to continue dealing with the present in terms of this past guarantees inappropriate behavior and action in the present? All people can grow. I believe the therapeutic process is the discovery by an individual that he indeed possesses a growth potential. Contemporary innovations in therapeutic practice concern new ways of making this discovery.

I see psychotherapy as being the official "behavior change art." It is called by many names: psychiatry, psychology, social work, school counseling, probation work, public welfare, pastoral counseling, occupational therapy, remedial teaching, and rehabilitation. These are only a few. Presumably, people representing the above are invested with skills for changing another's behavior. People whose behavior is described by themselves or others as undesirable, deviant, destructive, inappropriate, undeveloped, sick, bad, stupid, crazy, or childish become the legitimate charge of the psychotherapists. These people are called patients, clients, and counselees.

Since the therapeutic endeavor concerns itself with the change process, the crucial question is, To what shall human behavior be changed? We have yet to define the process for achieving the full functioning and integration of a human being. What needs to be changed (goal), how it can be done (the plan), and the doing of it (the action) make up the flesh, blood, and bones of the therapeutic process. The depth and breadth of this process is an individual matter between the persons involved, and the burden is on the therapist. His conviction of the value of what he is doing, his hope for the outcome, his awareness of himself, his sensitivity to others, his skill in communication, his willingness to experiment, his knowledge about human growth and development, his theory of deviancy, his theory of achieving health, and his image of the fully functioning person are all powerful shapers of the treatment outcome.

Therapists fall roughly into three categories: (1) the "open" therapist, who is continually available to new knowledge and to experimenting with its use; (2) the "closed" therapist, who has found the *answer,* and who must then show that everything to the contrary is wrong—he comes awfully close to sitting next to God—, and (3) the "student" therapist, who must find, and blindly follow a leader with status, thus violating his own sense of creativity. Innonvations can come only from the first.

The knowledge areas in modern-day psychotherapy concern man's body, mind, senses, relationships, place in time and space situations, survival, learning, intimacy, productivity, and procreation. I have been referred to as one of the founders of a recent innovation in psychotherapy, namely family therapy. Simply stated, I have discovered ways to use the family as the unit for treatment when one of its members manifests deviancy.* I do not feel like a founder of anything, rather I feel that coming upon using the

---

* Deviancy is used here generically to mean any kind of difference from the expected social norm: delinquency, psychoses, neuroses, underdevelopment, mental retardation, psychosomatisizing.

family as a treatment unit is the natural outcome of an evolving process in me, what has gone before me, and what is going on around me. As I look further and experiment more, I will go beyond where I am now. The last word has not been spoken, nor will it ever be. There is no *one right way*. The tyranny of the single anwer has retarded our growth for many years.

For me at this point in time, there are several areas that are commanding my attention: developing a more holistic model of maturity, deepening my knowledge of human interaction, clarifying the process of evolving a self, developing a fuller use of communication, clarifying a goal of life, developing new models for intimacy between human beings, developing new models for making changes in behavior, and finding and making connections between and among the information which is now widely scattered in different disciplines, different fields of knowledge, and obscure journals. For me, the family, looked at in the system and in an interactional frame, provides the most fertile ground for searching.

Specialized knowledge inadvertently has built walls of separation and consequently ignorance among various disciplines. Therefore, any one speciality contains only partial knowledge about the behavior of man. How long has it been, for instance, since we have known that man's body is influenced by his thought, and conversely, that man's mind influences the way his body works? What is gradually becoming obvious is that we have knowledge in depth about pieces, but little knowledge yet about how the pieces connect with each other to form an operating integrated whole. Not all of behavior can be explained by the operation of man's body, by his internal processes, his interactional processes, his system, his role, his place in time and space, his history, or his values.

Present innovations also deal with working out a more holistic concept of man's behavior. This makes vast changes in the understanding of, and approach to, behavior. Approaches to therapy today can be understood in terms of what pieces of man's life are used to understand his current living. Limitations in a therapeutic approach can be understood similarly.

Psychotherapy has never been so rich in its potential for

change, nor have the forces requiring change been so strong. The statistics on personal casualities occasioned by divorce, alcoholism, crime, drug addiction, school failures, illegitimacy, and mental illness are mounting. The reality of continued war and the threat of extinction by nuclear means is ever present. The development of social psychiatry, community psychiatry, new developments in religion, the increasing use of audio and video equipment, community planning, development of the humanistic psychology movement, the growing emphasis on self-actualization, the human potential, a climate which rewards anything that will give hope in a very troubled world, and the emerging request for a positive model of human interaction are all factors which bear on current change in psychotherapeutic theory and practice. Many old questions are being reasked with some new answers forthcoming.

The current picture of the practice of psychotherapy, which has evolved largely in the last thirty years, has many faces. The setting could be almost anywhere: a room in a private home, church, institution, neighborhood center, or abandoned building, under the trees somewhere, or an official treatment office. The persons to be treated could be a single individual, a related pair of individuals, a group of unrelated peers, a whole family or groups of unrelated families. The process of selection of persons can be elaborate or nothing at all. Therapy can be done by a single individual, cotherapists of the same sex, a male-female team, or multitherapists. The change session can last anywhere from fifty minutes to twenty-four hours. Sessions can be scheduled on a regular time basis or as needed. Costs vary from nothing to one hundred dollars. Operating models can be growth, pathology, or behavior.

The therapeutic gown of the therapist ranges from the authoritarian expert to that of a participating member. Techniques employed are myriad. The therapist may work with the intrapsychic part of the person, the interactional part, as well as body movement, art, music, or any combination. The interesting thing is that all approaches work for some individuals. Some methods seem to work for more individuals than others. Some take longer than others. All therapists claim successes.

There must be a common factor to these methods and approaches. If we are not trapped by *the single answer,* we may discover the common thread more easily. When I grew up in my professional life, *being eclectic* was a "dirty" label. One was supposed to have one method and stick by it. Recently, being eclectic has come to mean more competence and progressing in a growth direction.

Basic phenomena relating to all human beings are relatively small in number. There are many semantic styles of expressing them, and many may look like a total phenomenon when they are in reality only a piece. Unless one translates this to its basic phenomenological meaning, one would miss this duplication. There is a difference between a hash house and a gourmet restaurant. Phenomenologically they are both places in which one can get food. The difference is in degree, not kind. I think many similar things exist in the social sciences.

As an example, the physical anatomy of any human being is now universally phenomenologically predictable. Any well-trained doctor now could operate on any human being. He would always know where to look for the esophagus, the heart, or the liver. This would not have been possible before the discovery of the basic universal anatomical makeup of man. There is something equivalent in man's relationship to himself and to other men. Yet, we have not found the key. The last fifty years have produced a variety of styles and techniques on therapeutic approaches, representing for the most part the innovations of a particular individual.

Psychoanalysis, group therapy, psychodrama, sensitivity training, role playing, gestalt therapy, transactional analysis, existential analysis, family therapy, reality therapy, rational therapy, operant conditioning, peak experiences, total encounter therapy, body movement therapy, art and music therapy, hypnotherapy, drug therapy, and various forms of self-help therapy represent names of methods of approach. All of these have one end in view: a change in current behavior. Some also hope for a change in the self concept as well. Some, in addition, aim for the growth in self-actualization and the development of creativity. I aim for all three—a change in behavior, a change in self concept, and a direction toward self-actualization. Currently on a phenomenological level, several concepts have been introduced that are new in the application of psychotherapy.*

CONCEPTS OF BEHAVIORAL CHANGE THROUGH THERAPY —A NEED FOR INTEGRATION

The first concept is the application of the system concept to human behavior. It simply means that all parts related to the same whole have an order of relationship among them. Further, anything that affects one part, affects every other part. The parts are continuously in motion and a balance is constantly sought. The selection of the parts is for the purpose of developing a whole. Any one part can be viewed as a whole in itself, but can also be part of a whole greater than itself which then has altogether different outcomes. I see this most obviously as it works in a family.

A man and a woman are each wholes in themselves. To produce a baby they have to get together. Since babies come into the world as undeveloped adults, the man and woman are essential to bringing the child to adulthood. How a man and a woman treat each other and experience each other and themselves becomes the basis for how the growing child will treat and experience them and himself. Over a period of time, this develops into a set of predictable actions and interactions among all of them—their system. The question is, Do these provide experiences in growth or in distortion?

At a point in time, an oversimplified description of the smallest family unit system is as follows: adult female (wife-mother), who does the talking, the adult male (husband-father), who is silent, and the child (son or daughter), who does the acting. The experience of these individuals would be entirely different if the adult female was silent, the adult male did the talking, and the child did the acting. To the individual in that family, the awareness would be experienced in terms of how that person *was*, rather than the expression of that person's ideas of how he was *supposed* to be to maintain himself in that system.

---

* For a fuller discussion of my theoretical approach see *Conjoint Family Therapy.* Science and Behavior Books, Inc., Palo Alto, 1964.

Changes in the system are made by changes in the experience of the individuals in those interactions. Changes in the self concept follow these new experiences. With the concept of system comes the idea of *reciprocal* growth processes, ways in which a member of the system can bring out the growth potential as well as the pathology of others, thereby enlarging or constricting his own sphere of healthy activity. In a very real sense we get sick together, get well together, and grow together. The notion of system has been well known and used in the natural sciences, the physical sciences and technology, but it has been introduced only recently into human behavior.

The second phenomenon has to do with measuring man's change as growth rather than as the absence of pathology. The therapeutic model has been a medical-disease one, which essentially treats the symptom as something to be destroyed. The growth model gives new meaning to man's behavior and treats this behavior as a manifestation of adaptation, rather than as the crux of his disease. Successful change primarily concerns itself with changes in man's adaptation rather than the eliminating of certain behavior. The medical model provided us with a useful starting point, but the essence of its limitation is that it refers to the mobilization of resources for survival. As therapists, we are not and cannot be restricted to this. We deal with adaptation not only in the sense of self-protection but also in the sense of reaching out and taking risks. In this way, the person defines the ways in which he is *not* like others, and once he thus crosses into the realm of individuality the medical model can contribute nothing.

Change is an inevitable outcome of living; differentness is an inevitable outcome of change. Therefore, the process of living inevitably brings differentness. It is, therefore, mandatory that we human beings know how to use differentness constructively and creatively. In differentness lies the aliveness in life, the stimulus to creativity, and the excitement of growing and learning.

All change is either neutral, destructive, or constructive. The successful therapeutic process enables the open, aware acknowledgment of change and promotes its constructive use. It is then feasible to evolve from destruction to construction, from despair into hope, from unreality into reality, from pain into growth, from stagnation into movement, and from separation to intimacy. The techniques in therapy are the literal means by which the therapist uses himself to initiate new ways to experience change and use differentness.

A third concept concerns the emphasis on the present. The present has ties to the past and to the future. If the present is experienced only in terms of the past, there is no new experience from the present to give new shape to the future. For me, the response to a report of something painful from the past is, How are you using it now? Does it fit now? What needs to be changed so it does fit now?—instead of spending time on the *why* of it. The *why* is useful for academic research, but it is wasteful in time and money for behavioral change.

In practice this means that one works from what is immediately happening among people present, and one uses the past only to illuminate the impasse of the present, for the purpose of *changing*, not buttressing the *status quo*. Dealing with what is immediately there among the persons present serves two purposes: to heighten the impact of the emotional realization, and to enable the therapist to carry the persons through the risk-taking process and the discovery of new ways of behaving. Thus, the therapist facilitates a process of synthesis, instead of just analysis.

A fourth concept is the use of the communication process as a diagnostic and change tool. My definition of communication is "the process that makes meaning between two people." This process can take five major forms: words, voice tone, facial expression, body tones and gesture, and dress, including style of hair and makeup. If the meaning from all five sources goes in the same direction, there is a congruent message which easily can be understood. If the meaning is contradictory within the five sources, then the perceiver gets an incongruent or double-level message. This calls on the perceiver to bridge the gap meaningfully between the levels. The way in which this is done influences the kind of interaction which, in turn, has its effect on the self concept and the happenings that ensue.

People who have blind spots in their awareness or who have rules of behavior that inhibit or prohibit them from honestly saying what they feel and think, or asking questions when there is a puzzle or a contradiction, almost always give double messages themselves and privately decide without checking it out what the real meaning is when a discrepancy exists. If one observes communication between people, it is easy to use the discrepancies and note how they are dealt with. This provides clues to how the individuals continue their distortions of themselves and others.

The therapist attempts to enter this dysfunctional system, to become an active participant in it, and by his communication to change this system. He does this in two ways. Specific therapist communications focus on points of potential change within the system; this kind of therapist activity is common to most therapies. Also, and more distinctive of my approach, is the therapist's use of his own self: the therapist, by his own example, demonstrates a healthier mode of communication. There is no double message in which the therapist prescribes directness and sharing of feelings, but models self-protection by clinging to his professional inscrutability.

A fifth concept has to do with the development of techniques to use the body as an instrument to develop awareness and a more direct way to get at individual integration problems. This grows out of a conviction that human problems, sexual and otherwise, result in part from disowning the body and body feelings. Relegating the body exclusively to the medical profession is but one form of this disowning. But neglected or not, the body also speaks, and learning one's own body language can help us contact the neglected parts of ourselves and make them our own.

Attitudes toward the body have been shaped by taboos, especially sexual attitudes. This has resulted in alienation of the body from the self. If one feels shame or rejection regarding a part of one's body, one cannot have a fully acceptable, positive self-image.

The senses—hearing, seeing, smelling, tasting, and feeling (tactile), are basic equipment of the body. Complete experience of the self depends upon developing the fullest possible use of the senses. Techniques for developing sensory awareness are already in use. The movement of the body parts is related to a positive self concept. Giving training in how to move body parts results in a change in the self concept.

The form of the body itself is important. For instance, a caved-in chest on a person would affect his breathing. Air is a necessary ingredient to body function. The freedom of the body parts to move separately from other parts as well as in harmony is reflected in a feeling of self. Muscles and ligaments that are not aligned constrict movement and reflect a constricted behavior.

Currently there is a growing awareness that we need a positive concept of mental health for man which seems to me a recognition that he has a soul, a body, senses, a mind, a relationship to others and to the world about him. The fully functioning, integrated human being has harmonious connections among all his parts. A theory of therapy that does not include all these parts will, by definition, be skewed in its outcome. It stands the chance of destroying one danger and creating another.

For me, at this time, given our knowledge and experience, it is not a matter of choosing one way, but of integrating what there is now available. It is with this *process of integration* that my theory of therapy is primarily concerned. For this, my primary tool is communication within an interactional, self concept, system frame, and working with and from the family as the basic treatment unit.

I operate on the belief that all behavior is learned, and the family members are the most impressive teachers. I further operate on the belief that what has been learned can be unlearned. The quickest and most effective way to work at change is in the family unit where the learning took place. I have become aware that all that the child learns does not represent what the adults were aware of teaching him or intended to teach him. Yet, what the child perceived whether intended or not is what he uses for his self concept.

I believe that *human processes* are universal. They just occur in different forms and manifestations. For me, the processes are the following:

> Man in relation to his body
> Man in relation to his beliefs and values
> Man in relation to time and place
> Man in relation to his commitments
> Man in relation to life and death.

These human processes have physical, sensory, intellectual, social, and spiritual components.

The desired goal for me is to help each person discover his processes, understand how each works now, and how they work together. And in the communication frame, help him to become aware, then to discover his expression of his awareness, and finally, to extend or change his uses to be more fitting to his hopes, ideas, and to his survival and continuing growth. He is then openly in touch with all his parts.

In the final analysis, it is the integrated wholeness (self concept) of an individual which shapes interaction, develops systems among human beings, determines communication, and which, in turn, shapes the manifestation of behavior that then gets translated into happenings and events.

SUMMARY

This chapter represents an attempt to trace the historical transition of theoretical concepts applied to explain the causes of deviancy or "differentness" of human behavior and the resultant treatments. I then described five concepts of behavioral change which I have attempted to integrate as an operational system of psychotherapy, namely conjoint family therapy. The five concepts of behavioral change which were utilized are the system concept (all parts related to the same whole have an order of relationship among them); measuring man's change as growth rather than the absence of pathology (growth model); emphasis on the present; use of the communication process as a diagnostic and change tool (by focusing on points of potential change within the system and using the therapist's own self as an example); and the greater utilization of the body and body parts as a more direct means of achieving individual integration.

I operate from the frame of reference that human processes are universal, that all behavior is learned, that what has been learned can be unlearned, and the family members are the most impressive teachers.

IX

INNOVATIONS IN GROUP PSYCHOTHERAPY WITH PREADOLESCENTS

Haim G. Ginott

C HILD therapists of different orientations make use of play materials in the treatment of young children. For the most part, the toys are in miniature, and the materials are soft and pliable, *i.e.* water, sand, clay, and paint. These play materials enable the young child to communicate vividly how he feels about himself and his world. He can express hidden feelings, rehearse forbidden dramas, and resolve interpersonal dilemmas. For the young child, activity is a native tongue; play is his talk, and toys are his words.

This statement does not hold true for older children. Toys lose their therapeutic effectiveness for children entering their teens. Baby bottles, family dolls, and similar toys cease to serve them as media of catharsis and as symbols of communication. On the contrary, such toys become psychonoxious in effect: they induce resistance against self-disclosure. In "Age and Suitability for Nondirective Play Therapy," Lebo (1956) stated, "The sight of 'baby' toys dissuades twelve-year-olds from speaking. They seem to feel such toys are beneath them and that the playroom is not theirs" (p. 236). And Dorfman (1951) observed that "A young adolescent may be quite humiliated at finding himself compelled to occupy a room where everything is in miniature" (p. 265). She suggested "to allow those of approximately eleven years and over to choose between the playroom and an office, after inspection of each" (p. 265).

Dorfman's choice does not solve the problem; for neither play nor interviews are suitable therapeutic media for preadolescents.

272

They giggle themselves to death about the mere idea of sitting in one room with an adult and playing a table game while that adult desperately pretends that this is all there is to it. . . . They find it funny that they should try and remember how they felt about things and . . . [be] constantly expected to have worries or fears—two emotions they are most skillful at hiding from their own self perception, even if they do occur. Most of these youngsters seriously think the adult himself is crazy if he introduces such talk. . . . They naively enjoy the troubles they make and they would much rather bear the consequences of their troubles than talk about them (Redl, n.d., pp. 4-5).

The question remains, What is the treatment of choice for children who are too old for play therapy, and too young for interview therapy?

GROUP PSYCHOTHERAPY WITH PREADOLESCENTS

With disturbed children, ages ten to thirteen, this writer has used a specific method of group therapy, exclusively or in addition to individual therapy. While the conceptual framework is derived from psychoanalytic theory (Ginott, 1958; 1961; 1965), the practice is designed specifically to meet the needs of preadolescents. Many of the preadolescents seen in therapy fall into one of two categories: the acting-out and the overinhibited.

The acting-out children are those who in their manifest behavior can be described as tense, restless, excitable, impulsive, hyperactive, angry, aggressive, provocative, domineering, verbose, critical, rebellious, and disobedient. Their greatest defect is their proneness to discharge emotional stress in physical acts, and their greatest need is for a decrease of inner tensions and an increase of inner controls.

The overinhibited are children who, according to their manifest behavior, can be described as withdrawn, submissive, silent, fearful, shy, isolated, uncommunicative, inarticulate, overcompliant, constricted, meek, passive, emasculated, and ineffectual. The greatest affliction of these children is social isolation and their greatest need is the opportunity for free, safe, and respectable interpersonal communication.

Inhibited children usually prefer quiet and safe activities in therapy, while the therapeutic aim is to lead them to more vigorous forms of expression. The acting-out engage in boisterous and destructive activities, while the therapeutic objective is to lead them to more focused and more modulated forms of expression. The therapy setting must contain activities and materials conducive to development of controls in the overactive and of spontaneity in the overinhibited.

EFFECTIVE SUBSTITUTES FOR AGGRESSION

In the clinical experience, traditional materials have proven more appropriate for inhibited, than for aggressive preadolescents. Painting, model building, woodwork, and similar activities provide fearful and withdrawn children with safe channels for communication and socialization. Aggressive youngsters, however, find it difficult to accept such activities as substitutes for direct acting-out. They fail to use the equipment for its purpose: they turn all tools into torpedoes and all materials into missiles.

> A group that met in an office building almost tore down the place during the first few months. The boys invaded the dozen or more private offices, ransacked desks, appropriated candy, toys, and other objects, pulled telephone plugs, shouted profanities into dictaphones, clogged toilets, broke the panes of glass in doors and windows, hid paper and window poles, scratched walls and burned paper and wood on the floors (Slavson, 1943, p. 226).

The conclusion is that disturbed preadolescents who cannot bring themselves under control in the traditionally equipped room, need a different kind of therapy setting, one that allows for safe and respectable expression of direct aggression. A setting that does not provide them with *absorbing substitutes for aggression* can lead to uncontrolled acting-out and to further disorganization of personality.

In the course of searching for a solution to the problem of belligerent preadolescents, a setting was developed that meets the needs of both the aggressive and the inhibited youngsters. The new setting contains, in addition to suitable traditional equipment and activities, also unorthodox ones: facilities for fire making and wood burning, modern communication devices, and penny-arcade-type machines.

Fire in Therapy

Fire is a most therapeutic agent for aggressive preadolescents. It holds a magic fascination for them. They can spend hours absorbed in lighting matches, making fires, and burning wood. In the process, they burn up a great deal of hostility which ordinarily is directed against parents, siblings, teachers, and society.

At the end of a therapy session, Andy's mother said to her ten-year-old son, "What are you burning there? I bet you have burned your brother and sister and me and Daddy."

"Oh, never Daddy!" exclaimed Andy.

Safety is, of course, a prime consideration. The wood is burned in an enamel basin, half-filled with water, and set on a large asbestos pad. A pail of water is nearby in case of emergency. Three or four children sit around the basin, feeding the fire on the floating piece of wood. Fire making is limited to the basin. The rule of the room is "Fire over water." Only wood and small candles are for burning. For the sake of safety, paper, plastic, and other quickly consumed materials are banned from the fire. The therapist oversees the fire at all times. While the wood or candles are burning, the therapist does not leave the room even for a moment. The box of matches stays in his possession at all times, and no child is allowed to take a match out of the room. The therapist is keenly aware that the price of fire play is eternal vigilance.

From the first session, the therapist establishes himself as a giving person. He holds the matches and the candles (birthday) and he hands them out one at a time on request. The children react with utter disbelief, because whenever they ask for a match or for a candle, the therapist graciously complies. Never before have they encountered such a responsive adult, and they are bewildered. They take many sessions to test the therapist, until they are convinced of his friendliness and strength.

One eleven-year-old boy who never said anything to the therapist except, "May I have another match?" stopped his activities during one session, turned to the other boys and said, "Our Doc is nice." The same boy was overheard saying to his father, "You won't believe it, but he let us use a million matches."

Fire can be used beneficially by most children: the aggressive and the fearful, the gifted and the slow, the social and the silent. The aggressive use the fire daringly. They hold the lit match in their hands until it is consumed, and their wood burning becomes a bonfire. Often, the fire stimulates them to express their hostile fantasies: "No school tomorrow," said twelve-year-old Bruce. "It was burned down today. Pity! It was such a n-i-c-e disgusting school! See the ashes? The teacher was burned too. S-o s-o-r-r-y!"

Inhibited children are initially afraid to light matches. They stand at a safe distance, not daring to approach the fire. Yet they follow with eager eyes the activities of the other children. They are frightened by the permissiveness of the adult and fascinated by the daring of the other boys. In time, they move from passive observation to active participation. First, they ask the therapist to light a match for them and put it on a piece of wood they have chosen. Slowly, they gain courage to light the match themselves. Finally, they feel free to start a fire by themselves and to cooperate with other boys.

It cannot be overemphasized that growth is always grounded in relationships; only when he comes to trust the therapist, does the fearful child venture into new media and new relations.

Sexually inadequate boys especially may benefit from fire play. The symbolic meaning of the activity is not lost on these children. Like music, it talks to the unconscious. They encounter an adult male who allows them to use a big match with a red top, that lights up when rubbed. Dramatically, many boys choose to light the match on the zipper of their fly. Symbolically, they are granted potency, and they sense it.

In summary, fire play is readily available, inexpensive, captivating in process, and therapeutic in effect. Yet, few therapists make use of it. The reluctance may stem from realistic fear of possible dangers or from personal discomforts and restrictions. However, under proper safeguards, fire play is a most valuable therapeutic tool. It attracts the withdrawn and the insulated, it appeals to the sexually inadequate, and it offers the belligerent the most absorbing substitute for direct aggression that a therapy setting can provide.

Modern Communication Devices

A tape recorder, a walkie-talkie, and a typewriter have a useful function in therapy with preadolescents: they directly encourage conversation and communication. Few youngsters can resist the temptation of broadcasting over a walkie-talkie, recording on a tape, or typing on a typewriter. It is easier for a therapist to make contact, even with resistant children, when they need his help in activating these fascinating devices.

The very presence of this type of equipment reflects permissiveness. Such gadgets are usually associated in children's experience with parental restrictions and punishment. Many children have been scolded for tampering with mother's typewriter, fooling with brother's transistor radio, or playing with father's tape recorder. The availability of these machines for their own use communicates, loud and clear, the permissiveness of the setting and the tolerance of the therapist. The author can still recall the look of amazement on the face of a preadolescent, the son of a writer, who exclaimed in disbelief, "What! A typewriter for children?"

The communication devices allow preadolescents to experiment in safety: they can type or tape infantile and hostile wishes at one moment and erase them the next. They easily can conceal what they do not want to reveal. They can do and undo with impunity. The reversibility of the media makes it safe for them to explore their inner world. They discover that they can express forbidden fantasies without dooming themselves and destroying others.

Penny-Arcade-Type Machines

Every therapy setting must provide media for relationship, catharsis, insight, reality testing, and sublimation appropriate for the patient's age. Penny-arcade machines offer such media for disturbed preadolescents. The machines are interesting and absorbing. They are neither too easy nor too difficult to operate, thus being a challenge but not an insurmountable obstacle for preadolescents. Each machine is chosen with a specific therapeutic purpose in mind.

A rifle gallery provides both the aggressive and the timid with safe outlets for hostility. It allows the belligerent child to discharge aggression without becoming overstimulated and without interfering with other group members. It allows the fearful child to stay away from threatening group activities, while offering him a target for repressed hostility. The hyperactive child finds in the shooting gallery an activity that demands attention and focus. Since his hits and misses are electrically recorded, he is motivated to greater concentration. The impulsive child learns to postpone reactions when he discovers that better results can be achieved with concentrated effort.

A boxing machine provides energetic boys with a much needed chance to use their muscles vigorously. Some children, who in the past expressed themselves by annoying groupmates, find in the machine a means of showing their might without infringing on the rights of others. The machine records the strength of each boxing blow, a fact that motivates the boxers to further efforts. However, after a period of boxing, even an aggressive child becomes ready to engage in more sedentary activities. The boxing machine is of special importance to anxious and fearful preadolescents who happen to possess physical strength. Their powerful punch, reflected publicly in high scores on the electric panel, makes an impression on themselves and their groupmates, conferring upon them unexpected recognition.

An electric bowling table has a socializing effect on withdrawn preadolescents: several children can play the game at the same time. It involves taking turns, obeying rules, evaluating outcomes, giving and taking advice, learning from experience, perfecting skills, and achieving success. Even an isolated child cannot long resist an invitation from groupmates to join such an interesting enterprise. The game allows children who cannot sustain close contact to become a part of the group without having to go beyond their depth in personal relationships.

Penny-arcade machines are of special value to children who are too suspicious or too fearful to relate directly to an adult. The games enable them to play by themselves until they are ready to relate to other children and the therapist. The machines minimize failure because almost every trial results in a score. This fact diminishes the boys' fears and encourages them to participate in the group. Similarly, the machines have a beneficial effect on children whose self-image is damaged and who therefore expect nothing but defeat. Such children are apathetic toward the usual materials and activities. However, their interest is aroused and challenged by the electric games, and they react with curiosity and sustained efforts. Practice brings greater skill which is reflected in higher scores and increased self-confidence. Many children discover that they possess abilities that they have never known. As one boy who scored high on the rifle gallery said, "All my life I was an expert shot and didn't know it." The consequent enhancement of self-image cannot be underestimated.

Belligerent preadolescents, who are unable to participate peacefully in ordinary group activities, play these machine games in a comparatively calm manner. Even impatient boys exhibit considerable frustration tolerance while waiting for their turn. Impulse control is promoted by the emergence of group mores, or "a primary group code"; the boys themselves see to it that the law is enforced and that group members play according to the rules.

The machines are necessary primarily during the initial phase of treatment; subtly and successfully they direct the children's aggression from people to objects. In due time the children's aggression subsides, their security increases, and their interest turns toward group members and the therapist.

As treatment progresses, some of the machines and equipment may be taken out of the room or "out of commission." The purpose is to have more time for discussion of problems and exploration of personality. The group may spend the first part of the session in work and play and the latter part sitting around a table for refreshments and discussion.

The special setting for group therapy described here is designed primarily (though not exclusively) for aggressive preadolescent boys. Preadolescent girls, aggressive as they may be, are not so physically destructive or belligerent as boys. They are able to express their aggression verbally. Depending on clinical indications, they can be seen either in regular interview therapy (individual or group) or in activity group therapy (Slavson, 1943; 1947).

CRITERIA FOR SELECTION OF PREADOLESCENTS
FOR GROUP THERAPY

Not all disturbed preadolescents can benefit from group therapy; some require individual treatment. However, for the majority of them, group therapy is the treatment of choice. Some preadolescents are not accessible to any other type of treatment, and for some, individual treatment is contraindicated. The point is that group therapy is not a substitute for individual therapy. It is beneficial only in specific cases which are clinically selected and grouped. When composed haphazardly, groups can be not only ineffective, but psychonoxious.

Because of recent popularity of group methods, valid criteria for selection in grouping are urgently needed. Yet, there are few, if any, such criteria. The writer knows of no convincing experimental studies in this area. Personal communications from colleagues brought little clarity: for each therapist who found certain children unsuitable for treatment in groups there was one who reported success with just such children.

The following guidelines for selection of preadolescents for group therapy are derived from theoretical considerations and practical experience. They are based on informal experimentation and *post hoc* study of clear successes and definite failures in group treatment. The criteria are educated hypotheses—to be tested and revised in light of new knowledge.

The Basic Criterion

The basic prerequisite for admission to group therapy is a capacity (actual or potential) for social hunger—a need to be accepted by peers and a desire to attain status and maintain esteem in a group. In return for peer acceptance, the child is willing to modify impulses and change behavior. He begins to play, talk, and behave like other group members.

The desire for acceptance stems for satisfactory primary relations with a mother (or substitute) who, by fulfilling the infant's needs, imprinted him with the value of and craving for affection and approval.

Children who in infancy missed sustaining contact with a

mother figure are not suitable candidates for group therapy. Because their first relations have failed them, they suspect all relations. Having had no experience that made delay or sacrifice worthwhile, they find it difficult to delay gratifications and modify behavior in exchange for acceptance. Anna Freud stated, "If infants are insecure and lacking in response owing to a basic weakness in their first attachment to mother, they will not gain confidence from being sent to a nursery group. Such deficiencies need attention from a single adult and are aggravated, not relieved, by the strain of group life" (1949, p. 60). This statement holds true also for therapy groups.

Information about a child's social hunger should be available before his assignment to group therapy. This information cannot be obtained from tests alone. Complete case histories are also necessary. They should contain detailed descriptions of the complaints and symptoms for which the child was referred, his physical size and appearance, his level of maturity, his typical modes of reaction to frustration, his adjustment to school and peers, and his characteristic use of leisure time. The assumption is that the child will show toward the therapist and group members some of the same behavior which he shows toward his parents and siblings. The case data enable the therapist to anticipate each child's behavior in the group and to plan specific remedial situations and responses.

INDICATIONS FOR GROUP THERAPY

What follows are brief descriptions of preadolescents for whom group therapy is a treatment of choice.

Immature Preadolescents

Some preadolescents have been so overindulged and overprotected as children that they are unprepared for the realities of life outside the family. They have had little opportunity to develop sensitivity to the needs and feelings of others. They find it difficult to share possessions or to delay gratifications. They are spoiled and want what they want when they want it. They show excessive dependence upon parents, siblings, and playmates, and they annoy everyone with their constant demand to be waited on and catered to. Preadolescents who remain infants are constantly involved in conflicts. They create tension at home, turmoil in school, and quarrels in the neighborhood.

Group psychotherapy is of particular value to immature preadolescents. The group offers motivation and support for growing up, as well as a safe arena for trying out new patterns of behavior. In the group, they learn what aspects of their behavior are socially unacceptable, and what behavior is expected. As a result, they make an effort to adjust to the standards of their peers. In the group, they acquire a variety of essential social techniques: they learn to share materials and activities, as well as the attention of a friendly adult. They learn to compete and to cooperate, to fight and to settle fights, to bargain and to compromise. These techniques prepare them to deal with peers on an equal footing.

Withdrawn Preadolescents

Group therapy is the treatment of choice for withdrawn preadolescents with varied psychodynamic etiologies. They are extremely ill at ease in all interpersonal situations. They are unable to express ordinary feelings of affection and aggression, have no friends or playmates, and avoid social give-and-take.

Withdrawn preadolescents find it difficult to relate to a therapist in individual treatment. They continue their habitual withdrawl patterns in the therapy setting. They spend many hours working silently in the corner of the room. They choose quiet and safe activities and avoid spontaneity and risk.

These isolated preadolescents are reached more readily in group therapy than in individual therapy. The friendly adult, the enticing materials, and the groupmates make it difficult for them to stay within their shells. The mild pressures of the therapeutic group accelerate their emergence from isolation. By demonstrating that self-expression is safe, the group lessens their fears and induces them to participate in peer activities. An optimal group for withdrawn preadolescents is one that is active but mild.

Overreliance on Reaction Formation

Some preadolescents are referred to therapy because they are "too good." They are obedient, orderly, and neat. They are concerned about mother's health, father's finances, and little sister's safety. Their whole life is oriented toward pleasing others.

A frequently noticed symptom in such children is chronic fatigue. Under the "goody goody" mask, many a bad impulse is hidden. The effort of transforming hostile impulses into angelic behavior and the eternal vigilance required to maintain this facade consume the life energy of these children.

Preadolescents who overrely on reaction formation need group therapy, at least at the beginning of treatment. In individual therapy, they may continue their established pattern of "altruistic surrender." They act meek and gentle, and spend much of the time propitiating the therapist, whom they fear. They bring him gifts, sing him songs, draw pictures for him, and volunteer to clean up the room. They tell him how nice a person he is, and how much they like him. This is their way of saying how afraid they are of their aggressive impulses and of the therapist's expected retaliation.

Group therapy provides an effective setting for modifying reaction formation behavior. By observing the aggressive behavior of groupmates and the consistently nonretaliatory reactions of the therapist, these preadolescents slowly begin to allow their own impulses to gain some expression. First through spectator therapy and then through actual experience, they learn that there is no need to be ingratiating and self-effacing. They feel safe to give up dutiful compliance toward adults, and to assume normal assertiveness.

Overreliance on Projection and Rationalization

Preadolescents who use projection and rationalization as their main adjustment techniques are best treated in groups. In individual therapy, they may continue for a long time successfully to resist facing any unpleasant truth about themselves. They are experts in excusing failure, in blaming others, and in deceiving themselves. Any attempt by the therapist to deal with these defenses will only reinforce them. The therapist himself would become a target for accusations, projections, and blame.

In a group, these mechanisms are effectively unmasked by

other members. Their reactions are often powerful and penetrating as illustrated in the following example.

> George, aged ten, is always complaining that the teacher picks on him, and makes his life miserable.
>
> David, (aged eleven): What does she do?
>
> George: She says my homework is sloppy, and she sends notes to my mother.
>
> David: Is it sloppy?
>
> George: She doesn't like the special handwriting that I use, and she picks on me.
>
> David: You are full of shit! You're asking for trouble, and gettin' it. Don't write sloppy, and she'll leave you alone.
>
> For a minute George stood dumbfounded. The words hit him like a bolt of lightning.
>
> George: You are right. Anything to get her off my back!

Many preadolescents who resist insights from adults are willing to accept them from other group members.

Phobic Preadolescents

Preadolescents whose anxiety is expressed in specific displaced fears benefit greatly from group therapy. Some youngsters are compulsively clean. They fear any speck of dust on their hands or clothes and become distressed if they cannot wash it off immediately. Other children are afraid of loud noises, high places, dark rooms, or small insects. They handle their anxiety by avoiding places and activities that seem dangerous to them.

In individual therapy, a phobic youngster can continue to escape his anxiety by avoiding frightening situations and objects. He may restrict his mobility and confine himself to a few safe activities. In group therapy, however, other children are likely to engage in activities that will require the phobic child to do something about his neurotic fears. They may shoot loud guns, spill paint, turn out the lights, or make fires. The group makes it hard for the phobic preadolescent to escape facing his problems. The therapist can then deal with the fearful reactions as they occur. He strikes while the iron is hot. He helps the child to talk out his frantic fears and to master his vague anxieties in the very situation that aroused them. In individual therapy, it may take a long time for the child even to confront his problem.

Effeminate Boys

In psychotherapy one encounters some boys who have been brought up like girls. They usually come from matriarchal households, where father is either weak or absent or where they were the only boy in the family of many females. Since their primary identifications have been with nonmasculine models, these boys cannot help but assume some feminine roles. They may lack the characteristic aggressiveness expected of boys in our culture. They may shy away from rough games or be unable to mingle freely with other boys. They feel more comfortable in the company of girls. Such boys usually receive rough treatment from other children. They are nicknamed, attacked, and abused. They are socially stigmatized and emotionally scarred, and they often grow up to be inadequate adults.

Group therapy with a male therapist is the recommended treatment for such boys. Individual therapy is contraindicated because a close relationship with a male therapist may activate latent homosexuality, while a female therapist cannot meet the boy's needs for masculine identification. A nonintense relationship with a male therapist, masculine toys and activities, and the company of boys provide the optimal curative elements for treatment of effeminate boys. The group therapist serves as an identification model without strong libidinal ties. The materials and group members call forth the masculine components of personality without arousing anxiety. The setting as a whole encourages assertiveness without fear of retaliation.

Aggressive Preadolescents (Conduct Disorders)

Many preadolescents are referred to therapy because of conduct disorders such as fighting, cruelty, truancy, and general misbehavior. They engage in aggressive behavior only on a part-time basis; it occurs at home, but not outside of it, or vice versa. Their hostility is reactive. Their core problem is an unconsciously retaliatory way of life against real or imagined mistreatment by parents. Because their parents failed them, they are suspicious of all authority.

The most difficult task in treating these children is the establishment of a relationship of trust. They fear the therapist, distrust his kindliness, and cannot tolerate his permissiveness. They aggressively avoid close relationship with him by acting obnoxious and hostile. The directness of individual treatment is too intense for children with conduct disorders. Because of its diluted relationships, group therapy is the more appropriate treatment method. "The group acts as an insulator for them, diluting much of the tension that would otherwise exist if the children had no means of escape from closer contact with the worker."* At the same time, mild pressures from group members and the therapist's timely interventions help these preadolescents to achieve self-control.

Habit Disorders

Some preadolescents exhibit persistent mannerisms and behavior that are annoying to adults. They squint, sniff, grimace, pick their noses, bite their nails, crack their knuckles, and tap their feet. The contortions and mannerisms may be so obvious and grotesque that they compel attention. There is no escape from the discordant sounds of nose, throat, knuckles, and feet. In addition, there may be vocal displays of temper.

When these are the main difficulties and there is no evidence of more serious pathology, these habit disorders are symptoms of thwarted strivings towards independence. In most cases these difficulties did not begin in infancy but appeared at a later stage as a result of parents' inability to cope with their children's emerging independence.

Children with habit disorders readily benefit from group therapy. Their strivings for independence are encouraged by the permissiveness of the setting, the tolerance of the adult, and by identification with more autonomous group members.

Children with deeper pathology may also manifest habit disorders in addition to other symptoms. For such children, the treatment of choice will depend on the differential diagnosis.

---

* Schiffer, M.: Special Group Process in Guidance, (Unpublished manuscript, n.d.).

Preadolescents Without Siblings

Group therapy is recommended for disturbed preadolescents who are "only children" in their family. (Some of them may also need individual treatment.) Pampered by parents, they expect immediate gratification from the rest of the world. They are deficient in their ability to share possessions and feelings with their peers. They are narcissistic, grandiose, and conceited. They expect the world to be their oyster.

The group offers them a corrective experience: it confronts them with a reality where sharing is expected and compelled. In the group they learn to surrender self-centeredness in exchange for acceptance and camaraderie.

CONTRAINDICATIONS FOR GROUP THERAPY

What follows are brief descriptions of preadolescents for whom group therapy is unsuitable as the sole treatment method.

Preadolescents With Accelerated Sexual Drives

Some preadolescents seen in therapy evidence maladjustment that stems from impaired psychosexual development. They show premature and persistent preoccupation with sexual matters. They dream, think, and talk sex. They masturbate habitually and try to engage in sexual explorations with other children including brothers and sisters. They peek and peep, and attempt to catch their parents in sexual relations.

These are children who have been exposed to sexual overstimulation. They may have slept in their parents' bedroom, shared a bed with brother or sister, or been fondled erotically by a deviant adult. At any rate, sex is on their mind too much and too soon. Children with such libidinal distortions need treatment in depth, and should be seen in individual therapy. They need the strong transference relationship, the direct interpretations, and the insights that only individual treatment can provide.

Perverse Sexual Experiences

Preadolescents who have actively engaged in homosexual relations are excluded from group therapy. They may activate latent homosexual tendencies in others or initiate groupmates in undesirable practices.

Psychopathic Preadolescents

In clinical practice one encounters preadolescents who act as though they had no conscience. They are shallow, selfish, impulsive, and capable of committing extreme cruelties without apparent guilt or anxiety. They seem to lack the capacity for empathy and are strikingly unconcerned about the welfare of others. They may appear charming and solicitous, but they are cold and distant. They are, as one mother put it, "all take and no give."

Psychopathic preadolescents like to come to group therapy. They seldom miss a session. However, they make life miserable for the group; they bully groupmates, monopolize materials, and attempt to manipulate the therapist. They block progress in therapy by preventing other children from autonomous activities. Neither reflection of feelings nor direct interpretations have any effect. They resist introspection and are quick to change the subject when their behavior is discussed. Limits (Ginott, 1959) are also ineffective with psychopathic preadolescents; they sneak past them and continue their corrosive acts. Even direct censure and criticism have little effect on these children. They are indifferent to what others think of them.

To prevent group disruption, psychopathic preadolescents must be excluded from permissive therapy groups. Individual therapy that calls for close interpersonal relations, is also unsuitable for them. Because of their rejection of all authority, they cannot accept the therapist either. Slavson (1947) suggests that psychopathic preadolescents should be seen not in a clinical setting but in a group "of an authoritarian nature such as institutions provide" (p. 106).

Destructive Preadolescents

Group therapy is contraindicated if aggression stems from deep-rooted hostility, homicidal tendencies, or a masochistic need to activate punishment. The permissive atmosphere of the group only encourages the destructive impulses of such preadolescents. They cannot be allowed even the usual leeway for acting-out, as free discharge of aggression brings them neither relief nor insight. It only results in further disorganization of personality. Therapeutic restraints must be put on their acting-out to compel them to "look before they leap" and to think before they act. This policy cannot be carried out in a permissive group setting because of the detrimental effect that it may have on other group members.

Habitual Stealing

Preadolescents with long histories of stealing need individual treatment. Persistent stealing is a serious symptom representing intense hostility against authority. These children show total disregard of property rights; they engage in petty and not so petty pilfering whenever an opportunity presents itself. They may steal at home, school, supermarket, or from neighbors. Therapy may be a prolonged process because such deep hostility is not so easily dissolved. Group therapy is contraindicated because these children carry over into the miniature society of the group their deep resentment against adult society. They steal from group members, the therapist, and the room. They may also initiate group members into the art of thievery.

Preadolescents who steal only at home may be placed in group therapy. Stealing at home may just be a bid for affection or an act of revenge for unkind treatment. The stealing impulse subsides when the group (family substitute) meets the child's needs for acceptance and approval.

Recent Trauma

Preadolescents exposed to severe trauma or sudden catastrophe may develop acute symptoms even in the absence of underlying personality disturbance. A child may react with overwhelming anxiety to a fire, an auto accident, or the death of a beloved person, and he may develop dramatic symptoms that differ only in etiology from the symptoms of neurosis or psychosis.

Prompt individual therapy is the preferred treatment for these traumatized preadolescents. Anxiety generated by recent traumatic events can be dissipated by the child's repeated symbolic reenactment of the events. Resolution of intense anxiety and recession of acute symptoms occur more readily when the child can focus his talk or symbolic play on the content of his trauma. This can best be accomplished in a setting where there are no distractions from other children and where the therapist can give his undivided attention to the frightened child.

Intense Sibling Rivalry

Some preadolescents evidence intense hatred towards brothers and sisters. Their jealousy pervades their whole personality and colors their life. They abuse their siblings both physically and verbally. They seem unable to share the attention of a friendly adult be it a parent, a teacher, or a therapist. Neither are they able to share "worldly goods." At a party or at home they do not hesitate to appropriate for themselves most of the ice cream, candy, cake, or toys. They would prefer to hide what they cannot use, rather than to share it.

Preadolescents with such intense sibling rivalry are excluded from group therapy. They see all group members as substitute siblings and treat them accordingly. The permissive atmosphere encourages them to act out openly their intense hostility. In a thousand and one ways they victimize their groupmates: they grab their materials, interfere with their activities, and even abuse them physically. Such relentless hostility cannot be worked through in group therapy. These children must first be seen in individual treatment before they can relate to children in groups. Less intense sibling rivalry, however, can be treated in group therapy.

COMPOSITION OF GROUPS

The effectiveness of group treatment depends on the harmonious combination of patients. The presence of even one misfit in a group may create enough discord to block therapy. What follows is a discussion of factors to be taken into account in the composition of preadolescent therapy groups.

Corrective Identifications

Preadolescents must be so grouped that they exert a corrective influence upon each other. The group should consist of children with dissimilar syndromes, so that each child will have the opportunity to associate with personalities different from, and complementary to his own. An effeminate boy may derive ego strength from associating with an accepting masculine playmate. An overprotected child may become more independent by identifying himself with more autonomous group members. The tendency to withdraw into fantasy, so characteristic of the schizoid, is likely to be dispelled more by reality-oriented members. (When he builds castles in the air, the schizoid boy may be quickly brought back to earth by the prosaic question, And how much is the rent?) Hyperkinetic children may become less active and more introspective under the neutralizing influence of calmer groupmates. Withdrawn children should have the opportunity to model themselves after outgoing groupmates. Fearful children should be in the company of more courageous youngsters. Infantile children should be placed in a group with more mature children. Aggressive preadolescents must be put with others who are strong but not belligerent. Every therapy group should contain a variety of identification models to encourage corrective relations.

Optimal Tension

Groups, like individuals, have their limits for tolerating tension and anxiety. Groups that are continually in a state of agitation are psychonoxious in effect. The tides of hostility and acting-out in a therapy group must ebb and flow. A group composed only of aggressive preadolescents is contraindicated. It creates excessive tension because belligerent children reinforce each other's aggression. A group composed only of quiet children is also contraindicated. It fails to create sufficient tension to bring out each child's dynamics. An optimal group arrangement calls for several quiet children and not more than two who are aggressive.

A Haven From Ridicule

Another important consideration in grouping is to prevent children from experiencing in therapy the noxious influences of their outside life. Thus, an undersized, submissive boy should not be put in a rough group in which he will be dominated. In a wild group he will be stamped a "sissy." In a mild group he may be able to stand his ground. A child who has been defeated by more capable siblings should not be put in a group with highly intelligent children. Children who have been stigmatized because of physical appearance, or racial background should not be put in groups in which they are likely to reencounter ridicule. Therapy must be a haven from persecution that fosters freedom from fear.

Siblings and Friends

Siblings should not be assigned to the same group. In therapy, a child should not have to be concerned with taking care of a younger sister or being bossed by an older brother. He should be free to pursue his own activities and not have to keep up with or hold back for a sibling.

Likewise, friends should not be placed in the same group. One of the aims of psychotherapy is to replace old attitudes and relationships with new ones. The presence of familiar persons sometimes tends to freeze one in old patterns of behavior, thus blocking reorientation of attitudes.

Delinquent Heroes

Special care must be exercised to prevent antisocial children from becoming dominant figures in a group. Delinquents may glamorize criminal behavior, attain hero status in a group, and serve as undesirable models of identification. To minimize his influence, a delinquent boy should be put with children two or three years older than himself. To maximize the therapeutic impact, it should be an ongoing group not a new one; there should be only one such boy to a group.

Group Size

The number of preadolescents in a therapy group should not exceed five. A large group becomes too lively and makes it impossible for the therapist to observe the minute-by-minute activities of all the children and to react to each child in light of his dynamics.

Age

Chronological age is an important consideration in assigning preadolescents to therapy groups. Group members should not differ in age by more than two years. However, other considerations may take precedence over age. An immature preadolescent rejected by his peers may first be placed in a group with younger children. An oversized or belligerent preadolescent may be assigned to a group of older children. As they grow in maturity and social adaptability, such preadolescents can be transferred to a group of their own age.

Intelligence

The IQ is not a crucial factor in grouping preadolescents. Their facility to use tools, materials, and colloquial language masks their low scholastic ability. Preadolescents with extreme mental retardation are excluded from ordinary therapy groups. They are seen in a more intellectually homogeneous group.

Open Groups

In open groups, new patients are accepted during the course of treatment. In closed groups, patients begin therapy at approximately the same time, and no new members are accepted thereafter. The rationale for closed groups is that children who are far along in treatment may be disturbed when newcomers with deeper pathology are added to the group. In practice, preadolescent therapy groups tend to be open because children terminate or drop out of treatment and have to be replaced. To avoid anxiety, termination of treatment or the addition of new members should be discussed openly in the group.

Same-Sex Groups

Same-sex groups are indicated for preadolescents. During this period of life sexual identification of boys and girls needs to be intensified and reinforced through provision of models, interests, and activities that are culturally differentiated as masculine and feminine.

SUMMARY

The chapter attempts to answer the oft asked question, What is the treatment for preadolescents who are too old for play therapy and too young for interview therapy? A novel therapeutic setting is described that provides media for relationships, catharsis, insight, reality testing, and sublimation appropriate for children aged ten to thirteen. Basic criteria for selction and grouping of preadolescents in group therapy are formulated; indications and contraindications are described at length.

REFERENCES

DORFMAN, ELAINE: Play therapy. In C. R. Rogers: *Client-centered Therapy.* Boston. Houghton, 1951, pp. 235-277.

FREUD, ANNA: Nursery school education: Its use and dangers. *Child Study,* 27: 35 ff., 1949.

GINOTT, H. G.: Play group therapy: A theoretical framework. *Int J Group Psychother,* 8: 410-413, 1958.

GINOTT, H. G.: The theory and practice of therapeutic intervention in child treatment. *J Consult Psychol,* 93: 160-166, 1959.

GINOTT, H. G.: *Group Psychotherapy with Children.* New York, McGraw, 1961.

GINOTT, H. G.: *Between Parent and Child.* New York, Macmillan, 1965.

LEBO, D.: Age and suitability for nondirective play therapy. *J Genet Psychol,* 89: 231-238, 1956.

REDL, F.: Preadolescents—What makes them tick? (Pamphlet), New York, The Child Study Association of America, n.d.

SLAVSON, S. R.: *An Introduction to Group Therapy,* New York, Commonwealth Fund and Harvard, 1943.

SLAVSON, S. R. (Ed.): *The Practice of Group Therapy.* New York, Int. Univs. Press, 1947.

NAME INDEX

295

SUBJECT INDEX